SCRAPBOOK *of a* TAOS HIPPIE

Scrapbook *of a*
Taos Hippie

Tribal Tales from the Heart of a Cultural Revolution

»»»»»«««««

Iris Keltz

Introduction by Edward Sanders

CINCO PUNTOS PRESS El Paso, Texas

For further information, write Cinco Puntos Press, 2709 Louisville, El Paso, Texas 79930; or call 1-800-566-9072.

FIRST EDITION Printed in Canada
10 9 8 7 6 5 4 3 2 1

Library of Congress Cataloging-in-Publication Data

Keltz, Iris, 1946-
Scrapbook of a Taos hippie : tribal tales from the heart of a cultural revolution / by Iris Keltz.
p. cm.
ISBN 0-938317-50-4 (alk. paper)
1. Taos (N.M.)—social life and customs—20th century—Miscellanea. 2. Subculture—New Mexico—Taos—History—20th century—Miscellanea. 3. Hippies—New Mexico—Taos—History—20th century—Miscellanea. 4. Keltz, Iris, 1946- 5. Hippies—New Mexico—Taos—Biography. 6. Taos (N.M.)—Biography. I. Title.

F804.T2 K45 2000
978.9'53—dc21

00-023963

Book and cover design by Jeff Bryan, La Alameda Press, Albuquerque, New Mexico.
We couldn't have done it without you.

This book is dedicated to my two children Minka and Eli and to all the children who have ever asked, "Mom, Dad, tell me about the hippie days." I wish to thank everyone who generously agreed to share their experiences in the oral histories and their photographs from personal collections.

The vignettes I wrote are fictionalized recreations of actual events. They are woven from conversations with friends and from the mists of 30 years worth of memories. If anyone reading these stories and oral histories remembers these incidents another way, both versions are probably true. For if there is one thing I have confirmed in researching and writing this book, it is that there is no such thing as a true history told by one source. We must listen to several versions from different perspectives. Where the stories dovetail, we can suspect a mustard seed of truth. Where the stories diverge, we must accept the contradictions.

I thank my husband Marc, who has been a listening audience for the past 25 years, and my mother who went to speak to my fourth-grade teacher to patiently explain that I really did write the story I handed in. Hopefully, the stories, articles and photographs will linger in your mind and come together to paint a picture of a most exciting and unique moment in America. As this book finds its way into the wider world, our wondrous tales of those times go out together, tribal-like, none of them alone.

Iris Keltz

Contents

HELLO Forever....

Noli in Spiritu Combueri
The answer is not to be laid back
not to be cynical
not to be hesitant
not to be shy
not to be uninformed
not to be beaten down
not to be isolated
not to be frightened
not to be threatened
not to be co-opted
not to be lied to
Noli in Spiritu Combueri
Refuse to be burnt-out
Refuse to be burnt-out
Refuse to be burnt-out

The Fugs
(Edward Sanders)

Introduction
by Edward Sanders

Life Magazine had a cover story in July of 1969 entitled "The Youth Communes." Thus *Life*, representing the semi-liberal wing of the Luce publication empire (*Time*, *Life*, *Fortune*), gave its critical and tentative assent (as it had done in the late 1950s to the Beat Generation) to the phenomena of the communes. The idea of the commune of course is very ancient, but the idea of an egalitarian, non-patriarchal, non-authoritarian commune has elements of newness. For ancient communes, you can check out, for instance, the Russian communities of artisans called Artels which existed all the way back to the 12th century. You can probably go on the internet (or to your local library) and find oodles of information about, say, Brook Farm or the Oneida Colony of the 19th century. To learn about some of the American communes of the 1960s and early '70s, you can begin by reading Iris Keltz' *Scrapbook of a Taos Hippie*.

There are more than 30 sections to this interesting book, just about evenly divided between Keltz' biographic essays on her personal experiences in the commune scene in Taos, and sections she wove together based on the recollections of communards. In between the written sections she has placed clippings from the newspapers of the day, as well as photos and posters.

Keltz has an eye for detail, and her honesty reinforces her arguments that the commune movement has something to say in 2000 and beyond. She does not shy away from the flaws, the weaknesses, and the down times of the communes just as she does not neglect the thrills, the fun, the dancing, the highs, the eros, the communal physical work and the spirit of sharing she rightly urges us to celebrate.

A Hunger for Sharing & Peace

A generation grew up during the Korean War and the fumbly '50s which had a hunger for peace, creativity and

The Fugs at the Peace Eye Bookstore 1967 (left to right): Ed Sanderrs, Tuli Kupferberg, Ken Weaver— Lower East Side, New York City.

Photo courtesy of Edward Sanders

sharing. The very idea of preparing vigorously for a 60-year career in the suit-and-tie world followed by a few years retirement, then a terminal illness caused by pollutants, did not appeal at all to quite a number of young Americans in the 1960s and early 1970s. The hunger had a number of causes. Part of the hunger was based on things like actually trying to live according to the scriptures of the great religions. Part grew from the principles of the left: that a just nation could be created where sharing of the wealth was embedded permanently within its laws and mores. The word "greed-head" had arisen in the parlance of what was called the counterculture. Greed-head denoted something to be avoided. It was a sickness, a malady, a malformation of the soul that those who hungered for communes thought they might be able to escape.

The War & The Draft, Rebellion

Speaking of escape, the Vietnam war those years lay like a multi-decade curse upon the nation. The draft was sucking up the sons, mainly of working families, and hundreds of thousands wanted no part of a war that featured napalm, unnecessary body bags, fragmentation bombs and defoliation.

The nation became highly agitated over the war, both against and pro. It must be remembered that throughout the 1960s, until well after the Tet Offensive of early 1968, a majority of the great American television-gazing populace was not against the war. A younger generation, however, began to organize. To the horror of the military and the control class, the dinners of Americans those years were punctuated with ghastly visuals from Vietnam of blood and gore. There were literally tens of thousands of protest rallies all over the nation, teach-ins at colleges, and even an underground network to help soldiers flee from the war of napalm and televised slaughter.

As it happened, those were the years the use of drugs spread among youth. Available throughout the counterculture, abundantly and affordably, were marijuana, hashish, LSD, mescaline, peyote, various

"I see a vision of a great rucksack revolution, thousands or even millions of young Americans wandering around with rucksacks, going up to mountains to pray . . ." —Jack Kerouac, *Dharma Bums* (1958). Photo by Paul Dembski

varieties of uppers, and also strange ones like ibogaine, DMT, DET, and the most American drug of them all, tranquilizers. The years of drugs more or less dovetailed with a new sense of sexual liberation, spurred in good part by the mass availability of birth control pills since around 1961. Albert Camus' *Rebello Ergo Sum* became almost tattooed on the eager body of the age.

On the Road-ism & the Interstate

During the 1950s, the Beats crisscrossed the continent in fossil-fueled jalopies of literary seekers thirsting for a kind of transcendence. By the 1960s crisscrossing seekers had grown from a handful to thousands. We could call it On the Road-ism. Eisenhower's huge Interstate highway system, originally conceived as a way of getting troops and supplies around the nation in the event of a swarm job by the Russkies, facilitated the roaming of the 1960s. The spirit of roaming both helped and harmed the commune movement. When key people left a 'une to go somewhere else, they sometimes took a lot of the soul, organizational ability and expertise with them. On the other hand, a stable commune could get chaos'd by the constant arrival of interstate visitors and, let's face it, by mooches, ingrates, lazy-heads, spiritual parasites and even the violent and insane.

All this roaming across the beauty and insolence of America gave a sense of turbidity to the communes. It reminded me of the folk song verse I learned on a peace walk in 1961:

Passing through! Passing through!
Sometimes happy, sometime blue
Glad that I ran into you
Tell the people that we're only passing through.

"Passing through" brought impermanence and dislocation to a movement that ought to have been desperately striving to lay down permanent structures of sharing in the electric forests of the cities and the suspicious zones of the countryside.

Workers of the World Relax—The Concept of Goof Time

A key partof the communes was their celebration of Fun and Goof Time, emblemized by a fine poster Gilbert Shelton once designed called "Workers of the World Relax." Why not conspire to stand in the way of the Rat Race? Our grandparents' generation worked hard to lower the work week from 70 to 60 to 50 to 44 to 40 hours? Why not lower it to 20? Why not waste time, for is not time itself the biggest waster of them all? Allen Ginsberg's brilliant *Howl & Other Poems* changed many lives by the early 1960s, especially on the question of Goof Time and the abandonment of money-lust. His great poem "America," for instance, in the same book, thrilled a generation with goof lines such as these:

America I've given you all and now I'm nothing.
America two dollars and twentyseven cents
January 17, 1956. . .
America when will you be angelic?
When will you take off your clothes?...
I smoke marijuana every chance I get.
I sit in my house for days on end and stare at the roses of the closet

And the Spirit of Free

Another line from "America" spoke to the issue of Free:

When can I go into the supermarket and buy what I need with my good looks?

When indeed? Why not right now, in my own life time! For money, after all, is an hallucination, and banks create it, poof! out of nothing when they write a loan. I think that the spirit of Free provided much of the fuel of the communes, whose inhabitants wanted more than to "feel" free. They wanted Genuine Free! When the San Francisco Diggers served free food in Golden Gate Park , when the Free Store opened up first in San Francisco, and then in New York's Lower East Side in 1967, when free bins and community switchboards appeared by the thousands across the nation, the era was speaking its wildest desires: True Free—a world without profit, yet where everybody profited.

Communes Around the Nation

True Free was a message as inimical to the control class as the Ghost Dances had been in the 1880s. Yet it was an unstoppable spirit that spread in the late 1960s around the nation. Communes brought their hunger for sharing and social justice to just about every state. California, Colorado, New Mexico, Oregon and Washington had a bunch. There were 'unes in New York City, in upstate New York, in Illinois and the Midwest, in Kansas. Some tried to hide, but all had pride.

And in Taos

The movement found particular grace (as well as strong opposition) in the mountains near Taos, a town of a few thousand souls in north central New

Mexico at an altitude of about 7,000 feet, and 55 miles north of Santa Fe. The ancient Pueblo Indian village of San Geronimo de Taos lies north of the town. Taos is one of the oldest frontier settlements in the United States. It was a place where people talked openly about being in "God's country"—where boundaries seemed numinal rather than those recorded on deeds at the County Clerk's office. There was a kind of spiritual topography to the placing of roots in God's country, and somehow the curves of the brain flowed out and fit in with its contours, escarpments, shapes, smells, seasons, flora and fauna, drainage and heritage.

The Commune issue of *Modern Utopian*, published in 1971, listed nine communes in the vicinity of Taos. They had such great names! New Buffalo, the Hog Farm, Lama, Reality Construction Company, Morningstar, and others.

Since the early 1900s, Taos has been what they call an artists' colony. People mistakenly think that if a place is an artists' colony then it's automatically a liberal or leftist zone, shown not necessarily to be so, judging from the way the Taos area treated the communards and hippies.

As traced in Iris Keltz' book, certain Taos business interests and a number of locals strutting with self-importance rose up against the "influx of hippies" in the spring of 1969, just about the same time as the ghastly stories on the American rapes and slaughter at My Lai, Vietnam were being published in the establishment press. Nudity, drugs, unbathed youth, and "fuck you!-ism" were what they moaned about in Taos, but on another level, it was the Cold War being acted out in a think globally/act locally circumstance.

A similar situation was occurring in Woodstock, New York, an art colony like Taos, which at the very same time as Taos was experiencing the "hippie influx." In Woodstock in the spring of 1969 there were angry meetings called by conservatives at which it was proposed that hippies be met as they got off the bus from New York City, and forced back onto the Trailways. As in Taos, there were public forums between "hippies" and concerned locals, during one of which a commune was arsoned and burned to the ground. Woodstock had operated a public camping ground where visitors could stay overnight. To keep out the hippies, the Town Board passed a law banning camping out on land, closed the public camping place and banned use of a beautiful swimming hole on town land because it had become frequented by occasionally nude, loiterous and boisterous youth. So Taos wasn't alone among art colonies in its hostility to the communards.

Aspen Meadow—"high" above Santa Fe, the First (and Last) Annual Summer Solstice Great Bus Race where Bus Further lost to Bus Road Hog. *Photo by John Stearns*

The Great Society

Lyndon Johnson, president from 1963 through 1968, had many bad qualities. In some ways he rep-

Out of frustration with politics and war, in protest of a 9-to-5 capitalist agenda, there was much talk of what we'd all be doing after the revolution. There was a lot of talk, but many ideas were seeds that took root as real alternatives. Even today we're still fighting the same old system, still trying to live a philosophy that emphasizes peace, freedom, love, and respect for others and the earth.

Photo by Rich Jamison

resented the worst aspects of American civilization. On the other hand, Johnson had some good qualities also. To his credit, he did not entirely forget his early years under the influence of Franklin Roosevelt and the New Deal, and used his leadership ability as president to get a number of important legislative acts through Congress that have been grouped together as the Great Society.

War was a key word of the control class, and so in a speech in 1964, Johnson called for a "War on Poverty." Johnson said that housing, income, employment and health were, in the end, a federal responsibility. So, while he escalated the maiming of Nam, he escalated the drive for Great Society legislation. Medicare was voted into place in 1965, and Medicaid in 1968, plus a Fair Housing Act banning discrimination, and an Executive Order in 1965 requiring government contractors to prepare affirmative action plans.

One point of contention in Taos was the Federal Food Stamp program, inaugurated in 1964 as part of Johnson's War on Poverty. During those years, those with modest moolah purchased stamps which allowed them to buy much more food than if they had used their cash. Though a federal program, the State of New Mexico ran it on the local level, such as in Taos, where conservatives trembled with angst over possible hippie moochers taking advantage of the food stamp system. Communes had to select a manager who would add up all the communards' "income" and apply for all the members of the 'une at the same time.

Hostility of the Überculture

Fear of nudity, fear of pot and acid, fear of dissolved property boundary lines, fear of disrespect for Christ and Jaweh, support for the war ("my country right or wrong"), and fear of orgies and ambisexuality—these were some of the fears that convulsed through God's country in '69 and '70. It was particularly difficult in the Southwest for a commune to put down roots and establish long term tradition. Part of it might have to do with what they call karma, especially with the spiritual blood of the Indians still fresh in the land-grab psyches of the region. It was difficult to hold on to the communal dream, for instance, when longhairs would never know what the sharp nighttime shutting of a pickup truck door might bring—beernecks wanting to fight with hippies after a dance, a delivery of sacks of rice and produce, or guys just wanting to learn.

Across the nation the überculture stomped down hard on leaders of the counterculture—on Tim Leary and Ken Kesey for possession of ridiculously small amounts of pot, on Joan Baez for refusing to pay taxes for war, and on countless heroes and heroines across the nation who faced eviction, pot harassment, attacks on their underground newspapers, raids on their living space, etc.

After the Kent State shootings, ten students were stabbed by National Guardsman with bayonets on their rifles during a demonstration against the Vietnam War in Albuquerque, May 8, 1970. *Photo from the* Fountain of Light *(Summer 1970)*

In the Lower East Side of New York City, say from 1967 (the summer of Love) through 1969 (the year of the moon walk), there was incredible hostility by the New York Police Department against the setting up of a system of communes and crash pads. Dr. Benjamin Spock, Marcus Raskin of the Institute for Policy Studies, and others were indicted in early 1968 for counseling young men to evade the draft. It was a deadly hostility also. Look what happened to the Kennedies, to Martin Luther King, to Fred Hampton, to the "Four Dead in Ohio" in the spring of '70 and other martyrs to the making of a Better America.

The communes of New Mexico of course grew up not far from the most secret and guarded facilities of the military-industrial-surrealist complex—the nuclear research labs at Los Alamos and Sandia, and possibly at other places we still might not know about. Military intelligence agents, on the look for Russkie spies, international trouble makers and Mossad agents, undoubtedly kept an eye on the communes of New Mexico. In addition, the communes of the Taos area grew up at a time when the FBI was putting into action its Cointelpro program against the New Left and the underground community. It was around then that the CIA domestic Chaos program targeted the underground press for destruction. It's not known what, if any, military intelligence, FBI or CIA operatives were present in the Taos communes, perhaps stirring up strife and discomfort. They were masters at strife-stir. It's a field of investigation—now that the Cold War is over for now—that's ripe for researchers.

Interesting Innovations

The communes brought certain ideas and concepts to their daily routines which, taken together, offer a paradigm for the future. The first was the breaking of new ground in the architecture of living quarters—the genius, for instance, of having a "drumming room" at New Buffalo. The communes were in the vanguard for the creation of the Community or Alternative School. Iris Keltz went to work for such a school, and wittily notes in her book that the single question asked at her employment interview was, "Are you certified and do you know how to build adobe walls?"

The commune movement supported the Alternative or Underground Press, a very vital function in a nation where the right has controlled the media throughout the century. The communes knew more than anyone the need for alternate modes of communication: how the exigencies of the street and the mountainside sometimes called for instant communication such as the street fliers and posters put out regularly, within minutes after the need arose, from the free mimeo at my Peace Eye Bookstore in New York City during those years. And let us not forget the Hog Farm's newspaper, the *Daily Hogtopus*. Out of the mind of the communards and their supporters came the concept of the Switch-Board and the bulletin boards, packed with information, at health food stores and community centers.

Perhaps the most important legacy of the commune movement was the system of Free Clinics set up in the late 1960s. There was the Taos Free Clinic, the Haight-Ashbery Free Clinic; and even, for a while, a Free Clinic in New York City. It wasn't trumpeted at the time, but it brought us a true paradigm for the universal health care system that America desperately requires: the Free Clinic. Free Free Free Free.

Passing on the Vision

Without passing on the Vision of a movement, there is no movement. How is it done? Alton Ellis' reggae tune "Set a Better Example" always comes to mind. Ultimately the artifacts, images, writings and memories of a something like a commune BECOMES the commune. "Who digs LA IS LA," Allen Ginsberg noted in "Footnote to Howl." It's the same way with communes, because the communes of Taos came and faded so quickly! Just a few years, then "poof!"—though a number of communards stayed in the area, had families, put down roots, and found ways to survive in the increasingly laissez-faire economic climate of neocon America.

One of the interesting themes in Iris Keltz' work is the bonding of women in communes, and the problems of raising children in relative safety while passing on to them the seeds of the culture. It's an issue that will need to be addressed in the future.

Meanwhile, the complex of concepts known as "Communes" will always rise again, because they speak to a profound hunger in the minds of millions. It's not a hunger for "utopia," but a hunger for just plain old Topia. Something real, something now, and something always. One of the assets of this book is that it might help those in the future who would attempt to form a commune in the American landscape. The pathway to a Better World requires a lot of study, and this living book can be one of the courses.

Edward Sanders
Woodstock, New York

Why Taos

While it may be said we are fleeing the deplorable conditions of contamination of the urban areas, both physical and spiritual, the real motivation seems to be a quest for a more natural way of life. Away from the plastic and putrefying conditions in the cities. We mean to establish for ourselves new life styles that are basically simple and agrarian. Our concern is with the real— real food grown by ourselves for the most part, real and useful products produced by heads and hands and hearts, expressions in art forms that manifest individual energies of human beings rather than the faceless and soulless work of mechanized existence. To plant and cultivate and to ultimately harvest worthwhile things from joyous labors, this is what we are about. Some of us come to Taos because it is a real place, with real and meaningful history and traditions, isolated in a sense and abounding in nature. It is a ruggedly beautiful place that offers us a chance to reacquaint ourselves with the Planet Earth. Sure, some of our ways are different. We are a definite, if not distressing, change from the ways things are. Perhaps, though, a little patience and tolerance will reveal that we are, above all, people of good will and much of the change we wrought is positive and welcomed. We are not reformers and do not seek directly to influence social or political order, but only to be unmolested and live our lives in peace and let these lives speak for themselves. Words change little, action changes everything.

Fountain of Light • 1969

The Rio Grande rolling through the Pilar Valley, south of Taos. *Photo by Iris Keltz*

Preface
by Iris Keltz

My friends and I are becoming grandmothers and grandfathers, but when I wrote the first story for this book—"The Rainbow Gathering"—in 1973, I was a young woman, single and without children. Somehow I imagined that through some miraculous sliver in time, we would not grow old. In fact, people over thirty were generally mistrusted. After all, wasn't it the old men who had made the decision to send the young men to war? We had precious few elders to whom we could turn for advice.

At the time of the gathering, I was living with my housemate Cynthia in an old adobe house, half of which had already melted into the earth. I remember sitting in front of the cook stove in the light of a kerosene lamp, writing down my experience. That Rainbow gathering in Wyoming was a moment of epiphany for me—I was always on the hunt for a mythological explanation of the world. We were reverting to an old form—tribalism—but in a very new way. We would not be a tribe because of lineage, race, language or tradition. We were a rainbow of people becoming a tribe because we had a collective belief in an alternative to materialism, greed, military power and an unpopular war fought using our brothers, schoolmates and boyfriends. I understood that when we climbed that mountaintop in the Grand Tetons, we were praying for a miracle to change our world. We still are.

When I left New York City I was an idealistic twenty-something filled with the roaring slogans of my generation—"Hell No, We Won't Go," "Give Peace A Chance" and "Make Love Not War." I had been to the Democratic Convention in Chicago in '68 and watched as the tear gas and billy clubs came down on our heads while we innocently faced the TV cameras yelling, "The whole world is watching!" and believing that Eugene McCarthy would be

A friend (the guy with the backpack on) is getting ready to hit the road, leaving behind his friends and lovers. This photo was taken in the early '70s when I was living in Seco.

Photo by Paul Dembski

elected because it was right and just. When he wasn't nominated by the Democrats, our only recourse was a protest vote for Pegasus the Pig, the candidate from Abbie Hoffman's Yippie Party.

Timothy Leary advised us to turn on, tune in and drop out. The way to peace was through inner peace and the way to societal change was to change oneself. And so I headed to Taos, New Mexico, believing that we would create a new culture in America. We were the critical mass that could change the direction of our capitalistic society.

Northern New Mexico became a gathering place for young Americans and a microcosm of what was happening across the country. *Scrapbook of a Taos Hippie* documents those rebellious times. The complexities of the era are told as eyewitness accounts through personal vignettes, oral histories, photographs and newspaper articles from local, alternative and national presses. Each story deals with basic life issues—birth, death, educating our young and ourselves, food, shelter, entertainment, religious practices and ritual gatherings. The local community's response is best told through articles in *The Taos News*. *The Fountain of Light*, a hippie newsletter with a brief publishing life, extends the counterculture perspective. There are stories about the dark side as well as the joyful side of life.

The oldest old hippie around, Alfred Hobbs, celebrated his 70th birthday a few summers ago. People came from all over the country. Bands played all night, a sheep was roasted in the ground—we ate it without the benefit of plates or utensils. At sunset, a man played "Happy Birthday" on the bagpipes to the darkening skies. We knocked hips and danced with no one in particular on the hardpacked earth speckled with sage and cactus.

The party was on the west side of the Rio Grande River, somewhere off the grid—a place where people collected the sparse rain and snowfall, where people converted sunlight into electricity. Maybe if we knew how to live off the grid and without the food stamp/welfare dole in the '60s, the original communes would be thriving villages by now instead of vivid memories.

Some wiser and more knowing people could look back in time and think that our dreams were built on quicksand but in gathering up the stories for this book, I realized that in the most profound sense, the communes were successful—not that they lasted—but that over and over, people affirmed that the experience of living in them altered their perspective forever and, in some cases, saved a life. There are countless stories of scruffy vagabonds and lost souls who wandered into these refuges without a dime, sometimes without the ability to articulate a coherent sentence, but who left ready to take their places in the larger world. There was no "therapeutic program." There was acceptance.

The commune scene evolved as our needs changed. Since many of us had children, we grudgingly acknowledged our need for jobs, privacy and stability. But our makeshift institutions harbored a deep mistrust of "for profit only."

We were chronically straddling a paradox—rejecting our capitalistic roots while depending on rich hippies with money. We mimicked the ways of Native Americans without admitting to the waves of generations behind their traditions. We created capitalistic ventures like restaurants, grocery stores, newspapers, and schools and wanted them to exist without profit. In short, we were unafraid of our inconsistencies, a people who embraced paradox as the slippery road to a glorious future.

Over thirty years have passed since "the summer of love." My life's dream has always been to become a village elder telling stories to the next generation. And in that sense, this collection of stories is the fulfillment of that dream. These stories are to be shared with our friends and children around the campfires of time.

Alfred Hobbs 70th birthday party out on a barren piece of sagebrush towards Tres Orejas, jokingly referred to as Hobbsville. Hundreds of people showed up, some traveling from as far as Hawaii and Japan to be there. At sunset, a kilted man standing on an old school bus played 'Happy Birthday' on the bagpipes. Aging hippies came to see old friends and get gushingly nostalgic. The most wondrous sight was the young people, curious and hungry to taste the past at a gathering only an old hippie like Alfred could conjure.

Photo by Iris Keltz

Taos Pueblo *beneath Taos Mountain. It is one of the oldest continually inhabited communities in North America and epitomizes the word* ancient. *It would have looked very similar to this during 'pre-conquest' times, divided into the* Hlauuma *(north house), and* Hlaukwima *(south house) and set apart by the westerly flowing Rio Pueblo de Taos. Its watershed, Blue Lake, is one of the most sacred ritual sites. The restoration of it to Taos Pueblo in 1970, after being incorporated into the National Forest lands in 1906, was an extraordinary event in recent history and a victory for tribal elders who continue to struggle for the spiritual health of the community. Blue Lake is off-limits to all but Pueblo members.* *Photo by Marcia Keegan*

Taos: A Brief Portrait

by Bobby Byrd, publisher

"You cannot come to Taos without feeling
that here is one of the chosen spots on Earth."
—*D.H. Lawrence*

In the dark and mysterious underworld (the womb of the earth itself) the people and animals live with their kind and loving mother. But there comes a time when they must move to the next world, which is this world. To the north, near the sand, there is a blue lake. It is here, in the mountains high above Taos, the first people climb the great fir tree and emerge to populate the earth. With them come good and bad spirits who can dwell in everything (rocks, trees, animals, plants and people.)

The village of Taos is huddled up into a beautiful niche on the western slope of la sierra del Sangre de Cristo, mountains so named because they turn blood red in the sunsets. Many snow-fed rivers and streams flow from those mountains, like the one fed by the Blue Lake that tumbles down through the canyons to wander through the ancient Taos Pueblo. West of Taos, beneath an enormous sky, a wide plain—the dry flat basin of a lost sea—stretches like the hand of God into the translucent distance. A river, which has had many names through the centuries but is now called the Río Grande, gashes a huge black gorge into the plain. These are the eternal elements —the mountains, the sky, the plain, the gorge —that appear in the myths, legends and stories of all of the peoples who have wandered through northern New Mexico, the land of Taos, only to make it their home.

But it's not simply beauty that makes Taos unique. It's the history of the place, a history that doesn't begin with a band of religious exiles anchoring the Mayflower at the eastern edge of the so-called "New World." Nor does it begin with Columbus or Coronado or Hernando de Alvarado or any of the other conquistadors who fed the ravenous hunger of the European Renaissance with the riches of the Americas. The history of Taos stretches deep into the dark past of what our scholars call "pre-history" because it was not written down in books.

Thousands of years ago early peoples—hunters and gatherers—roamed the mountains and plains. They hunted mammoth, bison, and other large mammals. They gathered wild plants, and they built fires and watched the huge skies turn into night. Centuries passed, and then somewhere around the beginning of the previous millennium, peoples began to build great multi-storied dwelling places in the Rio Grande Valley, dotting the rich river plains in the midst of the desert. They planted crops of maize and beans and melons and squash. The stories, myths and oral histories of these peoples—stretching way back into subconscious time—are still told in the Native American communities that are alive and well in and around Taos.

You can feel this ancient history when you walk around the Taos Plaza. You can see the mountains, you can see the enormous skies, you can see the history in the faces of the Hispanics and Native Americans who wander past or sit in the shade of a cottonwood tree watching you, or you can walk the few miles up the road past the Allsup's to the Taos Pueblo that is almost 1000 years old.

You can also begin to understand the more immediate history that began in 1540. That's when Coronado sent Hernando de Alvarado, an artillery captain, to explore to the north and east. On the invitation of Pueblo representatives, he and his soldiers traveled up river, going from town to town. Upon reaching an impassable canyon, they climbed to a high plain, and on the edge came to a large pueblo divided in two parts by a river. This was the Taos Pueblo.

The Spanish colonized the area. They brought their priests to convert the pagans by whatever means necessary. They brought colonists and soldiers to guarantee their sovereignty, they brought sheep and goats, and they brought the horse. Time passed like it does for all colonized peoples under the yoke of an invader. Then, on August 10, 1680 all the Pueblos up and down the Rio Grande revolted against Spanish rule. Popé, a native of San Juan Pueblo who had been hiding at Taos, orchestrated the revolution. In Taos the revolutionaries killed some seventy settlers, as well as the priests. The combined Pueblo forces drove the Spanish out of New Mexico until 1692. The Revolt of 1680 is still very much a celebrated event in Pueblo and Native American History.

In the 1700s, the village became a trading center. In the summers the French traders, who were the first of the notorious mountain men, came to trade for furs. The Comanche, the Kiowa and other Plains Indians also crossed the mountains, looking to trade their captives for horses, grain and trade goods from Chihuahua. Unlike Santa Fe, its elegant and sissified cousin to the south, Taos becomes known for its rugged and sometimes wild ways. Life didn't change on the northern Rio Grande when the 13 colonies declared their freedom from England, nor did it change much when Mexico declared independence from Spain. But in 1821 the Santa Fe Trail was opened following the Louisiana Purchase, and the trickle of newcomers from the East became a floodtide. Still, because no train track reached up north, Taos remained in the backwaters of "Manifest Destiny."

In 1898 the first Anglo artists, Ernest Blumenschien and Bert Phillips, arrived in Taos. They established an artists' colony that attracted others to the rugged beauty of Taos. In 1917, only five years after New Mexico became a state, Mabel Sterne moved to Taos. She married Tony Lujan of Taos Pueblo, thereby becoming the legendary Mable Dodge Lujan. Already well known among New York and Paris literary society, she invited a variety of artists and writers to visit, among them Georgia O'Keeffe, D.H. Lawrence, Marsden Hartley, Willa Cather, Carl Sandburg, and many others. Thus, Taos became known in the popular imagination for its spiritual beauty and as an oasis where a "different" way of life is preserved.

When the hippies began wandering into Taos during the '60s, it was a small town with three cultures—the Pueblo, the Hispanic, and the Anglo. The Pueblo and Hispanic cultures were conservative and traditional. They kept to themselves and they maintained their customs. For the most part, the families of these communities were poor. The Anglo population was a potpourri—mostly middle-class outsiders, ranchers and farmers, retirees and budding tourism entrepreneurs, with a small contingent of artists and intelligentsia.

Taos Plaza, 1900. *Photo from the Museum of New Mexico, negative #104337*

Now, at the beginning of the 21st Century, Taos finds itself under siege from the nouveau capitalism with its rootless corporations who want to Aspenize the area. Land prices have sky-rocketed, skiing is a big-time industry, tourists wander the streets with cameras like they bought a ticket to Disneyland, a senator wants to put in a new airport for jumbo jets to bring in more walking dollars, the Pueblo has opened a casino, and Wal Mart wants to plug a superstore into the landscape. Ironically, Taos' hippie culture, which still has a strong presence in the community, has become one more photo-op for the carpetbaggers to sell.

Still, there are young people—feeling the same ennui and frustration with their lives, as all of us old hippies did 40 years ago—who come to Taos looking for answers to the emptiness they feel in their souls. They come from Europe and Asia and from American suburbia. They want to go find New Buffalo and the Reality Construction Company, and they want to hear stories about Baba Ram Dass, the Lama Foundation, Little Joe and the Native American Church. They believe there is romance and information in these memories.

Then maybe in another 40 years, after all of the folks in this book are dead and scattered as ashes to the winds, a new generation of young people may come to Taos. If they are lucky, the beauty will continue to flourish. The mountains, the sky, the wide mesa, and the Rio Grande Gorge will be the same. These young people will wander out to the Pueblo at daybreak on a New Year's morning. The temperature will be way below zero. They will wait, like we have all waited at one time or another, for the Turtle Dancers—naked except for breechcloth and moccasins—to rise like ghosts out of the smoke holes of the mud kivas. The dancers, repeating the vital rituals of centuries, will move from place to place around the Pueblo, stamping on the earth to the beat of ancient drums.

N.
LILA
LORIEN
MTNS.
QUESTA
12,723
W.
Hot Springs
GRANDE
Magic Tortoise
LAMA
CRISTO
Eagle Nest
E.
13,161
Arroyo Hondo
Arroyo Seco
Reality
Morning Star
New Buffalo
DE
To Cimarron & High Plains
Taos Pueblo
General Store
Fountain of Light
RIO
Taos
The Family
Angel Fire
Mabel Dodge Lujan House
Ranchos De Taos
Pilar
Pilar Hill
SANGRE
Peñasco
Dixon
To Santa Fe
Llano
Hog Farm
S.
Guadalupita

First Encounters with New Buffalo

by Iris Keltz

Faisal and I liked to have our photos taken at the game arcade in Chinatown, N.Y.

It was 1968, between the Summer of Love and Woodstock. Faisal and I had been married for one year. We were returning to New York City after a three-month migration across America. The highways were filled with young wanderers. Our vehicles identified us. Volkswagen vans and bugs, painstakingly hand-painted with psychedelic landscapes and designs, were popular. So were pickup trucks with funky rooms built in the back. We drove a '56 Chevy station wagon, dubbed Bella Blue, fitted with foam pads and sleeping bags.

After a lifetime in Jerusalem, Faisal was adjusting to life in the States. His English had improved but he still said things like "the fingers of your feet" and "breast socks." In Berkeley, he had had a reunion with Aunt Dina, his mother's sister, who'd left the Middle East twenty years ago. They reminisced in Arabic with unabashed happiness—crying, laughing and occasionally translating for me. He left his aunt's house homesick for Jerusalem. Even watching the war protestors in Berkeley take over a park didn't cheer him, so we decided to take a diversionary detour through the Sonora Desert in Mexico. Big mistake. It was like the inside of an oven. We couldn't drink enough water to urinate. Our fan belt melted and snapped. After waiting in the unbearable heat most of the afternoon for a new fan belt to be installed, we took the next main highway heading north. Interstate 25 took us to Albuquerque, Santa Fe and Taos.

Central Avenue in Albuquerque was hot enough to fry an egg on, so we continued to Santa Fe. The northern New Mexico landscape reminded Faisal of home. Transparent light engulfed expanses of semi-arid desert, home to twisted cedars instead of gnarled olive trees. The New Mexican peaks were higher, more jagged than the round Judean hills. The cool mountain air revived us. While sitting on a park bench in the Santa Fe plaza, someone handed us a newsletter called *The Fountain of Light*. It contained information on the local counterculture, including crude

Two wings of the pueblo and courtyard at New Buffalo. The pueblo blended with the landscape. Chance grasses and weeds took root on the roof.

Photo by Paul Dembski

handdrawn maps to communes in the area. "Let's check out the New Buffalo Commune," I offered as a possibility.

Following the Rio Grande through the gorge, we passed lush orchards and sleepy towns hugging the river. The uninhabited sections were walled in by craggy hillsides with barely any vegetation. Cresting Pilar Hill an hour later, we saw the canyon walls open onto a mountain valley looking like the dawn of creation. The map directed us to the village of Arroyo Hondo, ten miles north of Taos.

My dream of living in a village had been born when Faisal took me to Samour, his village, linked to the outside world by a bus that ran twice a day to Hebron. Chagall might have painted there. The stone and mud homes clustered along the only road, trafficked by camels, donkeys, dogs, chickens, people and one bus. When Faisal returned home after years of wandering, his father slew a sheep and invited everyone to a feast. The old man dreamed his son and new daughter-in-law would stay and raise their unborn babies here.

The rhythms and intimacies of village life were seductive. For a while, I dreamed of settling there and living in the primitive but comfortable stone house, in time becoming a village elder, and sharing the stories. But I was American and doubted I could accept another wife into the family, or wait until the men finished eating, or be kept in a constant state of pregnancy to prove my worth.

As we drove up the rutted New Buffalo driveway my vision was rekindled. This could be my village. But who were the bare-chested women ambling near the parking area? I tried to act blasé as they sauntered by, titties floating freely in the breeze over ankle-length skirts. Two mountain men engrossed in conversation were bent over a pickup truck. The barrel-chested guy with long matted black hair and matching beard scowled, seemed to withdraw inside himself when he saw us. I thought he was going to ask us to leave. The other wild-looking guy in gray coveralls smiled a sly but inviting grin.

"How ya doin? Where you guys from?" He looked like Davy Crockett, king of the wild frontier.

"We just drove in from Berkeley where this People's Park thing was happening," I said, trying to sound cool. He was not impressed. City dropouts swarmed like flies around here.

"I'm an Arab from Jerusalem," announced Faisal in his thick Middle Eastern accent. That got their attention. There weren't many Arabs passing through the communes.

"My wife Joyce is Lebanese," said the barrel-chested guy, no longer scowling. "She was born in New Jersey but her parents are from Lebanon. I'm George." His grin came out from behind a cloud.

I looked past the two men to the adobe buildings and courtyard.

"Why don't you hang a while and stay for lunch? I'm Justin," said the Davy Crockett look-alike. Life seemed simple here, at first.

Lunch was rice, beans and vegetables. So was dinner. Those in front of the line got more vegetables and those to the back more beans and rice. A macrobiotic diet suited the economics and ideology of the day. No longer were we the meat-and-potatoes people of America exploiting the land for the love of hamburgers. I was willing to go along with their ideals but not Faisal, who carried his culture with him like a turtle carries his shell. Without asking, he emptied a bag of charcoal, poured on the starter fluid and set up our camp stove in the courtyard. Before you could finish smoking a joint, the succulent odors of shish kabob went wafting through the courtyard. I expected our makeshift kitchen to be shut down, but learned that when one is culturally intact, as in "shish kabob is my native diet," one is invulnerable. Faisal threw on the spices, and doors began opening as more and more people gathered around the stove waiting for a taste.

"Where you guys from?" asked one of the inhabitants.

"I am an Arab from Jerusalem," Faisal proudly answered.

"Groovy. You guys gonna be around for a while? We got an extra tipi."

"Sounds great," I said, accepting their offer unhesitatingly.

The night was cold considering the heat of the day. Carrying sleeping bags and backpacks, we stumbled towards the tipi with a cornucopia of stars lighting the way. Each step felt like the edge of a precipice. Faisal let me know that night that there was no way he'd live on rice, beans, vegetables and oatmeal. We couldn't afford to feed meat to the entire commune, so I agreed to regular town trips for cheeseburgers.

The early morning air carried the sounds of wakening life. The squawking, mooing and bleating of animals mixed with crying babies waiting for their mother's comforting voice. My eyes took a moment to adjust to the windowless yet welcoming kitchen. Two doorways, one to the drumming room, the other to the outhouse, gave the only light. A fire already roared in the cook stove. An unpretentious wooden plank table flanked by two benches sat in the middle of the room. A guy in a remarkably white tunic handed me a tin mug of cowboy coffee and made room on the bench. I hadn't met any of these guys the day before.

"Mmm, this coffee's really strong," I commented. The guy in the white tunic introduced himself as Aquarius Paul and offered to share the recipe.

"Boil some water in a large coffee pot, throw on the grounds and let them settle. Then ya throw on some cold water to help them settle faster. To make another pot just boil more water and throw on more grounds. Continue this for at least a week before starting a fresh pot."

"Thanks," I said. "I'll remember that."

With its ebb and flow of people, life in the

Drumming up the sun in New Buffalo courtyard after a very interesting trip through the night.

photo by Paul Dembski

kitchen was endlessly fascinating. A woman wearing only an ankle-length drawstring skirt smiled at me as she fed cedar logs to the cook stove. "Can I help you?" I asked.

"Some visitor once built a fire in the oven instead of the wood box and smoked everyone out of the kitchen," she laughed. "My name's Moe and you can cut apples for the pies tonight."

"What's that white stuff oozing from that sack nailed to the beam?"

"You're looking at future cheese. Some of the cow's milk is saved to make cheese and butter. That dripping bundle is separating the curds from the whey." I finally understood what Little Miss Muffet was eating.

"A bunch of us are going pea pickin' this morning. Wanna come?"

Cultivating new attitudes towards modesty, I self-consciously took off my shirt like the other bare-breasted young women. Hidden by ripening peas under a hot sun with sweat dripping between naked breasts, we chattered like a flock of magpies and returned to the kitchen with full buckets. Moe was from Baltimore and had a ten-year-old daughter. She had no plans for their future and that was okay.

The four-seater outhouse near the kitchen was filled with flies and torn newspapers. At any moment, you could be joined for a moment of intimate sharing. Everyone mutually did their business while admiring the colors on the western horizon.

In the kitchen, bare-chested women were making a salad from vegetables that only an hour ago were in the ground. The sound of a gong announced lunch. People held hands in the courtyard for a prayer circle to bless the food. The number of people who appeared for lunch was well out of proportion to the people I had seen working in the kitchen, the gardens or with the animals, but as far as I could tell, no one questioned anyone's right to eat.

During an afternoon siesta, Moe took me to the swimming hole in one of the western fields not under cultivation. It was too hot to garden, too early to milk Chloe—a brown Nubian goat—or start dinner. Languidly, we lay on the muddy embankment next to the sinkhole, getting hot under a blazing sun, listening to the hum of the afternoon.

"Did ya notice that cute guy at lunch today? He's the serious type, a real hard worker. Hardly ever smiles. Well, I'm gonna make him smile." Without warning she jumped into the icy pool, swam three strokes across and surfaced on the other embankment. I followed. Drip-drying in the late afternoon breeze, I pulled my new green drawstring skirt over my head.

"Dy-no-mite! What a score you got in the free box!" Moe shouted joyfully.

As the weeks wore on, the difference between those who meant to settle here and build a life and the transients who came to marvel in this corner of the Aquarian Age became apparent. The struggle between the workers and the party faction was pervasive. Bob, the "Philosoper King" of the New Buffalo kitchen, spearheaded the party crowd. While people worked in the fields and gardens, the renegades crowded into Bob's room for electric Hawaiian Punch and Led Zeppelin, played on the only stereo at the commune with electricity pirated from the power pole. If George asked a visitor to leave because there wasn't enough food or room, Buffalo Bob would counter with an offer of dope, food and a place to crash. Faisal and I ran into Bob at Taystee Freeze one afternoon and offered to buy him a cheeseburger.

"Hey man, thanks. I mean it. I really mean it. You're cool." Translucent skin hung over a skeletal frame. Owlish eyes, almost feverish in their intensity, seemed to stare into nothingness. After that day, he joined us whenever we went to town. We bought him cheeseburgers and he shared his visions of the white light and introduced us to local hippies. I didn't know then that he was dying of tuberculosis.

Between meals the local philosophers, renegades and minstrels held court in the kitchen near the

Goats were important to commune agriculture.
Photo by Rich Jamison

never-empty pot of cowboy coffee. That's where I met Rodney, the handsome cowman, who was as responsible to the cows as Moe was to the goats. Twice a day he brought buckets of fresh milk into the kitchen. One afternoon I went to the barn with him and watched his strong hands rhythmically milk Bessie and listened to his fantastic tales of anti-gravity flying machines, aliens and spy missions. His short hair, Texas drawl and clean clothes added to his credibility. Rodney didn't look or act like a hippie. For national security reasons, he said, he left out critical bits of information when telling his stories so they would remain confusing. He swore that everything he said was true.

One day a bunch of women decided to go currant picking down by the Rio Grande. Even though it was a warm afternoon, we left our shirts on because of passing pick-up trucks driven by the locals who were both shocked and curious about us. Also, there had been recent reports of violence between hippies and Hispanics in other parts of the valley. Thorny branches filled with tiny berries made currant picking painfully slow. Needing to relieve myself, I walked upstream using nearby leaves to wipe myself. Hours later, when the itching started, I discovered I had used poison ivy. I squirmed my way around the commune trying to scratch my private places, privately.

Many agricultural projects took place at New Buffalo. Raised beds were among the planting methods tried. *Photo by Seth Roffman*

After consulting the bible of herbal cures, *Back to Eden*, Joyce made a poultice of mud, cedar ashes and dried mint. Generous applications onto the afflicted areas stopped the itching, but not my longing for a warm bath in a private bathroom.

Knowing we would soon head back to New York, Faisal and Joyce decided to cook an Arabic feast together. No one objected when Faisal bought lamb and grilled kabobs with fresh zucchini, tomatoes, peppers and onions. A huge pot of brown rice was his only compromise. We met in the courtyard for an evening prayer circle as the sunset played a symphony of colors. Rose became blood red, mauve, and lavender streaked with gold. There was a temporary truce as the farmers, party people, transients, mothers, children, philosophers, workers and poets held hands to share moments of awe and thanksgiving. George started, "Thank you for this day. Thank you for the snow and for the water to grow the crops. Thank you for the food to feed all the people who come to us." Others chimed in and added their prayers, some for people who were gone. Would they remember Faisal and me when we left? A strong hand squeeze followed by a shout of "Amen, let's eat!" signaled the end of the circle.

A fire was lit in the drumming room. Faisal played his oud, joined by drums, flutes and tambourines. Joyce came forward to dance barefoot around the fire. Long dark hair circled her thin wiry body like wings. The arc of her arms obeyed the ever-changing rhythms. With the mystique of an Arabian princess, she faded into the shadows as other women came forward. Faisal had played his oud almost every night we were there. His music would be missed.

Except for the infernal itch, I was in love with life in New Mexico, but Faisal was not impressed by mud homes lit with kerosene lamps and outhouses filled with flies and torn newspapers. With my visions rekindled, we headed back to our New York City tenement. Even as I squirmed and wiggled in the car seat trying to scratch myself, I knew my love affair with New Mexico was just beginning. I would be back.

'Hippie' Problem Stirs More Local Groups to Investigate

by Keith Green

The "hippie question" became more of an issue in Taos this week, with the Taos Chamber of Commerce and at least one service club taking note of what they see as an increasingly difficult problem.

They followed the Taos Ministerial Alliance in discussing the problem. That organization of Catholic and Protestant ministers last week named a small nucleus for a "task force" to determine how best the Christian community can respond to the influx.

The group thought that fact-finding efforts and then interpretation efforts to Taos people might be the first step. A clergyman who has taken an interest in the situation said that he believes there is a need for a "response" to the influx, but not a "reaction." He said "response" inferred a thoughtful and reasoned approach, not an emotional, unreasoning "reaction."

He said, also, that he was concerned about some of the "frightened, uninformed" remarks he had heard from townspeople, indicating the need for opening communications.

Chamber of Commerce directors, meeting Monday, delved into the matter at length, but took no action.

President Manuel Gonzales reported that a self-appointed representative of the hippies would like to speak to the chamber board. After some discussion, the board moved that the man take the matter to the Town Council and County Commission.

Board discussion during the meeting also brought out a number of things the directors believe are central to the problem:

—The renting of a house to one couple, then finding many others moving into it; and, generally, an adverse impact on property values.

—The influence upon young people who have grown up in Taos, some of whom have "joined" the hippies.

—Efforts to open charge accounts for prescription drugs, and apparent quick refilling of prescriptions, raising the question of improper and perhaps illegal drug traffic.

—The possible impact upon the tourist business if there is a great influx this summer.

—The impact upon the county welfare rolls, and the food stamp program. It was suggested that the chamber obtain a report from the welfare department covering the amount of welfare during the past three years.

However, it also was brought out that legal decisions and legal actions rest upon whether there is a violation of law. As an example, it was pointed out that people living together is not a law violation and there's no zoning law to limit the number of persons per dwelling.

It was suggested that a remedy might by through ordinances by the county or the town, in the area of zoning, health and morals.

On Tuesday, the Rotary Club of Taos by resolution set up a committee to approach other organizations to see if they would cooperate in exploring ways to handle present and future "problem" elements of the population.

A major difficulty in assessing the "hippie" impact has been the lack of a definition, and the means of separating the desirable from the undesirable.

Another is the economic impact, whatever the long-range view, of the newcomers who have money to go with their long hair. A Realtor stated flatly this week that property valued at $325,000 had been sold by one firm to "hippies" of one kind or another in the past four months.

With reference to the welfare rolls and food stamp participation, *The Taos News* learned Tuesday that there are "none, or nearly none" of the hippie-type on the welfare rolls. Mrs. Mary Alexander, county welfare director, explained that the state's one-year residence requirement effectively bars transients from receiving welfare.

As to the food stamp program, Mrs. Alexander said her department—by law—can look only at eligibility in determining who may purchase food stamps. Referring to welfare department records, she stated that in March 1968, a total of 3,613 people in Taos County purchased food stamps. In February 1969, the total was 3,714, an increase of 101 in an 11-month period.

Mrs. Alexander stated the department is absolutely required by law to assist any eligible applicant.

Attempts to estimate the total number of hippies in the county elicited widely divergent figures. A state police officer guessed the total as 200; a social worker, as nearer 500.

Nearly everybody agrees that more may be coming this summer. Even the hippie groups—or those who see themselves as permanent, in that they have bought property—are worried about the "bad actors" who may be on the way. Some are actively seeking solutions.

Taos Police Chief Arthur Leach said Tuesday: "I can't, and won't, do anything about this unless these people break the law. They have the same right as any other citizen."

Mary Martinez, Taos County probation officer, said, "most of the young people I have talked to have been good, clean people."

State Police Sgt. Tommy Cantou said there has been "no problem" with the hippies as a group, and added that the legislature's action to reduce the act of possession of marijuana to a misdemeanor should actually help the task of enforcement.

This is Arroyo Hondo, a pristine farming valley and tiny village when the hippies started moving in. Photo by Russell Lee, Farm Security Administration, Library of Congress #F34-34252.

Founding Settler of New Buffalo

told by Joyce Robinson to Iris Keltz

"Max Finstein and I came to New Mexico in 1966 just to live, not to start anything. Max had lived in Taos before and left when his marriage broke up, but he always had eyes to come back. That's how Max's life was. He went from Boston to New Mexico to San Francisco to New Mexico to Israel and then back to New Mexico. He would always leave a place disillusioned.

"When I met Max, he was living with his daughter Rachael and I was living with my son Michael. We were both divorced. Max was doing what he always did—write poetry, get high, visit with people and work. If you had to label Max something, he was beat. But he really wasn't that either. He was always his own man. He had friends and acquaintances in every corner. He loved people—whenever he spent a lot of time alone he got depressed.

"I went back East to see an old friend who was getting married. The ceremony took place in Steve and Barbara Durkee's church in upstate New York. It was the first and only time I met the Durkees until I moved to New Mexico where they helped found the Lama Foundation. The ceremonies were based on the Native American Church. Steve and Barbara already had a communal thing going. I took a lot of acid that night and it triggered something inside of me. I thought to myself, I love a lot of people so why don't we all live together?

"It took months to adjust when I returned to San Francisco. Max and I lived on Haight Street with our two children, Michael and Rachael. It was before The Diggers came and the neighborhood was still quiet. By the time we left, there were cops on every corner and stoned people everywhere.

New Buffalo founders and visionaries, late '60s (left to right): Mary Mitchell, Buffalo Bob Wertz, Joyce Finstein holding baby Jamil, Max Finstein, Rick Klein, Susan Bandura, Pat McMahon, Steve Ranes, Julie Von Erffa, Robbie Gordon, Jason, Dhugal, Solomon; (back row): Lenny Goodman (back of his head only!), George Robinson, Robbie Goodman, Alex Robinson, Michael Reich, Denise Lassaw, Chris Robinson, Dave Robinson, Dave Gordon, Jessie Hinton, Rachel, Beatle, Beverly, Aleks Hinton, Jenna Hinton, Justin Case, Bill Berlin, Carol Hinton, Steve Hinton, Pabla, Freida, Brian Anderson, Judy & Paul Berner. *Photo courtesy of Alfred Hobbs*

"We came back to New Mexico in April 1966, and lived in a little village in the Pecos Wilderness called La Cueva. We were very high all the time, always stoned out on marijuana. I helped Max drink his daily bottle of wine. When we moved in, we threw a big party and invited all the local hippies. I only remember one of them—John, a New York artist, who did smashed automobile sculptures. He and Max had been friends in New York. Life was exciting.

"After a few months we moved to Santa Fe and started talking about living with some other families. I was a lot crazier about the idea than Max. He liked being around people but had his doubts about living communally. Around this time, Max heard from Rick Klein, a young poet from Pittsburgh. Somewhere along the line they had connected. When Rick arrived in New Mexico, he told Max, 'I have a sum of money that I'll put up to buy a place.' We thought, Wow!—this must be the thing to do.

"Friends of ours, George and Mary, showed up at our house with their three boys. They had just come from living in Mexico. They also had the idea of living communally. Someone knew about a piece of land in Arroyo Hondo, north of Taos—103 acres of sage and piñon with water rights. We went to look at it and everyone said, 'Wow!' Rick paid the $55,000. That is the present site of New Buffalo.

"People who knew Rick from Pittsburgh started showing up. Justin and his pregnant wife came from California in a bubble-top van. I'm not sure who knew them. Justin used to drive along the dirt roads with his feet on the steering wheel rolling a joint, while talking and waving his arms.

"We held a peyote meeting to consecrate our moving onto the land. At first we all lived in tipis. Buffalo was the sustenance of the Plains Indians. We believed that we'd live off the land and this place would be our sustenance. So we called our commune New

Buffalo. We had an ideal, a belief that people could live together in peace. I never missed city life and urban culture.

"With the help of a midwife, Justin's wife had her baby within a few days of living at the commune, a beautiful simple birth. Someone else had a birthday. The beginning days were festive. We arrived on a virgin piece of land, planted a huge garden and built an outdoor kitchen with a chunk of money from Rick and cooked like crazy.

"At first we ate lavishly, like chile rellenos for breakfast. We were not vegetarians and only stayed on the macrobiotic diet five days. No one could stand it. The diet we ended up with on the commune was due to the fact that our money ran out. A spirit of poverty was there, the desire to get along on as little as possible.

"We started building right away. We asked a lot of questions and figured out how to build with adobe. The locals were curious about what we were doing and used to drive along the ditch road all the time. Since we used to bathe in the ditch, there was often a naked person there, but for the most part we didn't walk around naked. Nudity was not one of the maxims. We liked loose clothes and long skirts from the free box on the commune.

"We were a bunch of spaced-out city people doing a lot of marijuana and trying to live in the country. We built an open kitchen and an open outhouse. We didn't believe in closing anything. That was one of the rebellions against our parents' generation. To put up a facade was considered hypocritical. Letting it all hang out was one of our philosophies, meaning, if you have to go to the bathroom, it's okay to do it in the presence of someone else. One of our mistakes was building the outhouse too close to the kitchen. We never considered the flies or the wind. Before the fall, everyone got sick together, too.

Watching New Buffalo burn, 1967—Mary Robinson and Chris, Jane and Dogan, Michael, Bob and Black Dog in foreground, and Joyce. *Photo courtesy Rick and Terry Klein*

"From the very beginning there were visitors. They came in cycles. The first winter was wonderful because the visiting stopped and we just had each other. It was not anarchy because whenever you have a group, some people are natural leaders like Justin and George. They were the most responsible of the men. I was an unacknowledged leader of the women. Justin's wife made it clear from the beginning that she didn't go for all this outdoor stuff. She was a self-proclaimed pad chick, but we got along well because you could always count on her to do her part of the work.

"One of the most interesting group meetings was the one on electricity—to have or have not.

Barefoot in the mud pits—making adobe bricks at New Buffalo. The hill in the background led up to a mesa that was totally wild and barren. That was the late '60s. Now, in the year 2000, it's covered with homes. *Photo by Lisa Law*

There were the purists and there were those who wanted to run power tools and a radio. It caused a bitter fight. One married couple was on different sides and didn't speak for days. The pro-electricity people finally won and we got our chain saw, power tools, a well and a radio.

"The first summer we built a kitchen and a huge round room with a sleeping loft. We never finished the west wall so we put up bails of hay. With the spring came the west winds. One day the kids were playing with matches and the hay caught fire. Within twenty minutes it was hopeless. We got all the kids out safely. The only thing we lost was a litter of kittens. The fire department came really quickly. The wind just tore through that building like it was nothing.

"The neat thing was that someone had given us a deer and some of the meat had been sitting in a pan in the kitchen waiting to be put in the oven. When the fire was over, the deer was perfectly cooked. There was a pot of chicos and beans on the stove that was also perfectly cooked. We had all this food to eat so we had a party!

"Nobody was hurt and so outside of all the work we'd put in, it was no tragedy. There was one piece of paper floating in the wind from the I Ching and it said Youthful Folly. Some friends were living in downtown Hondo and invited all twenty-five of us to come and stay at their house for the night. We ended up having a blast of a party. Everyone was stoned on grass as well as the experience.

"The day after the house burned down, we talked about what to do. We salvaged as many bricks as we could. We also had several sacks of wheat. We went through each grain and saved those that weren't too burned. The rest was ground into flour. For months, everything tasted like fire.

"The summer our place burned down, mattresses, blankets and clothing were sent to us from people from all over the country. Thousands of them came to see us. We put all able-bodied visitors to work. All of a sudden there was a large-scale migration of people and New Buffalo was one of the meeting places. People from all over the country were tired of the old order and longed for something else. We happened to be some of the first people to manifest the idea.

"The guys were out there every day making new bricks. That summer we rebuilt the kitchen and the circle room. Through that summer, fall and winter, we made seven rooms and two communal rooms. Rick left the commune that summer but gave us money to build. The money lasted exactly one year.

"My relationship with Max fell apart that winter. He lived at New Buffalo for one year before growing restless. He needed to be master of his time, socialize when he wanted, get high when he wanted, write poetry and work when he wanted. Max was not interested in becoming part of the evolving structure. He didn't want to be a chief, but he didn't want to be restricted by someone else. He was not a rural hippy and wasn't connected with the other men who had become the honchos.

"George and I got together and he broke up with his wife. In those days the phrase 'free love' was tossed all over the place. It meant people sleeping with whoever they wanted to sleep with. People not living communally thought we were terrible and immoral but they also thought, I'd like to do something like that but I'm not free enough. Being part of the group that believed in free love, I found out that this practice created hurt. There was always someone being left behind. When there were families involved, it was more complicated and hurtful.

"Living within the communal family, we had an inability to retain our family identity with all the distractions. Before I got together with George, the group identity was more interesting than being wife and mother. My whole being went into that place. I got up before the sun and washed in cold water, worked in the garden and cooked breakfast for huge numbers of people. At one point we had twenty acres of wheat growing. I didn't know I could work that hard. I enjoyed those traditional roles more than I thought I would, but there was also the freedom to not cook everyday. A great sisterhood grew among the women who lived there, a lifetime bond. Even when I stood for hours in front of the wringer washing machine, it never seemed like drudgery.

"There were two strong opposing factions—the family/work people and the party people led by Buffalo Bob. It wasn't until after his death that we realized what he was doing. His philosophy was eat, drink and be merry because tomorrow I'm going to die. We didn't know he had tuberculosis. We kept getting together and having meetings but he just didn't care. Bob was one of Rick's friends from Pittsburgh and one of the original members of the commune. In the beginning he would work sometimes, but he split when he felt like it. Towards the end of his life, he retired to his room. He drew people into his room, offering them dope and telling them, 'The heck with these people. You don't really have to work here.'

Group OM in the courtyard of New Buffalo led by Tom Law, a yoga teacher and follower of Yogi Bhajan (circa 1967). The whole time I was connected with New Buffalo, meditation was not a regular practice. Yoga and meditation were more common at Lama.

Photo by Lisa Law

"If 15 people came by in a bus at dinnertime, we always fed them. It was beautiful at first. I always enjoyed meeting new people, but after two years it became exhausting. I didn't care who was going to get off the bus. It became evident to those of us who had families that it was important to preserve our family identities. At this point, I was happily married to George and sharing a life with the children we had brought from previous marriages. This was something I had never been able to do before and it filled up my life.

"After the founding group, New Buffalo never attracted families. Part of what happens in a commune is a reconstruction of a tribal society—that is what drew me in the first place to the commune, the support system. People can talk about doing their own thing but it's impossible. People were made to share and interact. The commune replaced the support system we had rejected. The only communes I ever heard that worked were committed to religious or political ideals, but back-to-the-land isn't enough.

"The original settlers had dreams and ideals of communal living, but not at the cost of the dissolution of our families. After a few years, it became obvious that we were more interested in building and sustaining our marriages and families. When you live with twenty people from ages 12 to 40, you have to expend a lot of energy. My interest in relating to all those people every day faded. But we couldn't close the doors to the commune because we didn't believe in that. We were caught in the Catch-22 of our own philosophy.

"In the beginning we jumped into this new life feeling that each person who lived and ate there would be a contributing party. In the end, I don't see the planet surviving for much longer, but while we're here we must make the most out of each day."

Update:
Joyce is now a born-again Christian, active in a Holy Spirit-filled church. The basis of her life for the past 26 years is her relationship with Jesus. Her love for Jesus is manifest in a happy peaceful marriage and great relationships with her five children and nine grandchildren. She plays keyboard with a small band at her church. Her husband George has a Maps and Old Print Shop in Taos. They have secured a comfortable life style. In a fearful world, Joyce has found great peace. Everything she was searching for in the commune she found in Jesus.

'Hippie Problem" Answers Sought By Committee Set Up By Town

by Keith Green

Taos Town Council members Monday unofficially began an investigation of the "hippie problem" in a session with representatives of a number of organizations, and the upshot was the formation of a committee to continue the study—and primarily, to communicate with the newcomers.

Mrs. Ashley Pond, who chaired the meeting, emphasized the need for communication: "We've got to be able to let them know what the town thinks of them."

Among those named to the committee—scheduled to meet again next Tuesday afternoon—are Mrs. Tom Ward, Eliu Romero, John Quintana, Mary Alexander, Joe Martinez, Rene Oppenheimer, Olando Anaya, Rev. Robert Salazar, and two identified with the "hippie" element—Jane Urvach and Joseph Sage.

Working with the group will be Minor Van Arsdale, of Santa Fe, who said he had been employed by the State Department of Health and Social Services under its federally financed community services program to work with communities in handling such problems as are developing in Taos.

He said his own working definition of a hippie of the problem variety was: One who uses drugs, and who considers himself completely separate from the established order.

Van Arsdale also gave as a definition of the Taos problem that most present seemed to accept: "The hippies represent a threat to our established way of life."

That threat has many manifestations, according to those attending:

—Incidents of drug (marijuana) use in the schools. Supt. Joe L. Otero said about 14 Taos High School students had literally joined the hippies.

—Public nudity in areas such as Manby and Ponce de Leon Springs, and at least one reported incident of sexual intercourse in a public place.

—The health hazard posed by lack of cleanliness, the spreading of such diseases as hepatitis through handling of food in grocery stores, and the increasing incidence of venereal diseases. These health problems were confirmed by Dr. Reynaldo Deveaux, president of the Taos County Medical Society, and by Joe Martinez, venereal disease investigator for the state.

—Overcrowding of dwellings, without the knowledge of landlords, to the landlords' detriment.

Other incidents were touched upon by those present, including the matter of food stamps and welfare participation, and the consensus seemed to be that state, county and town have the authority and the laws to control the "hippie problem."

The question essentially is one of enforcement, they felt.

Asst. Dist. Atty. John Sanchez emphasized however that enforcement must be equally applied; that no agency could use harassment against a particular group. He said he had heard the Taos Police Commission had considered recommending that procedure, but Mrs. Pond—a Town Council member—said no such plan had been brought to the council by the commission.

Hanging over the whole meeting were restraining laws such as constitutional guarantees and civil right legislation.

The owner of Spivey's Café said he had ended his own problem of service to those he believes undesirable on health grounds by posting a sign stating: "We reserve the right to refuse service to those we consider a health menace." He said he had consulted his attorney about that approach, and had been assured it was legal. At least one other business place has adopted the same sign.

One woman, Jane Urvach, who said she was speaking for one of the hippie "families," met with the committee following the open session. She said many newcomers to Taos want to contribute to the community, and be self-supporting, and that they are willing to cooperate with authorities in removing the "undesirable" elements.

Letter to a relative

...When I last saw you, we spoke of my using my college background in some way. Social work or some connection with a university are paths with a future, you said. Perhaps I read the future differently. A voice within my heart directed me along a path quite different than that advised by my elders. I want to tell you about it, but it is so difficult to express what is so deep and obvious to me, and what must seem so weird and hopeless and far-fetched to you...It isn't so much that young people lack respect for our elders, as that we want to direct our energies along a different path. Rather than stay involved in a corrupt and dying society, we want to reestablish contact with the source of all value and creativity, and start anew. My only ambition is to do God's will.

The slogan now is REVOLUTION, a peaceful revolution through the evolution of the human species. So there are young people leaving the cities to get back to the land. "Farming!? There's no future in that." But here is the only possible, hopeful future for the earth...to give up our material 'progress' for the sake of the progress of the human soul. The land and its life have much to teach us, and what looks like a step backward may take us much further spiritually than a rocket to the moon.

Surely, we work for peace on earth. Some march and protest for peace; some pray and fast in silence for peace, and give up involvement with the great Machine that made the bomb. We each do what we can.

There is peace in these mountains, on this land, a peace that can reach into your heart if you let it. The luxuries and comforts we thought we needed in the cities never gave us the sense of being at home on the earth, which we have now. We've been learning all we can about conservation, organic farming, natural foods, herbal medicine, handcrafts, building—all that it takes to live simply and in harmony with our beautiful land, our animals, our bodies and spirits.

There is a great satisfaction in living in a shelter built by loving hands, wearing clothes made with love, eating food grown and prepared with love, warmed by a fire of wood gathered with love, and seeing by light of candles made with love; the experience is so full and continuous with life, with this earth which God created with Love. The sunset was beautiful tonight. This meadow, these mountains are a constant source of inspiration and delight. We don't want to exploit this land, these animals, these brothers and sisters. We don't want to go into business and make money. We want to live and grow, and treat all things with love and respect.

Keep faith in your heart,
Mara

Close Encounters with New Buffalo

by Iris Keltz

It was one year before I returned to New Buffalo. By then I was free, single and twenty-something, accountable only to the demands of my personal whimsy.

"Casablanca" played on television my last night in New York. When Rick and Louie were toasting to a glorious future, I wept with empathy. The pain of leaving my marriage merged with a sense of limitless possibilities.

I'd lived in my fourth-floor tenement too long. Summer evenings found me on the rooftop, watching science-fiction colors spew forth through a smoggy sunset while I herded my imaginary flock of sheep. Tribal rhythms beat in the night from the bongo players in Tompkins Square Park, giving the illusion that we were a heartbeat away from an African village. Chimneys belching black smoke from spiraling skyscrapers became less real than my vision of life in a commune.

That winter Faisel and I had gotten a letter from Moe, the New Buffalo goat lady, offering us a room if we wanted to come back. In my buoyant optimism, it never dawned on me that a vacant room meant an indication of drastic change. I remembered the New Age-extended families, bands of naked roving kids, orgiastic nights of drumming and dancing around fires, sleeping under a canopy of stars in a tipi, getting stoned and meetings with remarkable people. I couldn't wait to return.

Faisal did not share my enthusiasm for fly-ridden outhouses, kerosene lamps, the one group bathroom and no privacy. For me, the idea of going to graduate school or getting a permanent job

Posing in front of Bella Blue, the station wagon that took me to New Mexico. I quit my teaching job in New York, fixed up my '56 Chevy wagon, loaded my possessions, and headed out along the Jersey Turnpike singing "Cast Your Fate to the Wind." I cruised along Route 66 into Albuquerque—though I had to give Bella a quart of oil every 50 miles—never doubting my date with destiny.

Photo by Paul Dembski

at a moment when the world was in transformation felt like shackles on the heels of possibility. I was willing to embrace poverty if it meant building a new way of life. I was convinced we were fated to slay the dragon of American imperialism and greed.

I sang along with the Jefferson Airplane, "*We are all outlaws in the eyes of America.*" Faisal and I spent hours discussing our ideological differences. I always got stuck defending Western civilization in general and hippies in particular. Faisal called America decadent, confusing, and wished he could return to Jerusalem.

"You're lucky to have a place on earth to love. Look at me, I'm from Queens, New York. If someone told me I could never go back there, I wouldn't give a damn." Faisal said he loved Queens with its quiet neighborhoods and would be happy to live near my mother in Middle Village. The differences tore us asunder.

I asked for our tent, my sleeping bag and a brass candelabra that had been a wedding gift from my mother. It took a few minutes to divide everything we'd collected in our three-year non-materialistic marriage. I quit my teaching job, fixed up the '56 Chevy wagon, loaded my possessions and left New York singing "Cast Your Fate to the Wind" along the Jersey Turnpike, cruising along Route 66 into Albuquerque, never doubting my date with destiny.

A shock greater than the ruts in the driveway met me that blustery day in March. Most of my friends from last summer had left the commune. My optimism gave way to confusion as thick as the snow clouds enshrouding the mountain peaks. Only English Jane and redheaded Richard still lived here and they were anxious to rent their own house. They'd just had a baby and kept to themselves. Why did the people who built this place with the sweat from their dreams leave so suddenly?

Reggie the Hermit remembered me. I had barely noticed him last summer since he tended to become invisible in groups. Susan from the corner room still lived here and asked about Faisal—she had just ended a long-term relationship with her old man and was eager to have someone to talk to.

"We split up in New York and I'm traveling alone. Where's Moe?" I asked. "She wrote us a letter inviting us to come back with the promise of a room."

"A few weeks ago Moe and Ira rented a house twenty miles north of here, near Questa." After giving directions, she added, "And you're welcome to share my room." I thanked her for the offer.

A very pregnant Moe quietly greeted me at the door. Her effusive joy was subdued. She no longer walked around half naked, flashing a wicked grin, saying "far out" and "dynamite."

"Remember that cute guy I liked last summer? Well, we got together on Halloween. He works at the Moly Mine. Now we're havin' a baby." She never told me why they left New Buffalo but her energies were clearly focused on her family and their newfound religion. Taking out a handmade cedar box, she showed me her sacred hawk and eagle feathers. Her days were filled with rubbing cocoa butter on her belly to prevent stretch marks and beading fans for the feathers. In hushed tones she intimated the great power and mystery of the Peyote Church.

"You're welcome to spend the night," she said, clearly defining her boundaries. We had a great visit. In the morning I drove to New Buffalo and never saw her again. With deflated expectations, I moved onto the commune anyway but gone was the sense of collective purpose. Carloads of people came and went all spring and summer. The ballast and vision had left with the founding families.

Susan informed me when the sun moved into Leo and then Virgo or when the moon was conjunct with some celestial body. Otherwise the days rolled uneventfully off the calendar. Susan volunteered to work at DaNahazli, the local hippie school in Taos. Her corner room at New Buffalo was lighter than most because it had two windows, one facing the east and the other looking onto the courtyard. Two single beds lined the walls separated by a pot-bellied stove in the corner. Kerosene lamps stood on the hand-made wood shelves that held all her books and clothing.

In the morning, one of us would sprinkle water and rake the dirt floor to keep the dust down. In the evenings, we'd stoke up the wood stove to warm the room and make a pot of tea. Reggie the Hermit sometimes joined us for a cup of Mu tea, salad and a Milky Way. His blue eyes hiding behind wire-rimmed spectacles were usually focused on some invisible horizon or buried in a book. A scant beard covered his pointy chin. I'd heard from someone he was a draft dodger, but he never talked about it. His room was like an animal's lair. Old turds were thrown in the fireplace and an army blanket hung over the only window, leaving the space in perpetual twilight. He was a pack rat and piles of old newspapers and books lined his walls.

Susan and Reggie had lived here through the heyday of the commune, when the original settlers were still here. Now they were disillusioned burned-out hippies who didn't know what to do next. Although people still ate in the communal kitchen, neither of them did. They had little interest in farming, gardening or in caring for the animals, but no one asked them to leave. If I was ever to meet the other people living here, I would have to get away from them.

There was less partner swapping and sexual promiscuity than the outside world imagined. No one seemed anxious to get attached or make a personal commitment, but even if you were single you never had to be lonely. Being one of the oldest women living there—23—and owning a running vehicle gave me instant respectability. On Susan's food-stamp day, we'd go to Safeway. I chipped in for groceries, which we kept in our room, not in the communal kitchen. The commune had become a group of individual hoarders.

We cooked our food on an old wood stove. Cedar wood burnt hot and smelled sweet. It took a few tries before I learned to build a fire. I loved to smell a pot of chile and beans cooking on the wood stove.

Photo by Paul Dembski

Soon other women asked me for rides to the laundromat or to carry groceries on food-stamp days. Thus began new friendships. Kathleen, sinewy and graceful, looked like Diana the Huntress galloping across the mesa on her white horse naked from the waist up. Returning to the pueblo with rabbits and prairie dogs slung over her strong shoulders, she skinned rabbits near the woodpile, in full sight of everyone, flashing her emerald eyes and her knife. Her nakedness was untamed. She was haughty towards the men except for Taylor, her hunting and fishing mentor. If he wasn't hunting, he was in his room near the kitchen sharpening his knives or tying fish flies. Kathleen's love for Taylor was unrequited. He told everyone there was a woman waiting for him in California.

Kathleen had taken over Moe's job as the goat lady. She loved the animals and made sure they had food. I helped her by hauling sacks of grain from the Feed Bin or transporting Mama Goat when she needed to get pregnant. Kathleen encouraged me to eat some meals in the communal kitchen. Soon after, I volunteered to cook dinner there a few nights a week.

Elaine the Lovely was Kathleen's closest friend. Her perfectly shaped breasts were brown from her sitting in the sun while weaving belts on a Navajo handloom—wearing only a cotton drawstring skirt. Her waist and her age were 19. Everything about her was sensual and soft, like someone's dream of the perfect valentine. When Kathleen went hunting, Elaine and I would lean against an adobe wall in the courtyard and weave silences around our talk. The loudest noise in the world was the buzzing of flies. We discovered we were both from Queens and became instant sisters-in-exile. Carlos, her lover, was a handsome Chicano from California with a deadly weakness for cheap wine. He was a gifted writer and a vo-

One of the favorite all-time hippie vehicles, this Paradise Now/Hello Forever VW bus belonged to a guy named Carl. He arrived in New Mexico in it with an entourage of friends, lovers, an ex-wife and a kid.

Photo by Paul Dembski

racious reader, consuming books in the commune's library. Sometimes their screams of joy filled the courtyard, but at other times the courtyard echoed with sobbing, angry shouts, and broken bottles. Elaine the Lovely eventually found the strength to kick Carlos the hell out of her room.

Elaine, Kathleen and I were concerned about Sadira who was seven months pregnant and lived alone in a room on the western wing of the pueblo. Sadira's head was crowned with curly red hair and her face and body were covered with freckles. Her voice and mannerisms reminded me of my Aunt Betty from the Bronx. She sat naked on her wooden bed folding hand-me-down baby clothes. Wooden shelves strung from the vigas were already filled with baby stuff. An empty cradle sat next to her bed. She never spoke of the father but rumors floated that she'd gotten pregnant while visiting an ashram in Hawaii, which was believable since she meditated twice a day and smiled a lot in the midst of chaos. She planned on delivering the baby in her room with the help of a midwife. Kathleen and I placed our hands on her undulating belly to feel the unborn life. When Jamil was born, he looked like a little Buddha who told the world of a copper-colored daddy with dark almond-shaped eyes. I was disappointed that I was gone when she gave birth.

One evening in late spring, the weather turned cold again. Susan came home from town early and stoked up the wood stove. Reggie the Hermit wandered in; so did Elaine the Lovely. Snow whipped around the courtyard and thick clouds hung low over the mountains. Susan got to telling stories about the early days of the commune.

"Whatever happened to Buffalo Bob, the Philosopher King of the New Buffalo kitchen?" I asked.

"He died of TB last winter. One week he started coughing up blood. I don't think anyone knew what was wrong with him. Someone took him to Holy Cross Hospital, where he died after twelve hours. It was George who went to claim his body even though they'd fought constantly when Bob was alive. Bob was buried on the edge of an arroyo, overlooking the commune. A pile of stones marks the grave. His last request to his friends was to prohibit any bullshit ritual at his funeral. Over 200 people showed up. Everyone was high. Four friends carried his wasted body and put him into the grave. Someone covered his face with dirt before shovels all around started filling in the hole." I remembered his haunted eyes and hoped he was in the white light he talked so much about.

When spring broke through again, I went to visit Joyce who lived at the other end of the Hondo Valley with her family. I remembered her as the Arabian princess who'd danced around the fire last summer. It was about a three-mile walk along the river, past the post office, Selso's Bar and across the highway. Joyce was diapering her baby when I got there. With safety pins in her mouth, she smiled and gestured me to come in. I walked past the laundry flapping in the breeze. Her long hair was cut short. After admiring the baby—her fourth—and drinking a cup of coffee, I asked why she'd left New Buffalo, hoping she'd tell me it was a terrible mistake. Her energy and vision had helped start the commune. George, her husband, had laid the adobes for the pueblo and plowed the land. Now they rented a small adobe house with minimal comforts. It had a cold-water tap in the kitchen and an outhouse in the back yard. Humor mixed with rancor when she spoke.

"Someday we're going to take that place back." From whom, I wondered? It had been their choice to move away and they were free to move back if they wanted. We sat at her kitchen table while she cut meat off an enormous bone.

"Chile stew for dinner. Want to stay?" She was calm and centered in her home.

"Can't. Promised to cook at Buffalo tonight."

Her family were no longer rice-and-beans hippies. Eating meat was daring at a time when people believed that vegetarians ascended more easily into the spiritual realms of universal peace and love. Everyone knew that meat eaters were more exploitive to the environment, more aggressive with their fellow humans and definitely not as healthy. Closer to the truth was the fact that unless someone went hunting or slaughtered an animal it was expensive to buy meat at the supermarket for a large group. Like Moe, Joyce's family went to Peyote Church meetings that gave everyone a sense of spiritual community without having to live communally.

Joyce gave me baby blankets and clothes to take back for Sadira. When I went to her room, Cave Dave was doing a silent vigil over the sleeping mother and baby. In his chaste way, Cave Dave was devoted to Sadira and Jamil. Before moving to New Buffalo he'd taken a vow of silence while living in a cave for three months. He carried around a little chalkboard to write cryptic messages on. He lived in the greenhouse because of his need to be in constant touch with the plants. He was into "vibrational biology." I'd talk to Cave Dave instead of writing in my journal and my words bounced back to me across the silence.

The first time I heard him speak was at a peyote meeting. It blasted his image of deep, centered and wise. He confessed in front of everyone to having lustful thoughts about another man's wife. If only he'd lusted after Sadira who needed a father for her baby, but he thought of her like the Virgin Mother.

One day, we heard gunshots in the courtyard and hoped it wasn't Toby run amuck. Toby was a casualty from Vietnam who'd left an essential part of himself there. No one knew the extent of his delusions that became violent when he got angry. Maybe he was still fighting the Viet Cong in his mind. Guns were kept away from him because he was capable of shooting himself or someone else. Certain women, like Sadira the Virgin Mother or Elaine the Lovely, invoked the gentle side of this man, who treated them with southern civility saying "yes ma'am" or "no ma'am" to their requests. He had the confused look of a person whose main victim is himself. When I opened the door to the courtyard, Elaine was scolding Toby as if he were a naughty kid and Taylor had already gotten his hunting gun back.

When Jamil was one month old, Elaine and I went with Sadira to Black Rock Hot Springs for the baby's baptism. We followed the Hondo River two miles into the Rio Grande gorge where swallows' nests and stubborn weeds clung to slate grey volcanic cliffs. When we got to the John Dunn Bridge, there was only one car parked at the top of the hill where the narrow footpath to the river started. That meant the hot springs wouldn't be too crowded. We passed the cave where Dave once lived. Down at the river, a circle of black rocks held water flowing from the bowels of the earth. Baby Jamil floated contentedly between us as we passed around a joint and talked about nothing in particular. The day was cloudless. After a while, I jumped into the icy river and swam across the current to the other bank. People from all over the world somehow found this pool. When someone washed dirty socks and underwear in the hot springs, I lost hope for the peace and harmony promised by the Aquarian Age.

Towards the end of my stay at New Buffalo, the fire rarely burned in the circle room. Communal meals and prayer circles were occasional. One day some visitors showed up from California and gave everyone a hit of mescaline. That night the fire in the drumming room burned until dawn. People came out of their rooms and shared food and played music. We wandered down to the hot springs and made love under the full moon. The founding families were gone but on nights like this I dreamed that one day new people would drive up—wisdom disguised as gypsy-clad hippies—and revive the vision. When the drug wore off and the sun came up, the temporary unity crumbled like dry sod.

Meditating at Stagecoach Hot Springs. We all loved to go to the various hot springs, which caused much distress to the powers-that-were. People were arrested for nudity and Ponce de Leon Hot Springs was closed by order of the Health Department. Of course, some hot springs lovers couldn't resist and where there's a will there were ways.
Photo by Paul Dembski

New Buffalo nurtured me and became my home in spite of the disappointments. One day I heard of a dream fomenting on the other side of the valley—a dream of an experimental high school—a school of life—and I followed the sound of the piper across the valley and left.

LA RAZA & NEWCOMERS

Fountain of Light *(reprinted from* **EL GRITO DEL NORTE***)*

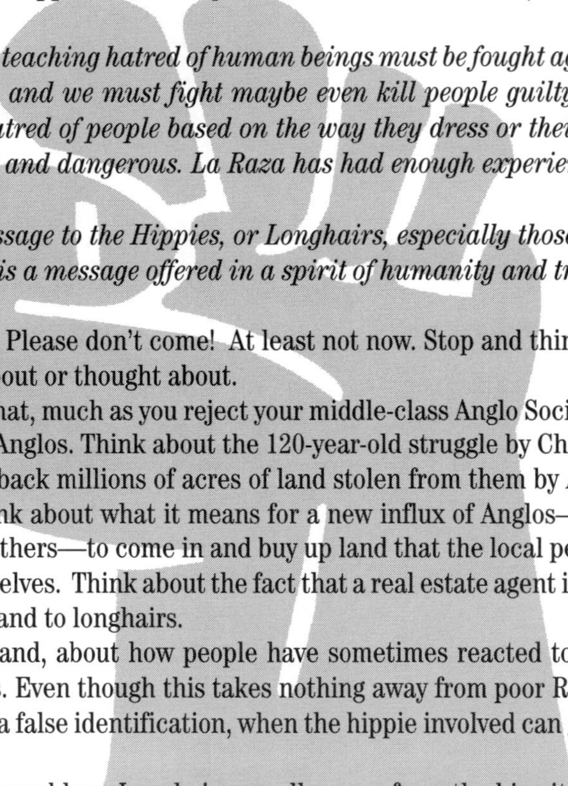

After talking with many people, EL GRITO has come to some conclusion about the Hippie Question.The first one is this: Any violation of anybody's civil rights is a threat to everybody. If the police are today arresting Hippies when they have committed no crime, they can arrest you tomorrow—in the same way.

The second one is that teaching hatred of human beings must be fought against. We can hate injustice or oppression or lies, and we must fight maybe even kill people guilty of these crimes against humanity. But to teach hatred of people based on the way they dress or their religion or whatever it is—this is dehumanizing and dangerous. La Raza has had enough experience of this, not to become guilty of it toward others.

The third one is a message to the Hippies, or Longhairs, especially those who are thinking about coming to New Mexico. It is a message offered in a spirit of humanity and truth-telling.

The basic message is: Please don't come! At least not now. Stop and think about a few things that you may not have heard about or thought about.

Think about the fact that, much as you reject your middle-class Anglo Society and its values, you are still seen here as Gringos-Anglos. Think about the 120-year-old struggle by Chicanos and the even older struggle by Indians to get back millions of acres of land stolen from them by Anglo ranchers with their Anglo lawyer buddies. Think about what it means for a new influx of Anglos—no matter how different their purpose from those others—to come in and buy up land that the local people feel to be theirs and cannot afford to buy themselves. Think about the fact that a real estate agent in Taos reports having sold almost $500,000 worth of land to longhairs.

Think, on the other hand, about how people have sometimes reacted to hippies who get welfare payments and food stamps. Even though this takes nothing away from poor Raza people, they have felt resentment. It seems like a false identification, when the hippie involved can get money from home or a decent job if necessary.

Think about the water problem. Longhairs usually come from the big city, not knowing that water here is precious and often hard to get. They see a stream and wash their feet or dishes in it. Hey! That's our drinking water. We are used to being abused, scorned, ignored—but that's too much.

Think about not only the land and the water, but also the culture. Longhairs come, often deliberately unwashed and ungroomed in their rebellion against a sterile, hypocritical middle-class society. They don't see that, for the Spanish-speaking people, cleanliness is a weapon of cultural self-defense against the oppressor. It is not a symbol of hypocrisy but part of the little pride and self-respect left to them, preciously guarded. So is conventional sexual morality: tight-knit family is everywhere a source of strength and unity against a hostile environment. Longhair values might sometimes be better—but they cannot be imposed. Especially when you are not joining the struggle of the people against the oppression which is the source of many Raza values.

Think about the educational advantages that you often have—whether you wanted to have them or not. You can come here and start a little business, and you will often succeed where Raza people fail (or would not even try). "Son muy vivo," Raza people say—"the hippies are very bright." It is often true, it is not your "fault," but it is important to remember how many millions of times the Anglo's education and technology helped to make him a successful oppressor. If you say, "I've come to learn from the people," excuse us if we sometimes remember: that's what the Anglos said when they came to the Sierra Nevada, learned from us how to mine—and then drove us out, even murdered us.

Think about yourself, and just how clear you are about rejecting your own society's values. Recent events here have shown that, when things get heavy, the longhairs sometimes act very much like the society they have fled. When a hippie woman was raped by a Chicano youth (because the Chicanos don't understand free women and because they have been taught not to see hippies as human beings), the longhair men called the cops—THE COPS. In another case, the longhair went out and shot the Chicano dead for supposedly raping "his" woman, and he got off, with a hung jury.

Think about this: the longhair has opted out—most of the Chicanos and Indians have no option, except revolution. People here cannot flee to islands of peace in a nation of horrors, this is their nation. It cannot be said too often: there is a long, hard political and economic struggle in these beautiful mountains, a struggle for land and justice. That struggle calls for fighters and supporters, not refugees with their own set of problems. You may see the scenery as relief from an oppressive America. We see a battleground against oppression.

Think about this: if you (rightly) condemn your own society, your own culture, so strongly—why not go where it is, and change it? And if your answer to that is "I can't" or "I won't," then think about what this answer implies—and whether you are then a person needed by people here, who can be useful here.

Now, finally, please think about this: If you must come, wait a while. Wait until things cool off for longhairs, wait until the speed freaks have (hopefully) left, wait until the longhairs who are already here can develop a better climate—if they can. While you wait, read and learn about this part of the country. Read what has been done to the people here by the white man, find out why they see Kit Carson and all those other frontier types as murderers—not heroes; find out what the U.S. Forest Service and Smokey the Bear represent here. Don't just put on a long skirt and beads, and think you understand "the Indians"; too many rich tourist ladies do that too. Learn Spanish, learn about the everyday culture, hang around some poor Spanish-speaking families. Learn about the tradition of courtesy, and why you must not presume on it. Learn some humility. Look in yourself for unconscious arrogance and selfishness.

Ask yourself, what do I know? Do you know how many Mexican-Americans there are in this country? Do you know that, in terms of education and jobs, they are worse off even than the blacks? Can you imagine what it is to speak one language as a child and then suddenly be dumped into a classroom where another is enforced on you—and fall behind in class, and then be told you are stupid?

Can you see the difference between being poor and being without money? Can you go to a demonstration by poor people and let them run it their way, and not impose your style as did some longhairs in Santa Fe recently? Can you show respect for another people's culture and not be disrespectful simply because that's the way you feel toward your own culture? Can you, in other words, do some hard thinking?

If you think, you won't come. Not now. Any when you do come, come as a revolutionary.

TLC: Better Known as Taos Learning Center

by Iris Keltz

It started as a dream: A school where our children would not be limited to the meager curricula of public schools. The teaching would be relevant—learning how to build shelters, grow food, tan hides, make tipis and survive in the wilderness—but this wouldn't stop us from studying ancient civilizations, literature, science and mathematics. The Taos Learning Center would value and celebrate individual differences while embracing our common humanity.

Kathleen Summit, a local storyteller who lived on the Seco rim road, invited me to live with her for the winter. *Photo by Seth Roffman*

Colin and Adela (not their real names) donated their home in Arroyo Hondo to create this utopian vision of a community school. Having two teenagers of their own, they understood the great need for this alternative learning environment. In return, they asked volunteers to help build a small adobe house on their land. Colin was a potter by craft, an architect by degree and head of the building crew. We had no idea the two loves of his life—pottery and architecture—were about to merge.

John Kimmey, who helped start the Santa Fe Community School, moved up to Taos to become the headmaster of the Learning Center. His pioneering efforts in developing a state-approved alternative school were well known in northern New Mexico. A freshman from Antioch College was recruited to assist John as a student teacher.

People found their way to this corner of the Hondo valley from all over the country, creating a steady flow of free labor all summer. We slept in tents, tipis, school buses, campers, vans or under the stars. A hodgepodge village emerged on what came to be known as the back hill, which was separated from the two-story schoolhouse on the front hill by a ditch running through an arroyo. A videographer from France took footage of the project in all its stages.

Colin's idea was to build a small adobe house connected to an underground "growhole" in order to lengthen the short growing season. In late spring, a backhoe dug a giant hole about the size of an Olympic swimming pool on the back hill. A corner of that hole became a mud pit where five or six half-naked men and women monotonously stomped straw, dirt and water into perfect consistency for adobe bricks. The mud was shoveled into wooden frames and left to bake in the sun. One time, while trying to balance a dirt-filled wheelbarrow along a narrow wooden plank, I almost went headlong into the mud pit, burying myself and fellow mud mashers. Remembering my ancestors— the slaves who had built the pyramids in Egypt—I left the mud pit before any plagues descended and went to work in the cook shack. Later in the summer we got a cement mixer to mix the mud.

Built of plastic and scrap lumber from the sawmill in Eagle's Nest, the makeshift cook shack sheltered the black Majestic wood stove and all our food supplies. Feeding such a large group would have been expensive were it not for government subsidies in the form of food stamps. Social workers who helped the hippies fill out the government applications were always frustrated by ungridable answers to irrelevant questions, like "Who is the head of your household?" In '60s slang, "a head" meant someone who did drugs. According to the "regs" each person receiving food stamps had to have their personal cooking facility unless they were part of a family unit.

We believed we were part of a gathering tribe but the government didn't have a category for communal endeavors. Small groups of us created cooking facilities—even if it was only a circle of rocks with a grill—for the occasional visits from confused social workers forced to confront these new forms of social evolution.

Dulcimer Dan was my co-cook and the main baker. We put out about two meals a day—breakfast and dinner—on an old Majestic wood stove. *Photo by Paul Dembski*

Dulcimer Dan was my co-cook and main baker. We put out two meals a day—breakfast and dinner—for about 30 people on the old cook stove. Day after day we rose at dawn, yawned into a cup of black coffee sweetened with honey and served huge bowls of oatmeal. Dulcimer Dan and I had major philosophical differences. I'd point out that everyone was starving and the sun was about to set so let's just get the freaken' food out! People would be milling around ready to eat straw. He would shake his shoulder-length golden mane, dismayed by my impatience, and roll his blue eyes heavenward.

"But the rolls still need a little browning."

In fact, Dulcimer Dan's eggless, dairyless, wheatless rolls were a triumph of form over matter. They smelled sweet and tasted divine. In the evenings around the crackling campfires, this self-proclaimed perfectionist often played first-rate music on his dulcimer, mandolin or guitar.

One morning Colin announced, "Enough adobes!" We might not have cheered if we had known that brick making would be followed by weeks of hauling river rocks and a trip to Chaco Canyon in hopes of becoming master stonemasons like the ancient Anasazi. We pooled vehicles, tents and food and were gone a week. Chaco Canyon walls were miracles of geometric designs that emerged on flat rock surfaces built without the benefit of mortar. When Colin said the walls of the growhole were going to look like Chaco Canyon, he meant it—except we had the benefit of mud for mortar.

"You mean we're going to build stone walls along the entire edge of that hole in the ground?" asked some brave soul. A week later, another rock wall emerged from the perimeter.

"What's this wall for?" asked an apprentice stonemason.

"That's going to be a meditation room inside the growhole. Meditating around plants is great for their growth." Colin must have read that popular book about the gardens in Findhorn, Scotland. It was midsummer and we hadn't even started to build the little adobe house on the edge of the growhole. But we were a volunteer chain gang and no one knew the master plan except Colin, and he never shared that information.

Adela, Colin's wife, looked like an Indian princess. Long black hair flowed along her slender body as she worked alongside us in the mud pit or cook shack with her baby, Papu, strapped to her back. In Tiwa, the language spoken at Taos Pueblo, papu means the naval of the earth. We took turns cradling and holding Papu, who became everyone's baby. Born and raised in northern New Mexico, Adela was as indigenous as we were imported. She taught us how to roast chile, make tortillas and speak Spanish. The

Adela teaching Spanish at the Taos Learning Center.
Photo by Seth Roffman

local Hispanics loved and respected her, although she lived a life style they did not understand. Caught between two cultures, she was determined to live the best of both.

Colin enjoyed creating his Chaco home in Arroyo Hondo. He also enjoyed the adulation of the young women in the mud pits, but after a long, hot, people-filled summer, Adela was growing tired. Raising two teenagers and a baby, working at the building site, and living in a tipi left little personal or family time. Everyone admired her. She was royalty, our own Jacquelyn Kennedy. She spoke the language of metaphor bathed in moonlight and howling coyotes. Her words smelled of cedar and sage carried on the wind. Her inspirational firelight talks gathered and soothed the group like a lullaby. She made me cry, even when I wasn't sure what she was talking about. Because of her, I would even consider stomping straw in the mud pits again.

John Kimmey, the gatherer of curricula at the

A house/truck parked on the back hill where a family of growhole workers lived. *Photo by Seth Roffman*

Taos Learning Center, took his job seriously. His inspiration for the curriculum came from a fervent belief in the Hopi prophesies and frequent trips to Hopiland to learn the wisdom directly from the elders. This left little time to haul rocks, work in the cook shack or slog it out in the mud pits. His vision did not always mesh with Colin and Adela's pragmatic curriculum—about learning to build shelters and grow food. But John had a very pragmatic problem—his wife and three children were about to move up from Santa Fe and he needed a home for them.

Tension and confusion spread throughout the once harmoniously chaotic encampment, testing our faith in the greater school of life. We decided to hold a peyote meeting to pray for guidance and a higher common vision. The volunteer labor force and teachers gathered in the kiva room of the schoolhouse. John prayed to the four directions for wisdom and clarity. He was eloquently long-winded that night, like a river endlessly meandering through a thirsty canyon. Colin sat on his haunches looking like he would rather be hauling river rocks.

Like a firecracker ready to explode, Gabby Mossman let everyone know she was having her first encounter with an hallucinogenic. Gabby had been a high school social studies teacher back East and actually had an official state-approved certificate in her files. Married to a doctor, she lived a life most Americans would consider respectable. In the morning, she had a rough time communicating her ecstatic experience to her husband who'd been babysitting their one-year-old son.

Windy, granddaughter of an East Coast stock market tycoon, sat next to me. At 18, she had been presented to high society at a debutante's ball. We were the English Department and had gotten to know each other while discussing our future program. Tonight she wore her usual L.L. Bean camouflage outfit, wire-rimmed glasses and hair tied back in a bun. For boogies, she let down her long hair, threw on a slinky dress and acted like someone named Lola. She'd just purchased 25 acres of virgin land in San Cristobal and planned to build an adobe house with the help of Juan, a handsome Hispanic man she'd fallen in love with. Teaching was her vocation of the moment and being involved with the Taos Learning Center offered a break from a self-imposed hermit life style.

The craggy-faced sea captain with a distinguished handlebar mustache sat quietly by the fire, reflecting the flames in his blue eyes. The mysterious captain had appeared sometime during the summer, offering to help with maintenance and repair of buildings and machines. His letters of reference, photos of boats he'd worked on, and an abundance of tools had impressed Adela, Colin and John. His camper shell, permanently parked on the back hill, became a sanctuary for the teenagers when they had problems. The captain's slow-paced raspy voice had a gravity that was hard to ignore when telling stories or advising the teens. Some of us wondered why the enigmatic sea captain chose to live in a land-locked desert.

The firelight dwelled on Adela who carried herself with dignity as she softly spoke to the group, admitting what we all suspected—it was a rough time in her marriage. There was nothing metaphorical about her talk that night. Normally a private person, she bravely revealed her vulnerability, which gained everyone's sympathy and inspired her husband and children to gather round her like a blanket.

Captain Larry. *Photo by Seth Roffman*

The meeting accomplished two things: the volunteer labor force was determined to finish building their house and the young women who actively admired Colin left.

Meanwhile the rock walls continued to grow until one morning we could see our breath in the chill air. Overnight, snow had fallen in the peaks, like it often did just before Halloween. The meditation room was done and we still hadn't started to build the walls for the adobe house. Colin and Adela announced they had rented a place in Arroyo Seco for the winter and were shutting down the construction site until next spring. A few determined people wanted to try

Working on the growhole house. The exquisite rock work was inspired by the walls of Chaco Canyon.

Photo by Seth Roffman

and winter in a tipi on the back hill but most of us scattered like fallen aspen leaves. Some left the valley, and others found homes nearby.

The transition from makeshift village to community school took at least a month. Every morning over coffee, someone announced his or her winter plans. Kathleen, a local storyteller who lived on the Seco rim road, invited me to live with her for the winter. In the evenings we would sit in front of her pot-bellied stove and drink tea with graham crackers and butter. She told me story after story while we watched the world turn white and then green again.

John's family did not have a home until a friend gave him $2000 to build a 1,000 square foot house on the Learning Center's property. By putting up posters around town, offering a free tipi and "all the adobe you could eat," he got help making adobe bricks from the dirt in the front yard. The crew started in July and John's family moved into the round house the day of the first major snowstorm, just before Thanksgiving.

The 15 or so local teenagers who attended the Taos Learning Center were a cultural mix of Anglo, Hispanic and Pueblo Indian. The two out-of-town students who boarded at the school had just graduated high school and became Nick's apprentices in the pottery studio and the building site.

Tuition was decided on a sliding scale. Parents were asked what they could pay in money or trade. Most teachers did not receive a salary, although I was offered $100 that winter so I could visit my family in New York. Many of the people who volunteered to teach at the school were recent arrivals in the Taos valley—societal dropouts armed with all kinds of degrees and incredible life experiences.

Every morning, the Antioch student teacher drove Colin and Adela's van along the Hondo-Seco Road, picking up students. Teachers who lived close to students car-pooled if possible. Others hitchhiked or got there however they could.

The school policy regarding absenteeism—If you weren't at the Taos Learning Center, you were probably expanding your mind somewhere else, so you could never be absent in the school of life. Home-

Interior of the growhole. This is part of the living space which leads into a lush greenhouse filled with plants.
Photo by Seth Roffman

work was what you did at home, like chopping wood or baking bread. Discipline was self-determined. Teachers were not required to take attendance, write lesson plans, or give grades.

Many times I found myself wishing that I knew how to do something useful—like make pottery, jewelry, weave, ride a horse or survive blizzards on mountaintops. I felt boringly literate in a culture that valued experiential learning. All that winter, I tried to create a cohesive program in the midst of crisis and confusion outside and inside my head. My first job as a teacher had been in the crowded classrooms of Harlem, New York. Now my classroom had views of extinct volcanoes, mesas, meadows, clouds—and hopefully—students.

One day I made copies of Rudyard Kipling's *How the Elephant Got His Trunk* and read the story out loud to my students while they wandered out of the room not waiting to hear what happened "by the banks of the great, gray, greasy Limpopo River all set about with fever trees." They never learned what onomatopoeia was and never wrote their own "pour quoi" story.

Early on, it was obvious that the kids were coming to school stoned. One of the teachers got parent releases to institute a course called Safe Drug Use. For several weeks—with supervision and in a safe environment—the kids were offered a different drug: mushrooms, peyote, LSD and marijuana. The students were required to write a research report before

The house that Colin and Adela gave up in order to create an alternative high school—the Taos Learning Center. It was a traditional old adobe structure with a portal outside.

Photo by Seth Roffman

and after the experience. They came away with a profound understanding of how drugs affected their minds and bodies and discovered that most ancient civilizations used some kind of mind-altering drug as a sacrament.

Much of the learning that year took place on the many field trips—to Chaco Canyon, Hopiland and the Four Corners Power Plant, the museums in Santa Fe, an arts festival in Denver, the Los Alamos Nuclear Museum and a nearby scrapyard that contained discarded non-radioactive equipment and stuff that was junked by scientists from various projects. It was an exploration of the tension that existed between traditional cultures, the creative arts, and modern technology and science.

The many meetings we had that year to solve problems concerning the school, the students and ourselves took an emotional toll. Each meeting became an encounter session. It was never clear whether we were an alternative community school or an alternative community in the school of life. School disbanded that spring and never reopened in quite the same form. For a number of years it became a decentralized apprenticeship program. Separate from that, Adela opened a Waldorf school for young children in the front schoolhouse.

Colin, Adela, their three children and assorted friends lived in the unique underground home for a few years. Open sleeping cubicles afforded little or no privacy, a small price to pay for togetherness. The growhole became a cluster of grapevines and vegetation, spreading moisture throughout this subterranean cave, a lush response to the surrounding desert sage, chamisa and piñon. They lived there just long enough to learn firsthand the joys and humidity of having unintentionally built into the water table.

Editorial • Fountain of Light • October 1969

If We Are To Build

"Who is the victim? Who is the slayer, speak!"—Socrates

The time has come for the irresponsible elements of the hip community to ask themselves if they belong in Taos. If the people are to learn from the past mistakes such as Haight Ashbury, they must look within and find what they want and expect from Taos. Certainly, many of the institutions here are as corrupt as those in the cities that many of us have left behind–but we will not change these products of a dying society unless we look beyond them to the New Age which is beginning.

No one helps the community by leaving behind housing in ruin, all it does is make things more difficult for the next person. It does not help our image to mirror the thieving minds of businessmen with shoplifting, all it does is help produce suspicion and doubt. It does not impress the overly puritanical if a person defecates on his lawn or place of business, it only supports his belief in our alleged lack of worth.

If we are to build, we must be discriminating in our actions, taking into consideration the long term effects they have on the community and our relationship to other folks. In California there is a group of people who walk around the streets picking up everything from trash to dogshit.

When I was in Europe I was impressed by the difference in the various cities, the cleanliness and ecology of the cities mirrored the minds of the people. In Copenhagen I found myself putting candy bar wrappers into my pocket rather than throwing them on the ground. In Venice the reverse was true, until one day I realized that the environments were teaching me. If we are to create a new environment we must live as if it already exists.

It would be wrong for me to condemn the "hippie tripper" since I was one as well. It has been a difficult struggle for all of us to overcome the mire of meaninglessness that the past generations have left, but we have stood at the void long enough. NOW is the time to fill it with the substance of a new way of life.

The time is growing short if we are to win the war, not "The War Across the Sea" but the war within the minds of people. Then we must move away from the "hippie tripper" and into the productive use of new energies we have discovered. Not to supply our egos with rewards, but to create the New Jerusalem. One of our wisest philosophers once told the straight world: "Don't stand in the doorway, don't block up the hall."

Students at Taos Learning Center learn video production. *Photo by Seth Roffman*

TLC and the Counterculture: A Kid's Perspective

told by Morgan Haynes to Iris Keltz

"When I was 11, I lived in San Francisco with my mom, her boyfriend, my little brother and some friends. One of our places was at the top of Castro Street when the gay community was just starting to move in there. Instead of going to school, I'd spend my days roaming the city with a student bus pass. You couldn't tell whether I was a boy or girl and I'd get hassled all the time but was always careful or at least I thought I was. Once I walked from the Presidio to half-way across the Golden Gate Bridge. Standing in the middle of the bridge, I felt it sway back and forth while the cars went roaring by, certain that a strong gust of wind could blow a 90-pound kid right off. I'd get lost in Chinatown at least once a week. For an extra 35 cents, I could cross the Bay Bridge to Berkeley and panhandle on Telegraph Avenue for lunch money. We eventually moved to Berkeley, a few blocks from the University.

"When no one was home one day, I snuck a half-hit of acid from the stash at our house and proceeded to scare the crap out of myself. It was my first trip and I was all alone. The physical part of the trip was as intense as the psychic. For the duration of the experience, I had persistent pattern hallucinations of triangular owl heads. I remember thinking that my perception of reality was off but I didn't know what was happening. Somehow that was okay. That was before I read books by Carlos Castañeda or Aldous Huxley. By the time Mom and her friends got home, I was fine and never told them about my experience.

"I did this intentionally before the acid trip that was set up as a mentorship by Mom and her friends. We drove up to Mount Tamalpais with me and another kid around my age in the back of the pickup truck. It was a twisty winding road and I started throwing my guts up. I spent the afternoon chasing lizards and seeing outlines of psychedelic dragons in the clouds. Mom believed that it was better for me to do acid in a controlled environment with her rather than go out in the streets alone, which was ironic since we hung out with Hells Angels, Black Panthers, radical Indians and psychopathic Vietnam vets.

"When we packed the red pickup truck that spring, I thought our family was just going on an extended camping vacation to New Mexico. I had no idea we were moving. Driving through Gallup at dusk and waking up in Taos with views of Wheeler Peak and Lobo Mountain, I wondered where the hell we were. I had pictured saguaro cactus and roadrunners in a sandy desert.

"By the time I moved to New Mexico at 12, I was already a drug connoisseur who had given up acid because it was too harsh on my body. I'd been doing it about once a week in California. The second day I was in town, I remember buying my life with drugs. Being used to Berkeley and the big city, I thought it was pretty safe to walk the main road in downtown Arroyo Hondo. I had no idea about the local social dynamic. A gang of Chicano boys about my age approached me, threatening to do great bodily harm to this no-account longhaired hippie kid. I had a tin of hash-ish in my pocket and asked them, 'Wouldn't you guys rather get high with me than beat the shit out of me?' And they said, 'Yeah, man.' I bought my safety but had to keep them supplied all through high school.

"We arrived in Taos in March just after a major snowstorm. Colin and Adela invited us to stay with them in their rented Seco house until my mother made a tipi for us. When I walked through the door of that house, a mirror image of myself stared back at me. The person was about the same size, maybe a little taller with long black hair the same length as mine. I couldn't tell if it was male or female. We kept staring at each other wondering, Who the hell are you? We bonded quickly. Manny, Colin and Adela's son, became my best friend.

Morgan, age 12, just before moving to New Mexico.

"Soon after I got there, a kid from the Learning Center asked me to go skiing and I said it was a little cold to be water skiing. I had never snow skied before and nobody warned me—of the beauty or the steepness. Getting stoned in the chairlift on my way to the top of the mountain, I thought 'Oh, my God, it's straight down!' When I survived that experience, all thoughts of California were gone for years.

"I went to the Taos Learning Center for what

Halloween has always been an important holiday in New Mexico, closely connected to el Día de los Muertos (the Day of the Dead) on November 1st. In 1972, teachers as well as students got into face painting to celebrate that day. John Kimmey is the smiling face with the wavy lined forehead on the left. *Photo by Seth Roffman*

would have been 7th and 8th grades. My mother, brother and me lived in the tipi Mom had made all summer and fall and moved into the goat shed in December.

"I sensed a lot of conflict among the adults who were the leaders—the top of the food chain—but had no idea why. They were so into expanding their consciousness, they didn't always consider their offspring who had to come along for the ride. A sense of idealism made me angry because it wasn't what I expected from a communal organization. I understood what the adults were trying to do but I didn't have the life experience to tell them how to do it right. The kids were like little shadow people running around—in the pottery shop, at the building site, in the cook shack. The adults didn't seem to realize that we were listening to everything.

"I think that the 'classes' part of the school had broken down by the spring when we first got there. There was always a lot of talk about getting the classes going again but I don't remember going to many—maybe one or two. John Kimmey seemed like a consultant with a lot of authority. The schoolhouse was more of a residence than anything. Most of my memory of the Learning Center is that I did a lot of physical work—making adobes, laying adobes,

There was a great sense of camaraderie among the students. Here on the roof of the schoolhouse, some of them are posing and play-acting for a student video.

Photo by Seth Roffman

hauling vigas from the mountains and loading the truck with river rocks. I was one of those naked people in the mud pit. I got very good at laying the adobe bricks. Slave labor is what we were. If we weren't working, we were avoiding work.

"I was hungry all the time and hated the food that came out of the cook shack, especially those muffins. The adults were into this organic health food thing. Chris and I started swiping olive oil, garlic and potatoes or pasta. We'd cook them up wherever we happened to be camped out, like our lean-to in the arroyo or sometimes Pierre, the videographer, let us stay in his camper when he was out of town. Starved for meat, we decided to assassinate one of the local chickens. We borrowed Captain Larry's gun and chased one of them into the arroyo near the fence. We shot this chicken five times but it didn't die. By then we were in total blood lust. I went berserk with a sharp slat of wood and whacked its head off. When we went to clean it and started plucking the feathers, the chicken was so full of holes, we decided not to eat it. So we buried it. Everyone was very upset with us.

"Except for Manny, I felt like an outsider. A few years younger than most of the kids, we were pretty much our own peer group. There was an intimacy I'd had with my friends in California that came from having grown up together. Going through puberty at the Learning Center was tough. I had all this knowledge but then came all these weird feelings and sprouting pubic hairs and all these naked people. I remember the first time I saw the adults take off their clothes and jump into the mud pits. I thought, *you're joking*! They were so wrapped up in themselves they didn't notice what the kids were going through. Stomping straw naked in the mud pits is not necessarily sexual unless you're a pubescent boy. I had to sit in the mud for hours because I just couldn't get out. Other times, I remember rolling around in Captain Larry's camper with one of the older girls I had a crush on and feeling petrified of being rejected. A sex education class or some adult guidance would have been helpful.

"We were brought up in a culture that gave us easy access to drugs, mainly pot and assorted hallucinogens, which we got from our parents. But I think I would have done drugs regardless. Now I can see

John Kimmey loved to talk about the Hopi prophesies that he had heard from tribal elders. Here, he is teaching in the kiva room of the schoolhouse. There was mutual respect and caring between him and the students.

Photo by Seth Roffman

that when you do drugs at a young age it stops you from developing emotionally and affects your motivation. Sometimes I wonder what all those drugs did to my brain.

"It's ironic that after working so hard to do everything naturally—with adobe bricks, river rocks and mud mortar—we were forced to make concrete cisterns in what would have been a round living room and storage area when it was discovered that the house had been built in the aquifer. The collected water that might have flooded the house was used to water the plants in the growhole.

"My family stayed at the Learning Center two summers and a winter. Then Mom enrolled me in 9th grade at the local public school, a year ahead of where I would have been had I not dropped out for two-and-a-half years. But I was not behind. Above and beyond the required curriculum that included the Kabbala, Carl Jung and Tolstoy, I read all the Hardy Boys and as much science fiction as there was time. I graduated from Taos High School with good grades in 1978 when I was 17. By then we were pretty well separated from the people at the Learning Center.

"A lot of people look at me and say, 'You don't seem like somebody who grew up like that.' And I tell them, 'I've got the pictures to prove it.'"

Update:

After leaving the counterculture environment, Morgan stepped into mainstream society to become a self-described "public servant, working as a paramedic, wearing a uniform and a flat-top haircut." At 39, he lives in Tijeras Canyon—east of Albuquerque—and is studying to be a doctor of oriental medicine. He has one foot planted firmly in mainstream society while stepping back into an alternative medical community or what is called New Age medicine. Interestingly, he dreams of building a self-sufficient solar home for himself some day. It will be partially made of stone.

Do Hippies Love Us For Our Food Stamps?

Food Stamps: Are they a factor in bringing the long hair traffic to Taos?

"Not likely" is the general consensus of those who are involved with food stamps, either in the distribution or on the receiving end of the program. The reasoning being used to support this conclusion is a valid one. Since the food stamps are federally funded, the requirements are basically the same in every state.

In California, the state from which many of the hippies are coming, foods stamps are just as easy, if not more easily obtained, than in New Mexico.

Even though the overall operation of the food stamp program is relatively uniform, states do have some fluctuation in setting requirements. Colorado, for instance, requires that recipients must be actively seeking employment in order to obtain stamps. New Mexico had a similar requirement until April 11 last year when employers who got tired of turning down applications for jobs asked the state Board of Health and Social Services to drop the requirement.

Eddie S. Martinez, manager of the local office of the N.M. State Employment Service, said the requirement for recipients of food stamps to apply in the employment service office was a waste of time.

"In the first place," he said, "there are so few jobs to be found in this area; also applicants of the new culture variety are very hard to locate should a job turn up, because they live in the mountains, have no phone and seldom stay in one place." Martinez also mentioned that very few employers would accept long hair types as employees. Martinez said his office currently has only four claimants of unemployment of the new culture type and they are drawing unemployment checks from their home states.

Since the Colorado and the New Mexico requirements for food stamps vary and since Southern Colorado is relatively free from what many consider a "hippie problem," it might appear on the surface that the difference in programs could be a factor in the hippie influx.

"Probably not," said two directors of welfare in two separate southern Colorado counties. "More than likely it is the difference in climate or surrounding." It was also mentioned that some counties in southern Colorado offer even more aid in obtaining food stamps than New Mexico in that their local CAP boards supplemented some needy incomes to make the initial purchase of stamps.

"If food stamps are not a drawing card for hippies to come to Taos, what is?" one might ask.

"To understand what is happening in Taos in regard to the hippie influx, one must understand what is happening in the large cities," said Bill Quinn, board member of Lorien Enterprises which is headquartered next to General Store on the South Santa Fe Road. "What is happening in Taos is happening all over the county," Quinn said. Many people are getting fed up with huge cities, the destruction of environment, and the fear that should revolution erupt they would be trapped in the cities. People are looking for a way out, Quinn said. Taos, with all its natural beauty, its unspoiled water and air, its climate, the ancient Spanish and Indian cultures, is catching much publicity in the cities as "the place to go," he said.

"There will probably be a greater influx of long hairs this summer," Quinn said, "and there will be many who will come without any concept or regard of this community, with no notion of supporting himself, and will probably be a burden on all the cultures in the community, Indian, Spanish, Anglo and Hippie." Quinn mentioned that many of their group were writing to friends in the cities trying to discourage them from coming to Taos this summer.

"Still," Quinn said, "we have to understand the conditions which drove him here and our actions should reflect this perspective to individual situations. How many hippies are using food stamps?"

Local retail grocery merchants estimate anywhere from 80% to 100% of the long hairs they see in their store are using food stamps. Minor Van Arsdale, Community Planning Specialist for the State Health and Social Service Department, and whose job is working directly with the hippie communes, estimates roughly 50% of the hippies he works with are using food stamps. Van Arsdale said approximately 60,000 people in the state receive food stamps; approximately two per cent of these recipients are hippies. He said of course Taos would have a higher percentage but he has not yet determined how much higher. He also said many of the communes are self supporting and that the majority of the permanent hippie types living in communes are working toward that goal.

There have been some cases of over-issuance to hippie groups in Taos County. In one case 44 people at the Hog Farm near Penasco were certified by the local board to receive food stamps. An investigation one week after certification revealed that 27 people were living at the Hog Farm and some were new and uncertified, officials said. There are cases where individuals receive food stamps from two or three counties, according to officials.

Foodstamps

Fountain of Light April #12

Gov. David Cargo, upon being confronted by a group of Taos citizens with a list of abuses of the foodstamp program, made certain remarks about cleaning up the program. Both conservatives and radicals drew the implication that the Dept. of Health and Social Services (Welfare) was preparing to harass and eliminate hippy and commune participation in the foodstamp program. They fail to distinguish between a politician making promises in order to win a few votes and a federally sponsored program whose broad regulations are not locally controlled. The foodstamp program will help New Mexican residents who want help.

Certain Dept. of Health and Social Service regulations have become more liberal and will continue to become more liberal. For instance, the requirement that foodstamp applicants register at the Employment office was dropped last year (at the request of the Employment office, which has no jobs for the applicants). In February 1970 the foodstamp standards were revised, nearly doubling the amount of stamps given to households. Finally, HEW regulations that take effect next July will make it easier to receive financial assistance (welfare money). Whereas previously the application for financial assistance was eight pages filled out by a social worker upon questioning the applicant, starting July 1st the applicant will fill out his own form of two pages.

However, the Dept. of Health and Social Services is taking steps to stop the misuse of foodstamps. To prevent anyone drawing stamps from more than one county, each county office is sending its roll of recipients to other counties. To eliminate the practice of using several names to get more stamps, proper identification is being required of applicants. Manuel Barela, head of the Taos county depart., says that a social security card, driver's license, draft card, or birth certificate is adequate identification.

The department is also tightening its investigations of who is and isn't a member of the household. The simplest way to avoid trouble is to obey the regulations. Each household should choose a leader who acts as manager for the household. This person is responsible for seeing that every member of the household is certified in the foodstamp program. This means that the income of every member is counted in the income of the household and that every member has identification. The manager must see that the welfare dept., at the time of drawing stamps each month, is kept informed of the present income of the household, the arrival and departure of new or old members and any change of address of household. The manager is accountable by law to see that the regulations are followed.

These regulations present no problems to the stable communes that have a basic family. Visitors may stay with the family, but not for long. If they stay on, they must become a part of the family, which means declaring their income and becoming certified for foodstamps.

Communes that have new people coming and going continually will have trouble drawing stamps because it will be impossible for them to know their exact number and income. Since the foodstamp program is designed to help residents, not travelers, the communes that are wide open to travelers will probably have to decide which they want more, the stamps or the travelers.

If you want to get stamps, it's very simple. Don't draw stamps at more than one place. Don't draw stamps for more people than are really members of the household. Identify yourself properly when you are certified to receive stamps.

Acequias, or ditches, are the lifeblood of New Mexican villages. They provide the water for crops and an element of social connection. Every year the ditches have to be cleaned from debris so they can flow properly. Organized by a majordomo, ditch cleaning days are always a major event. *Photo from the Museum of New Mexico, negative #55021*

Dixon Before Los Hippies

told by Dianna Valdez to Iris Keltz

"My family has lived in northern New Mexico for generations. My mother was from Tierra Amarilla and my father was from Dixon—which is where they met. The larger of the villages in that area, Dixon was a meeting place between Embudo on the Rio Grande and Peñasco and Mora in the mountains. When I was eight, Dixon already had electricity and plumbing whereas some of the smaller communities weren't as lucky. Dixon had two general stores, a couple of places to gas up, a post office, the Presbyterian Mission and they once had a clinic.

"My grandfather on my mother's side was the 'paralegal' of the area and had the school bus contract. My grandfather on my father's side was a farmer. He had a little ranch right in the middle of Dixon behind the church. He also did migrant work, such as picking potatoes in Colorado, to keep the family going.

"Though my father didn't finish his degree, he was a teacher/principal at the Dixon Elementary School. The big court case about separation of church and state was brought up at that time. He and Mom moved to Santa Fe for a few years, which is where I was born. Then they moved back to Dixon until I was four and then to Albuquerque so Dad could finish his degree. But most of my family still lives in the north—Santa Fe, Española, Taos and Dixon—throughout the Rio Grande Valley. Both my grandmothers died when my parents were young, so I only knew my grandfathers.

"Life was hard for my parent's families—sometimes subsistence level—but wonderful. In summer, I would help hoe the corn and chile fields and pick chokecherries in the fall when I went to visit.

"My cousins and I would go to Taos for the fiestas. It was a big treat because it meant not getting back home until ten o'clock at night.

Dixon was a meeting place between Embudo on the Rio Grande and Peñasco and Mora in the mountains. This is St. Anthony's Catholic Church in the old Dixon plaza where Diana's parents got married. Her grandad's house is a little way down a dirt road on the north side of the plaza.

Photo by Jeff Bryan

"I had a great aunt who lived in Taos. She always gave us fresh goat cheese from her herd. There were also distant cousins who lived in that area, too.

"When Granddad died around '57, the family was going to sell the house in Dixon. I tried so hard to get Mom and Dad to buy it, but there was no way. We were living in Albuquerque and it would have been too difficult to take care of. Dad told me, 'You didn't have to haul water from the ditch or chop firewood. You don't remember how much hard work a place like that is.' I think Dad was in high school before they got a hand pump inside the house.

"My aunt and uncle bought the house from the rest of the family a few years later. Another uncle worked the ranch that was down the road from his home. When my aunt and uncle owned the house, one of my cousins and I would spend vacations there. We both loved the house and dreamed about buying it for ourselves. My aunt and uncle tried to keep the house up, but it began to deteriorate. I heard that when it got rented to some hippies, the wooden floors were pulled up and used for firewood. Whoever was there couldn't or wouldn't go out and get firewood.

"I remember my grandfather's old adobe sitting on about two or three acres on the *otra vanda*, which is the lower pasture, near the river. That was their ranch. They had cattle, horses and livestock. On the stretch towards the river they planted corn and chile. It was a territorial house with a pitched tin roof and a veranda in front. The kitchen had a wood-burning stove. Off to the right was my grandfather's small bedroom. In winter when I visited, I would sleep there—the warmest room in the house and closest to the outhouse.

"There were six brothers and sisters and, as the family grew, Dad said that they kept on adding rooms. The floor was packed mud. I heard of families packing their mud floor with grease from their *metanzas*, melting down the pig fat and using it on the floors, but my family would sweep, pack and wet the floor with water. The walls had to be whitewashed with limestone once a year. It was almost like replastering.

My family would hang linen under the *vigas* to protect the house from dust. Once a year they took down the linens, so they could wash and bleach them and clean out the cobwebs from the *latillas*. Both my parents would tell me how hard it was to keep up the house when they were young. But both my grandmothers were meticulous about having the house clean and white.

"As a teenager in the early '60s, I would spend Easter, Christmas, summer vacations and whenever I could in Dixon. My cousins would warn me, 'Don't walk up to the northern end of the village because there are strangers there and you don't know what they're up to.' Aunts and uncles would talk about *esos hippes* moving in and buying land upriver. It seemed to be a point of resentment in the village because it was prime land, beautiful land, land that had been in our families for generations and sold for one reason or another. Maybe the owners had died and the children moved away to find jobs in Los Alamos or California so the land became available for outside purchase. It was hard for a village that was close-knit to have a lot of strangers moving in. The villagers didn't seem concerned about drugs or having our morals corrupted—it was more a feeling that the integrity of the village was compromised.

"We called them outsiders. Most of them were gringos. Most of them were in their 20s and 30s and I don't remember them having kids our age. Once they started having children and the kids interacted at school, they became part of the fabric of the village. I think that's where the integration took place. Until then they kept to themselves. I don't remember any violent confrontations between the villagers and the outsiders. Years before the hippies came—when my parents were young—there had been a Presbyterian mission so the people in Dixon were somewhat used to dealing with outsiders.

"The village post office was the gathering place. The women would get their mail and catch up on news. The men would hang out while the kids played near the steps. Few, if any of the strangers, knew the folks in the village, and besides, there was so little interaction, there was little to talk about.

"I never met them, never talked to them, only saw them in passing. But it was cordial. Dixon wasn't like some of the villages to the north where the strangers were ostracized. There are reported cases of people refusing to sell staples and firewood in other places.

"My great aunt owned one of the general stores in the village. Some of the hippies would come and buy supplies there. I knew they were hippies because they had long hair and they dressed differently and were gringos. We never saw them running around naked or heard they were having orgies, and marijuana was nothing new. It had always been around, but we knew little to nothing of heroin or LSD or any of the other drugs associated with the hippie movement. We expected that the hippies were probably growing their own marijuana out back in the hills away from the village proper but no one bothered them. As long as they didn't act loco and do crazy things, it was none of our business. It was more like, 'you live your life and we'll live ours and if you don't get in our way and cause problems, we'll get along.'

"If I had been interested in establishing a relationship with one of them it would have been considered improper. I don't remember any of my cousins interacting with them or having friends from the communes and one of my cousins was quite a character, a young teenage boy who was dating and hanging around. I don't think even he ever had an occasion to interact with the hippies. It seemed that the villagers stayed in their group and the hippies stayed in theirs.

Hippies moved into old adobes and became homesteaders, preferring wood stoves, kerosene lamps, outhouses, and wells to modern conveniences.

Photo by Paul Dembski

"They were young adults making their own way. Some were raising crops, some were on welfare, but they were independent. We were still teenagers living with our families and hung with the kids from Hispanic families who had lived there forever.

"It wasn't until I went to Highlands University in Las Vegas, New Mexico, that I connected with kids from the counterculture. My father had let me know that there were many ways of seeing the world other than the Hispanic viewpoint. He was educated and open-minded. My parents weren't as traditional as other families raised up north. Being Spanish-American and raised in New Mexico didn't mean we were all beans, chile and tortillas. I dated a few gringos during my sandals-'n-candles days at Highlands. It was my questioning period, a time when I wasn't as tied to the Church or family traditions and expectations. It was a time of getting to know different points of view. I didn't shy away from the hippies although I didn't buy into their ways. If they weren't wild and crazy and drugged out, I was able to establish a relationship with them.

"The first time in my life I felt prejudice was when I went to Highlands—it was from my own people. I could speak Spanish, knew Spanish history and had family up north. The kids I grew up with couldn't understand why I was friends with non-Hispanics—gringos, hippies, whatever you call them. Most of the kids tended to stick with kids from their area.

"We went through a period of time wondering if we were Spanish-American, Latinos, Mexican-American, Chicanos. I refused to be called Chicana because I wasn't from Mexico. My family's roots came from Spain and from the Indian culture up north. We were all struggling with our identity, with who we were.

"The kids from the counterculture that I hung around with valued the Hispanic-Mestizo culture more than the kids I grew up with. To those kids, our culture was everyday stuff, nothing new or especially exciting, whereas people from the outside valued the adobes, the pottery, the serapes, the food and jewelry. People used to say, '*Esos hippes*, they'll buy anything. We tell them that it's handmade or hand woven and that it's been around for a while and they want it. They snap it up and buy it. This is junk to us, but if they want it, let them have it.'

"When my grandfather died, his tools and implements were for sale. His old horse-drawn plow and wagon—*á carreta*—were sold for the price of junk, according to Dad. The wagon had been down in the fields since I was a little girl and it was nothing special, but all of a sudden everything that we didn't value was being sold. People came and bought the artifacts of our culture because they were unique. What we had taken for granted, other eyes saw as special.

"When I go to Las Golandrinas and see all the things that were in use during the Colonial Period, I think, 'My grandmother had an iron like that.' Where in the world did all the things go that were in my grandfather's house? I don't think the relatives have them. They've been sold by the families for a couple of bucks and now they're treasures, museum pieces.

"People my age now realize what we had. It was ours for the keeping, but no one wanted it and it was sold off. Some of the anger is directed at ourselves for not realizing how important all this was—the culture, the traditions and the land.

"My aunt and uncle sold the house around 1965. Although I know why they had to get rid of my grandfather's house, it still tears at me that it's gone from our family. The couple they sold it to still lives there and has renovated it. One Memorial Day, Dad and I went to the Dixon cemetery to clean the graves and take flowers. We went by the church and I talked Dad into stopping by Granddad's old house. We stood by the portal and the couple that lived there saw us and came out. Dad told them, 'I grew up in this house.' They welcomed us. 'Come on in and see what we've done.' We noticed all the changes.

"The couple had restored the wooden floors in the house. We came to a small bedroom and Dad said, 'This used to be my room.' It touched Dad's heart to see the kind of care they were taking. They asked us about the house and we gave them pieces of history that they didn't have before.

"We went into the fields. A connection between the main house and a little row of apartments where the *brujas* used to live had been knocked down. We went around the yard and saw the cherry tree we used to swing on as kids was still there, still bearing fruit. As kids we used to run from the plateau where the house sat to the irrigation ditch and then to the hill where the cows hung out, to the stables and to a great field by the river. My little legs had to work hard to get up that hill. When Dad and I visited, I was amazed at how small it looked. We saw the care the couple had taken to terrace the land. I don't even remember their names except that he's a wood carver and she's a paper sculptress.

"We left feeling that if we couldn't have the house at least these people were taking care of it. They valued it. My dad still doesn't want it. He has memories of too much hard work. But I want it and if they ever decide to sell, I would buy the house and land back in a heartbeat."

Update:
Dianna Valdez lives in Corrales, a village outside of Albuquerque, New Mexico. She shares her home with her cat Calisto. She works with student teachers as a clinical supervisor for the University of New Mexico in collaboration with the Albuquerque Public Schools.

Peyote bird collage by David Pratt. Photographed in the home of Michael Duncan in Arroyo Seco by Iris Keltz.

The Founding of Morningstar Commune

told by David Lee Pratt to Iris Keltz

"How did I end up at Morningstar Commune in New Mexico?" David Pratt mused over a cup of hot coffee. "I don't know where to start because it's a complex case of cause and effect, all tied in with many different things happening around the world.

"It starts off in New York City where I'd been living as an artist. It was a creative time for me. I met my wife the first time I ate peyote. I was in a bar and it was the day Kennedy was shot.

"In retrospect, I see Vietnam as the catalyst. None of the rebellious hippie movement would have happened without it. It was the straw that broke the camel's back. Something in society broke apart and we were the reaction.

"A year or two before the hippie thing exploded, I moved to California. When I got there, I couldn't believe how different it was from New York City. Californians are laid back and always tripping on the cosmic ethers. The environment is much softer there—it's easier to survive. I was an old-time hipster or beatnik and never comfortably fit with the hippies, but that's what was happening so I followed the movement.

"The hippie-phenomenon was created for the most part by middle-class kids who became disillusioned with the American dream. The kids from ethnic and lower socio-economic backgrounds tended to be less crazed. It's hard to reject what you've never had. They were fighting to get into the system.

"My wife and I were desperately poor. We used to go to Golden Gate Park on Sunday and watch the Diggers feed all these people. I admired them very much. They fit into my political, philosophical and religious thinking. If all these people had their basic needs taken care of, they would have more time and energy to explore the things people usually don't have time for.

"People are after two things: security or adventure. I always believed in adventure and admired the daring of the Diggers. They tended to be older. Many of them were transplanted New Yorkers. One day I saw a poster in the street inviting people to go and live on Morningstar Ranch in Sonoma County. I was desperate as usual, and tired of living off my friends, so my wife and I went to check it out.

"Lou Gottlieb, an ex-Limelighter—the number two folk group of that era—owned a ranch. It was 30 acres of land filled with apple trees. Gottlieb retired to devote himself to classical music, and wrote reviews for a San Francisco newspaper on the side.

"The ranch was named by the previous owner, a mystical Christian, who called it Morningstar after references from the Bible. The last words of Christ in Revelation had to do with the morning star. Christ said, 'I, Jesus, have sent My angel to testify to you these things in the churches. I am the Root and the Offspring of David, the Bright and Morning Star.' (Revelation 22.16 NKJ)

"There are references to the morning star in all the world's great religions and mythologies. Quetzalcoatl, from Aztec mythology, taught a doctrine of peace and love, very similiar to Jesus. He told the people to stop the human sacrifices and love one another. One day he told the people he was going to leave, but to take this as a symbol. 'I am the eastern morning star and one day I am coming back.' Cortez arrived on the day it was prophesied Quetzalcoatl would return. The people mistook Cortez for Quetzalcoatl and gave him everything. That's how the western hemisphere was conquered.

"Somehow the Diggers got wind of Gottlieb's ranch and posted a sign in the streets of the Haight Ashbury inviting hippies to move there. The summer of love in 1967 saw thousands of hippies pass through Morningstar in California. Some stayed and some didn't. I built a tree house there and always had apples to eat. The local people had never seen anything like this before. The health conditions were terrible and they tried to close the place down.

"Lou Gottlieb decided to deed his land to God. He ended up in court because they said he couldn't do that. The court said that land must be privately owned. He responded by saying, 'We belong to the earth, not the earth to us. Who can own the earth? If someone comes on my land I don't have to kick them off. It's my right.'

"The judges answered by saying, 'We have this regulation. Hippies carry diseases and we don't want them around.' The pressure got great. They kept throwing us in jail and fining Lou. As far as I know, we still do not have the legal right to deed land to God.

"One day I went to a party down in Sonoma County with the rich hippies who always had lots of acid and other drugs. They had this mansion with a swimming pool. Owsley was there passing out acid. The Grateful Dead were playing music. I was real high on acid in this large group of people and things started to feel wierd. People were breaking into small groups and hanging out in the shadows. There was a feeling of separateness. Suddenly I felt there wasn't much future in what was going on.

"My friend, a Digger who had just come from New Mexico, told me, 'New Mexico is where it's at.' I had nothing to lose—no money, no nothing—so I said, 'Okay, let's hitchhike to New Mexico tomorrow.'

"There were already a few people from Morningstar, California living in this ghost town four miles north of La Madera, New Mexico. We had problems with the local people. There were incidences of rape and violence against the hippies. The locals wanted middle-class life badly and there we were—a bunch of white kids from middle-class America flaunting those values. They thought we were the devil incarnate. In reality, we were a bunch of young kids trying to live right, the way we saw it. But we showed no respect for local culture.

"I had moved to an old adobe house in Truchas with my wife when my California friends started showing up. They'd found me through this incredible underground network. Some of the women were pregnant so I couldn't just throw them out. The local people started freaking out and attacking us. It was a violent place. Gunfights were not uncommon Saturday night events.

"We stuck out like a sore thumb. By now we were about 15 people living in this small adobe in Truchas. We bought wheat in the 100-pound bags used to feed cattle. It was difficult to go to the store and get food because every time we went out we were in danger of being shot. It became a life-threatening situation. We had to leave town or get killed. It was the only time in my life that I wanted to see a cop, maybe even be in jail. At that point we couldn't do anything but survive.

"One night some locals started burning the buildings. A kid who'd grown up in Truchas showed up and led us out of town through a secret route that he knew. We took refuge in someone's house on the north side of town. The next day I went down to the state government offices and said, 'You've got to help us or someone's gonna get killed.' There was so much violence against the hippies in this state at that time that the government had appointed a special liaison, Van Arsdale, who told us, 'I'll drive you around to a few places where rich hippies have already bought and settled on some land.' The group chose Larry Stein and me for this exploratory trip.

Building with adobe and farming took a lot of work.
Photo by Rich Jamison

"We ended up at Michael Duncan's place. He'd just bought 800 acres on the mesa in Arroyo Hondo. It turned out that Michael Duncan and Larry Stein were old friends from many years ago. They were involved with Timothy Leary and the LSD scene together. Larry says to Michael, 'You've got to help us out. We're in a desperate situation. We've got children and pregnant women.' Michael said, 'Sure, come on over.' However, he wasn't really prepared for us. We weren't just wanting to come for a week or two. We were looking for a long-term thing. We borrowed a truck from someone and loaded fifty pounds of rice, an old rusty hammer and all the people and moved to the mesa owned by Michael Duncan.

Visiting with friends who lived in the valley was my favorite pastime. Here I am with Catherine on the rim in Arroyo Seco.

Photo by Paul Dembski

"Reality Construction Company was already making their adobes when we arrived with nothing. Max Finstein, a visionary Jewish beatnick poet from New York, started Reality. He had helped to start New Buffalo, but the reality of it did not meet his dreams, so he started another commune that consisted of militant blacks, Chicanos and politically radical whites. They were bitter—their ethic derived from the have-nots. They had a strong political and self-sacrificing aspect.

"Reality had some sort of understanding with Michael Duncan. At best Michael tolerated us, at worst he tried to kick us off the land. Reality Construction Company was busy trying to set up systems while we were bent on breaking them down.

"We had no money and no experience with adobe. All we had were people and the will to survive. We observed how the Indians were building an adobe house for Michael. We watched the guys from Reality make adobe bricks and we started putting it together. We held meetings, nothing regular. There were no leaders. It was an anarchist expression. People would gather and talk. Since we all needed food and shelter, we talked about that.

"One night I went outside and lined up a dagger with the shadow of the full moon. We planned three rectangles lined up with the North Star. There would be three living quarters in each section and a communal space in between with a courtyard in the middle.

"We planted our first crops that spring and had a birth in a lean-to before we had permanent shelter. We didn't even have tipis. Sometimes there was an attending midwife, sometimes not, but we never lost a baby or a mother. We were so poor the hippies from New Buffalo looked down on us and sent us their rejects, derelicts, psychopaths and winos. We should have been paid by the government to take care of these people who normally would have been institu-

Since many people did not have running water—hot or cold—the nearby hot springs next to the Rio Grande was a popular place to bathe. Kids loved it.

Photo courtesy of Terry Klein

tionalized. We took them in and taught them how to grow food and build shelters. Some of them became whole again and were able to return to mainstream life. Some did not.

"Morningstar was a quest for freedom, a pure creative anarchy—hippie dippy, but live and let live. We were formless, which allowed anything to exist. The total freedom gave a person the chance to create new forms. Anything could happen and usually did. I used to think that—since we all have similar needs—if given the freedom to choose what to do with our lives, we would choose to take care of the earth and each other. That's not true. Lots of people just wanted to get drunk and stoned all the time, but that eventually plays itself out.

"Morningstar was a truly revolutionary experience. Without any money, the dregs, dropouts and rejects of society were able to build solid structures, feed lots of people and create a community. We made mistakes because we were naive and idealistic, but we were in the forefront of what was happening. In the Bible it says, 'The last shall be first.' And I believe it."

Update:
After living at Morningstar, David Lee Pratt whirred through life like a drunken wildfire. He spawned two boys both with angel hair of spun gold. Eventually he stumbled into Austin, Texas, where he frolics with a mermaid in a magic trailer, works as a security guard, helps run Alternate Current Productions, makes strange art that few people ever get to see and acts in the movies whenever they let him. He still walks the line between innocence and experience, art and life, reality and illusion, time and space, light and shadow, life and death and he often wonders—what's next?

from the Fountain of Light, 1970

Morningstar Rose

told by Rose Gordon to Iris Keltz

"In the spring of '67, my friend Barbara and I hitchhiked from New York to an address my sister gave me in California. I was dropped off in the parking lot by a traveling salesman. It was raining and the parking lot was a pool of mud and full of ruts.

"The first person I met was Superman, a tall guy with wild brown ringlets and matching eyes who walked as if he were on a pogo stick. He was the official self-appointed greeter for the farmhouse and diverted me from going to the creek. At the house, the hippies were gathered around a fire. They had stripped most of the building in order to continue feeding the fire. There were a couple of stuffed couches and one bed. Chair legs and tabletops were making their way to the flames.

"I was innocent and put down my purse with $30 and the Buffalo Springfield album I'd carried from New York. When I came back after having been shown the house, my purse and album were there but the money was gone. I considered this my initiation. If you were willing to stay after your illusions were crushed, you were accepted into the group.

"Lou Gottlieb's commune, about 70 miles north of San Francisco, was 32 acres of redwood groves, apple orchards and wild fruit trees. People lived in the farmhouse and all over the land. First I slept by the creek with the creek people. Later I moved to the apple orchard. Penny and David Pratt—who later helped to found Morningstar in New Mexico—lived in a treehouse in the redwood grove. They had built a beautiful two-story treehouse from found objects.

"I met Paul down by the creek. He was a free-floating, psychedelic minstrel. He played the flute. His long blonde hair was held in place with a headband, and a sash was tied around his purple homespun tunic. The creek, which was near the

Rose's baby Nova was the first baby born on the commune. Her father delivered her. A few weeks after the birth, Rose went into town and weighed Nova on a scale in the produce department of the supermarket.

Photo courtesy of Rose Gordon

parking lot, had become a scene for winos headed by Tex, a wild man with matted gray black hair and crazy eyes—the kind of man my mother would've said, 'If you see him coming, cross the street.' But there was a splendidness about him. When visitors came he was a showman of hospitality. 'C'mon down,' he'd yell, pointing towards the creek. He'd pull up a redwood stump and share whatever he had. That's when he'd make stone soup. 'Boy, this would really taste good, if only we could go to town and get some…' He'd sweet talk people out of their money to make a giant pot of spaghetti or something. Then he'd say, 'What's a pot of spaghetti without a few loaves of bread and a jug of wine?'

"Eventually everyone was forced to leave the land because the neighbors were offended by nakedness and drugs. Sonoma County issued a law stating that the police had the power to shut down something that was a threat to public health, safety or morality. After several confrontations with the community, the County declared the commune such a threat. It became illegal to live there. The police would come at dawn and arrest whoever they found. I woke up one morning to discover my friend Santiago jumping over my legs. Then I saw my friend Larry running naked through the woods. He jumped over me also. Chasing them were two cops the hippies called Rocky and Bullwinkle. They leaped over me. The cops knew who they wanted to arrest that day.

"More and more people were getting arrested. Finally Paul and I got arrested and stayed in jail a couple of days. The law stated that you couldn't live in a structure. Our lawyer argued that sleeping bags were not a structure and we were released. They fine-tuned the law until your physical presence was enough to have you arrested. If you were arrested twice you were really in trouble, and so we left for a time and went wandering in Big Sur. When we came back to Gottlieb's farm we found out he had deeded the land to God.

"Nova was conceived in an apple orchard there.

"An old couple named Mama and Charlie invited us to stay with them in Sebastopol. Mama had had a stroke and could only say 'hamburger,' 'oh shit,' 'wine' and 'hippies good.' Her husband played the mandolin and we'd all drink wine. There were about seven of us living there. One day some old friends from Gottlieb's farm showed up. Barbara and Reggie had just gotten back from Truchas, New Mexico. She'd just discovered she was pregnant and wanted to get out of California. Two days later, I discovered I was pregnant too. Paul and I decided to hitchhike to Truchas and meet them there.

"After adventures too numerous to mention, we found Jeffrey Horton's house on the outskirts of Truchas. My friend Barbara greeted me with, 'Oh, my God, Rose, I'm sure glad to see you, but I wish you hadn't come.' She told me Joe Cota had been stabbed two nights ago and someone from The Hog Farm had been beaten and tied up. Rumor had it that some developers wanted to make Truchas a tourist place and paid local Hispanics to shoot the hippies and drive them out of town. By now I was three months pregnant. Our first day there we went to a birthday party for some little kid. Everybody brought rifles because there were frequent shootouts in the streets. Thirteen of us lived in one giant room. We knew we had to move but we had no place to go.

"One day, a group of us were visiting our neighbor Bill Tate when 'the acid cowboys' from Reality Construction Company showed up. They were macho, wore guns and used psychedelics. They told David Pratt that they lived on 100 acres of land in Arroyo Hondo. David said, 'Ya know, we really need a place to live. We have two pregnant women and a lot of other people.'

"David was keenly aware that the full moon in Scorpio was drawing closer. There had been violence before on the full moon and now it was going to be a full moon in Scorpio. We knew we had to find a place to live before the full moon.

"The guys from Reality said, 'Nah, it won't work. It's really rough living up there and you people are from California. We don't accept nobody who hasn't lived in New Mexico for at least a year 'cause you just don't know how hard it is to make it.'

"Bill Tate sat there drenched in his turquoise jewelry listening to this conversation between the California hippies and the acid cowboys. The kitchen had huge wooden furniture with a little room off to the side that had been an old *penitente morada* filled with the original old whips and crucifixes.

"Meanwhile, one of the guys in our group, Larry Stein, had bumped into an old friend named Michael Duncan somewhere near Taos. You can't imagine our surprise when Larry came home and told us he'd convinced Michael to welcome us onto his land. The first contingency including the pregnant women could move up there right away so they would be there before the full moon in Scorpio.

"In order to avoid any violence, we believed our move should be secret. Thirteen of us, with all our belongings, walked down the road in the middle of the night. We went up and down canyons and through the woods, whispering. There was another pregnant woman besides several sentries and myself. The wind was blowing in the high trees as David moved silently along beside us, guarding us in our escape. We believed that no one in town noticed.

"I'll never forget my first visions of Morningstar. All I could see was sage and looming mountains, no houses, no structures, absolutely nothing. I thought, Oh, my God, I'm in the desert! We'd only brought sleeping bags. Everyone chipped in whatever money they had to buy bags of wheat and oats from the Feed Bin.

"Guess who comes to visit after a few days? The acid cowboys from Reality Construction Company had discovered that the California hippies they'd met in Truchas were living on the other side of the mesa. Now all of us were here—by the grace of Michael Duncan. They sat down on their haunches in a little circle and delivered a survival lecture. This was their good-neighbor visit. According to them, unless we had this, that and the other thing, we'd never survive the winter. We just laughed.

"We were cooking and hanging out when it snowed. Three days after we moved to the mesa, there was a cold, wet, late spring snowstorm. We had no shelter, no structures, nothing. We built a shack from plastic and scrounged wood. It was large enough for thirteen people to lie under, side by side. With plastic on the ground and all those bodies, the small space was warm. We erected the shack right where we kept our bags of grain. When the storm passed, we took off the plastic and discovered that much of the grain had spilled and was sprouting! There were baby oat and wheat plants growing everywhere we had slept! That was the start of our first garden!

"Michael wanted to build a house on the mesa and hired a Pueblo crew. The Indians needed help, so we women stomped in the mud pits and washed the adobe brick forms. In return for helping, Michael gave Morningstar a certain number of the bricks. We got thousands of bricks to build our pueblo. I was six-and a-half months pregnant, stomping in the mud pits. A year and a half later they used a donkey for the same job. Under the leadership of David Pratt, the guys figured out how to make the bricks.

We cooked on whatever we had. Sometimes that meant a camp stove—but it got the job done.
Photo by Rich Jamison

"I helped derock the road from Morningstar down to the bottom of the mesa, which was about three miles. One of the therapies for pregnant women was to throw rocks off the road to make them strong. Meanwhile, Paul built us a tiny, six-sided shelter near the *acequia*, large enough for sleeping but not for standing. It was made of rough-cut lumber from the nearby mill and had a narrow plastic strip nailed to an opening on the ceiling, so light could come through. The door had no hinges; it opened and closed like the lid to a cookie jar. I walked barefoot across the mesa that summer without ever getting stuck by cactus. When we needed water, I'd tie a couple of jugs onto a rope, sling them across my shoulder and walk down the steep trail to the springs. Coming back home, the whole world seemed filled with the sound of Om.

"My goat Priscilla had long curly hair and horns. Every time I went to milk her she acted like she was going to butt me in the stomach. She had me totally intimidated. Occasionally, she let me milk her.

"The day before my baby was born I laid the first course of adobe bricks on the room that was to be ours. It was important to me that I laid at least one row of bricks. Paul delivered Nova, our daughter, in the shelter—our resident midwife watched over him. A doctor who was visiting checked me out and gave my baby her first shots. He gave all the kids shots if their parents requested them. I washed my baby's diapers in the cold waters of the ditch. Nova was a healthy baby. Some weeks after the birth, I went to Safeway and weighed her in one of their produce scales, somewhere between the lettuce and zucchini. She was over eight pounds. A sweet old Hispanic woman came over and admired her with me. She thought Nova would be perfect for a nativity scene.

"Before the first snow fell that winter, the pueblo was built. We were at least 30 people now. The men made the bricks and the women cooked. One wild woman walked around naked with sunglasses on when she cooked. She'd buy boxes of Velveeta cheese with her food stamps. When the cheese was melted over the pasta, she'd screech, 'Come and get it!'

"When Paul and I moved into our room, my mother sent me money and I decided to buy a little cook stove. Driving down a country road in Des Montes, we saw a house with a big barn. I knocked on the door and asked if they had any cook stoves for sale? The lady sold me a beautiful cook stove, the littlest one I'd ever seen. From then on, I ground all my grains and made bread every day. I'd be hanging out in a friend's room, and suddenly I'd perk up, as if I'd just heard something. 'Oh, my bread is calling. Got to go stoke the fire.' I knew just when my stove needed more wood.

"We continued to have weekly meetings with Reality Construction Company. I was only there once. The guys had more contact with them. In fact, our guys partied with them and their women. I stayed at Morningstar until Nova was two. By the time I left, most of the people who'd gathered there before the full moon in Scorpio had built separate houses. But I'll never forget mornings when a bunch of us would watch the sun rise over the mountain and melt across the mesa. We'd lean against a warm adobe wall and drink hot coffee while Jason strummed his guitar. Kids and dogs ran around peacefully. We were far from the madding crowd, although some might have considered us to be quite mad."

Update:
Rose lives in a solar home with her son, a dog and a cat on the edge of a mesa overlooking the Arroyo Hondo Valley, just a few miles down river from where Morningstar once existed. She attends the University of New Mexico. Rose has added Buddhist practice to her Jewish roots and meditates at a center in Santa Fe. She is the director of a program where she trains volunteers to work with people who are dying. And she is still searching for a life style far from the madding crowd.

Vandalism, fights erupt...

Hippies Attacked

Numerous incidents of vandalism last week brought reinforcements of police into the area to prevent further trouble over the weekend.

Some 25 law enforcement officers were patrolling the Taos area last weekend to prevent a recurrence of acts of vandalism which were prevalent in the area on Wednesday and Thursday nights.

State Police offices weren't immune, either. Officer James Aragon found at 5 a.m. this Tuesday that someone had broken into the police building on Santa Fe Road, throwing down a typewriter and a number of small radios, upsetting files, and generally creating a mess.

Nothing was stolen, however, and officers theorized that the vandalism was of a "show-off" nature.

Earlier Monday night, occupants of a house near Taos High School reported to officers that their house was under a rock-throwing attack. When officers arrived, the rock-throwers had fled.

The only other reported incident was the firing of a fireworks rocket on Taos Plaza during the evening; lots of noise, but no damage.

At an opening party last Wednesday night, Modern Art on Cabot Plaza, an apparently intoxicated individual entered the gallery cursing the attendees. From the time the incident occurred until midnight, 19 fights were reported, three windows on business establishments were broken, and a window on the town police car was smashed.

Levi Esquibel of the Taos Police worked through two eight-hour shifts in an effort to control the vandalism, which appeared to be directed at various "hippie" establishments.

The "Hexagram," a craft shop, reported one window broken, and the Macrobiotic Restaurant reported window damage.

Esquibel said, "There were more fights than we could cover; when we got to one, they had broken up and started fighting somewhere else."

Fights were reported with hippies and juveniles involved, though no arrests were made and none of those involved was apprehended.

On Thursday night, vandalism continued. Five windows at the General Store were broken. Two windows at the Macrobiotic Restaurant were broken and the windshield of a bus was broken after the bus had been forced off Highway 240 while it was traveling west at about 9 p.m.

State Police Major Martin Vigil and new District Commander J.D. Maes were in the area and held an organizational meeting Friday to plan areas of surveillance for the weekend.

One police officer reported that gunfire had been directed at him in the Ponce de Leon Hot Springs area. Nobody was injured and there was no damage.

On Saturday night a window was broken at the Northern New Mexico Real Estate Exchange and two were broken at a residence. Francis Martin, owner of the Exchange, commented, "If people are afraid of losing tourists because of hippies, what do they think will happen when the tourists see all the broken windows in town?"

Another observer said, "Maybe things will settle down when the hippies catch on that somebody doesn't like them."

From Anthropologist to Native

told by Alfred Hobbs to Iris Keltz

We're sitting around the wooden table in Alfred's adobe casa in Cañon, where he's been adding and removing walls since 1974. His house is an ever-changing labyrinth. Sections of the house are 190 years old and were the old Cañon mill house. Pointing to a carved wooden star hanging over the refrigerator he says, "That's the original Morningstar sign. I pulled it out of the trash. It was the only sign ever to hang at the commune and look, it's been chopped on pretty bad." Two July's ago, Alfred celebrated his 70th birthday on a barren piece of sagebrush out towards Tres Orejas, jokingly referred to as Hobbsville. Hundreds of people showed up, some traveling from as far as Hawaii and Japan to be there. At sunset, a kilted man played 'Happy Birthday' on the bagpipes. Alfred gleefully handed out herbal butter on crackers. Rock bands played live music. Kegs of beer and cheap wine were still flowing plentifully when I left at midnight. Aging hippies showed up to see old friends and get gushingly nostalgic. Some old friends who had given up drugs and alcohol made a point of not going. The most wondrous sight was the young people, curious and hungry to taste the past at a gathering only an old hippie like Alfred could conjure.

Alfred Hobbs holding the original Morningstar Sign in his home, summer of 1999. Photo by Iris Keltz

"By the time I reached the communes, I was in my 40s and had traveled around Asia and Africa. In 1945—as a young man—I was a Marine in occupied Japan. Things happened that made me question why I had been killing these people. When I got back to the States and was studying at the University of North Carolina, I discovered a book called *The Perennial Philosophy* by Aldous Huxley. He believed that the material life was not important. You have to come to know yourself and accept who you are. It made a lot of sense. That was the first time I saw any alternative to what I had known growing up as a Presbyterian in North Carolina.

"When my graduate work in anthropology from Syracuse University was finished, I planned a trip to India for my dissertation on urban migration. I'd lived in Pakistan for two years and noticed that people were moving into the cities. I wondered how they adapted to city life. That idea—going to India—fell through for lack of funds and I found myself looking for another topic.

"One of my students mentioned he was going to bum around the country for the summer by staying in different 'crash pads.' In 1969 young people were migrating around the country. I began to research the traditional communes of the 19th century, which were extremely authoritarian. The new communes were anything but that. Could they even be considered communes if they were unable to maintain any kind of structure?

"I took off across the country to do the research with Carole, a woman I'd met in New York. We visited many communes before ending up at Morningstar in New Mexico. I told the guys up front that I was an anthropologist doing my dissertation on hippie communes. Nobody minded, so I took the camper shell off my truck and lived in it, right in the middle of the parking lot. Carol rented a house in Taos on Dragoon Lane. The guys from Morningstar and I used to stop at her house for hot showers during town runs.

"Every evening I took notes. It was damn cold that first winter. For three nights it went to 35 below zero. My dog slept in the sleeping bag with me. One morning, I woke up with a horizontal stalagmite of frost pointing right at me, stuck to the camper wall. It was from my breathing.

"There were three main groups—the winos, the peyote people and the communists who were obsessed with the idea that this shared lifestyle could somehow work. The winos went to peyote meetings to get stoned and the peyote people were hard-core communists. Morningstar was closer to the edge than anything I'd seen across the country. I think anarchy is something we all ought to be working for in the sense that everyone has to take responsibility to keep the thing going, but that doesn't include violence.

"There were two ways to arrive at Morningstar. You could drive up the road or just appear. Those who drove up usually never stayed long because they had possessions, like a car, which was seen by the inhabitants of Morningstar as something they had a right to appropriate. Those who just appeared were the ones who stayed the longest because they needed it the most. At first the newcomers might sleep in the bushes and stand in back of the food line when it was time. Then they'd get an attachment to somebody and start visiting their room and sleeping on the floor somewhere. Before you knew it, they'd move in. Those who lived in the room usually felt like they didn't have the right to kick anyone out.

"Once there was this guy who came from a wealthy family in the Midwest. At first he hid under a straw hat that was down over his face, and an army coat that hung down to the top of these old cowboy boots with loose heels that would slap back up at him with every step. He was filthy as hell. Late one night when the guys talked together in the darkened kitchen, he admitted that he'd been in one of those fancy mental institutions before he came to Morningstar. He left months later, wearing fine khaki trousers and a clean shirt with a paisley ascot, all from the free box. Down the road and back into the world he went.

"Years later he came to visit me in my house with his plump Midwestern wife, driving a big Pontiac. He was working in the family's rug business and had his act together. I told him Morningstar should have sent his family a bill for the thousands of dollars they had saved.

"A typical day would start by everyone hanging around drinking coffee and talking about who'd done what with who last night. We'd sit out there in the sun till lunch, which was usually beans and tortillas. The women cooked. After lunch, we'd go sit in the sun again. I usually drove the truck if the women wanted to go to town for a laundry run. The head of the winos would panhandle from the visiting hippies. With a running account in his head, he knew to the penny how much more was needed to buy the next gallon of Cabari. If there was enough money, we'd go to the liquor store. Drinking was a man's activity. Only Joe Cota could go into the liquor store off the plaza because he looked Spanish. If Joe wasn't with us we'd go to the Taos Supermarket.

"One day, Army Joe decided to take my truck to town for a wino run. I said, 'Like hell you are.' We got into a helluva fight. I couldn't see letting these hippie winos take my truck, the best-running vehicle on the mesa. Finally someone showed up with another vehicle—maybe it was Jerry with his VW van—and they all went to town to get their booze. I turned to my friend Patrick. 'Why in the hell didn't you stop that fight?'

"'Alfred, you didn't need to get in that fight in the first place. Fighting over a truck just ain't worth it.' He was right. To this day I keep the key in my truck. I figure if someone needs it that badly, let them just take it.

"Lots of people looked to David Pratt as an unofficial leader, but Patrick was an undeclared teacher at Morningstar. I hung out a lot with him and his wife, Clea. By the time I got to the commune they'd been living there a year. Clea found out she was pregnant

Rosie flashing the "peace sign" while climbing the school bus at Alfred's 70th birthday party, summer of 1997.
Photo by Iris Keltz

when they were living in the Tenderloin District of San Francisco and went cold turkey off drugs. After their daughter Baba was born, Clea took their last welfare check, bought an old van, loaded it with Patrick, the baby and some food and drove into the desert until it ran out of gas. It was Patrick's turn to go cold turkey. It took him two weeks to sweat it out. Finally he got it together to get some gas and drove the hell out of there. They joined the movement to Northern New Mexico and ended up staying at Morningstar for two-and-a-half years.

"Patrick was the best mechanic on the mesa. He kept the vehicles running, especially the old flatbed we needed for wood runs. Getting a wood run together was a monstrous activity. Nobody really wanted

Wood was always a chore—getting it, cutting it, splitting it into stove size. You had to be careful—Asa Hearts almost cut off his hand one time with a chainsaw, he was so stoned.

Photo by Rich Jamison

to go. Most of the wood was scrounged. We'd drive down the road and pick up pieces. The wood had to be cut by hand until we got our chainsaw, and then Asa almost cut off his hand one time, he was so stoned.

"Asa Hearts was my other good buddy. He got his name one night in a card game. Cowboy Bob, a macho, wino, cowboy-type wanted a room that had come open. So did Asa, who was then using his original name, David. Cowboy Bob said, 'Let's draw cards for the room.' The cowboy drew a jack and Asa pulled up the ace of hearts. Then Cowboy Bob said, 'Two out of three.' He shuffled the cards and got an eight. Again Asa pulled up the ace of hearts. After that he was always called Asa Hearts. He even got that name put on his social security card.

"Clea, Patrick's wife, also had a quality of leadership about her. She was the one who got town trips going. She didn't do this in the way of running things, but if she said she was going to do laundry or grocery shopping, a lot of people showed up at her house with dirty laundry and went to town with her.

"There was a lot of violence back then—sometimes among ourselves and sometimes between us and Reality, the other commune on the mesa, and sometimes between the hippies and the locals. Morningstar people didn't believe in violent revolution like the people at Reality so we usually stayed away from them—except when we'd get messed up at peyote meetings together.

"When Tom Brown was made hippie sheriff of Morningstar to stop the thieving and violence, his power came from how obnoxious he was. Nobody could put up with him. He lived in the goat pen—about a hundred yards from the pueblo—with Army Joe and an eclectic group of winos and druggies who just wanted to be left alone. The pen smelled so bad the goats stayed away. One of the things I learned from Patrick was that if you don't want to encourage people like Tom Brown, just walk away from them, don't fight them. Don't confront them.

"One afternoon David Pratt and his wife Penny were coming back from a peyote meeting and were jumped by some of the drunks at Selso's Bar. When they came home and told us, all the winos jumped into Jerry's VW van and headed to Selso's but only Joe Cota and Jerry were visible. Six or eight local guys were sitting in the bar. When they saw the van, they said, 'Oh, here come some more hippies. Let's jump them. Hey, hippie, come on over.' With that the doors to the van slid open and out popped four more hippies. Everyone had sticks. We beat the crap out of them. There was only one more fight after that.

"Michael Duncan's approach to the violence was different. We dealt with it the only way we knew how, by direct confrontation—they jump us, we gotta jump them back. Michael started giving out acid to the local guys, getting them hooked on the stuff. It mellowed them right out. First thing you know they were up on the mesa playing baseball with us. That was his version of 'chemical warfare.'

"One communal thing we did was to pile into my truck and drive to Colorado to glean the fields for potatoes, carrots and cabbages. After the machines went through, the farmers would let us have stuff for free. We'd fill burlap bags and empty them into the truck. It was easy. We must have been carrying 2,000 pounds of potatoes not including all those hippies—men, women and babies. How that truck made it up the hill out of Questa, I'll never know. We were going to dig a root cellar, but we never got around to it, so the vegetables were stored in the community room where a lot of them rotted.

"I left Morningstar that spring along with lots of the people I had gotten to know. I never finished my dissertation, although I still have my notes. All this happened almost 30 years ago, but walking through Taos the other day I saw a guy in the street who looked like he needed a place like Morningstar—a space without shrinks, rules or government sponsorship, a place that left people free to work out their problems. That was the real function of the communes, and in that sense Morningstar and New Buffalo were successful, although not everyone survived their madness."

Alfred eating some "herbal buttah" and crackers at his birthday party. *Photo by Iris Keltz*

Update:

For the past 20 years, Alfred Hobbs has been working on pipeline constructions as an archeologist and environmental inspector. He has recently returned from a nine-month trip around the world, starting in Europe, across Russia, China, Indonesia, Australia, Tahiti, Tierra del Fuego, Antarctica and up through South America and home. This was his third trip around the world. He is planning his 75th birthday on the full moon in cancer in 2001 and "you're all invited."

reality construction company

Fountain of Light ***April #12***

A member of Reality, Jasper Blowsnake, sent us this:

It is necessary at this point in history to be concerned with the common good of the people. All thought about self must be expelled in order that one may become individually responsible for the whole—the whole of humanity. The establishment of cooperative groups is necessary for the production of food stuffs and the perpetuation of the biological process—life on the planet. The prerequisite for selflessness is to begin the establishment of such cooperative groups—to begin—not to join an established order, not to step in another's gain. The whole damned world is over-populated. Find for yourself that which will bring joy to others. Don't expect it to be handed to you. We will not fail in the task we have set out to do here. We intended not to be interfered with by irresponsible people. You've got to do it yourself. This is an enormous continent with lots of available land. Northern New Mexico is an arid dry terrain. The wood is sparse. The people are poor and are being invaded. This is a plea for help. Don't come.

There has been here at Reality an establishment of regulatory factors such as—setting and maintaining a stable population of stable individuals—meetings of 40 and 50 people around a table built to seat 25 comfortably to decide who will have to leave—very unnatural—but necessary. We have regular meetings to lay out work projects and decide who is to do certain jobs. We are a family of 25. We have been together a year. If too many people are here sometimes you don't talk to your brothers for days and the family has lost track of itself. We are working together with 20 acres of very poor land to fertilize, compost, terrace, furrow, and irrigate in the best way we can. We are building a green house, hotbeds, goat pen, chicken coop, tool shed, work shop, garage, etc. and we need to know who the family is—to be strong and to get the job done right. What more do we need to offer a visiting brother but a good day's work, three good meals and a good night sleep and that's all! This is a way of life, not a scenic wonderland—a bridge, not the water flowing under it. Visitors are encouraged to find for themselves in another State, a family and begin themselves elsewhere. Plainly, frankly, openly and honestly—begin for yourself. It is a sin to step in another's gain.

We do not play any games of friendliness, unity, one humanity, cosmic cowboy bullshit—we all know that! We inform our brothers of the possibilities available to them elsewhere and encourage them to move on. This we all agree is the right thing to do.

We are striving to become self-sufficient. We are eating less and only what is available and/or grown here. The possibilities of global famine are imminent—soon there will be many more cooperative farming groups all over America. If you establish them—do it by our example if you like—but do it! This is one way of curing the illness of this earth.

The land we are established on is specifically designated for cultivation and game preservation. There is no room for more dwelling structures. The land has told us it cannot feed more people.

The time has come to adopt a way of life that will give meaning to the sojourn on earth. Begin now to establish cooperation community.

Buy land in every state and with vigilance put into operation this dream. But above all remember, Mother Cabrini says, "Don't come to New Mexico and if you are already here with nothing to do—LEAVE!"

Saturday Nights at Morningstar

by Iris Keltz

"Oh, yeah, every night was Saturday night at Morningstar!" Alfred emphatically stated during a nostalgic rap session. He should know, being one of the most legendary hippies whoever found his way up to that pristine mesa.

"Alfred, was that a true story about how you got to Morningstar?"

"Which story might that be?" he asked with his full-bellied contagious laugh.

"That you arrived wearing a suit and tie and carrying an attaché case. That you got out of your camper, took all your clothes off, and stood naked before heaven and earth and everyone on the mesa. That you proceeded to hand out pot, hash, LSD and mescalin to everyone who was present. Was that true?"

Grinning at me, he said, "Let's just say that some of the twists in the story have changed over the years, but never doubt the mustard seed of truth."

I first met the guys from Morningstar on their weekly water runs when I lived at New Buffalo commune across the valley. Irrigation ditches watered their fields but they had no drinking water. Getting water from the Buffalo well was an all-day event. They bounced along the rutted dirt road between the two communes in an antiquated pickup truck loaded with empty wooden barrels soon to be filled and full bottles of Tokay soon to be emptied. "Tokay, it's okay," was the chant that rang through the New Buffalo kitchen and drumming room. They rarely brought women with them.

Their costumes were more dramatic than the ragged farm clothes worn by the guys of New Buffalo. Those into the macho-bandito-pirate look had filthy, unkempt beards, matted hair and sweaty bandanas tied around their neck. Sometimes a silver hoop pierced an ear and if they wore a cowboy hat, it was torn. Those into the Native American look had shoulder-length braids lashed with leather thongs, hand-beaded earrings and turquoise necklaces. In a no-cash economy, jewelry was either made at home or you traded for it.

Although they drank cheap wine, these were the productive guys. The really bad guys they left at Morningstar. Relations between the two communes were friendly despite the differences.

One hot summer's day, I decided to visit the residents of Morningstar in their natural habitat. The drive would have taken me ten minutes, but it was better to arrive at Morningstar on foot. Stopping along the way to pick up my mail at the post office, to munch on wild watercress by the river, I made my weekly call home from Selso's Bar, and crossed the highway. Joyce was hanging laundry when I passed. We chatted.

She had been my first friend at New Buffalo. Now she lived in a rented adobe with her husband and children. Contentedly she diapered her newest baby—she already had three. Her husband had been a hard worker when they lived at the commune. Now *his* family benefited from his work—not indiscriminate wanderers in the Aquarian Age who showed up at dinnertime.

Up the road, past the curve, a secondary road took off into the sagebrush. A wind- spattered, hand-painted sign read: THIS IS NOT THE ROAD TO REALITY. I rolled some tobacco and contemplated this for a moment. A statement as well as a warning, the sign referred to Reality Construction Company, the Third World commune specializing in the needs of the disenfranchised. The barrel of a shotgun greeted uninvited guests. Both communities fought for territorial dominance over the mesa, which was legally owned by Michael Duncan.

I took the trail that didn't lead to Reality. The canyon narrowed as it followed the river upstream to a little delta. The scrub oak on the delta appeared to be in bloom, as if some poppies decided they were in the Elysian Fields. On closer inspection it turned out that the vermilion was puffballs of dyed wool drying on the branches. A woman with Medusa-like hair and saucer blue eyes sat spinning.

"Hello, Marilyn," I said softly, not wanting to intrude. "I've heard about your lovely island and your fine weaving." Actually, she was a squatter and I didn't know she was a weaver until this moment, but it seemed the right thing to say. "I'm just passing through on my way to the Morningstar mesa."

A tall blonde man was cooking macaroni and cheese in a black cast iron pot hanging over an open fire. They invited me to stay for lunch.

In the distance, two loin-clothed hippies sat warming themselves on the stone roof of their cave, doing beadwork. They waved. Through the treetops behind them colorful ribbons blew in the wind from the tops of tipi poles.

The scent of cedar mixed with sweat as I climbed the steep hillside. My legs were sore and I was thirsty by the time I got to the mesa top. In the distance, Morningstar stood like an adobe feudal manor with no master plan. While taking in the grandeur of the landscape, a mare came galloping across the mesa, tearing through barbed wire fences, heading in my direction. I stood transfixed and watched as a half-naked hippie rode bareback on a horse with a nose like a Buick. Several guys were chasing it. The horse saw me and veered away. The guys stopped running long enough to catch their breath. "We've been trying to breed that damn horse for a month and he's shown no interest in anything until Eddie Gaudet climbed on her back. And now she's wild, out of control. Not only that, Carmen's got colic and Alfred's going to shoot her."

"Who's Carmen, who's Alfred?" I asked in alarm.

"Carmen is Alfred's horse." I was a little relieved she wasn't a woman.

"Why does he want to shoot her?"

"He lost his watch and one of his gloves in her bowels, trying to feel her intestines because she hasn't shit in weeks." It sounded like a lot of horse trouble to me.

"Hey man, is anyone at home at the commune?" I asked unnecessarily. The more the merrier was the dominant philosophy in this anarchistic society. Winos, psychopaths, idealists, visionaries, thieves, druggies, children, mothers, fewer fathers and a midwife lived in a perpetual state of attempted harmony, eking out a very basic life style.

Walking towards the pueblo, smelling the aromatic smoke from the cedar fires, I saw a naked woman stooped over the ditch washing diapers. She didn't notice me. Near the communal kitchen that had suffered a fire, a woman was grinding wheat, her breasts bobbing about as she cranked the old grinder. Naked kids were running around playing with barking dogs. A group of men stood sunning against the western wall of the pueblo. Things seemed more peaceful than I'd expected.

"Hey, howya doing? I didn't hear a car drive up. How'd you get here?" It was Jason, one of the guys I'd met on a water run.

"I walked."

Before visiting, I'd been warned that my car and money could be liberated for a town run to buy booze for the local winos. I didn't want to seem uncool or uptight about possessions, especially when faced with hospitable people willing to share their last food stamps. Ethics here were confusing.

"Hey, man, is anyone home?" I asked unnecessarily, because doors were never locked and someone was always home. The more the merrier was the dominant philosophy in the anarchistic society at Morningstar.
Photo by Rich Jamison

"Wanna cup of coffee? David and Penny just made a fresh pot in their room. We're getting ready for a peyote meeting." He explained to me that Michael, the patrón of the mesa, had given an ultimatum. Either the thievery and the shoot-outs had to stop or everyone would be evicted, even if that meant dismantling the pueblo brick by adobe brick. Everyone knew who was behind the thievery, but nobody could figure out what to do. As for the shoot-outs, they had to defend themselves against the radicals living at Reality. The peyote meeting was to pray for peace on the mesa. Neither commune wanted to leave. Most people had no place to go to.

When my eyes adjusted to the twilight in David and Penny's room, I saw people sprawled on the bed, leaning against a dresser and lying on the floor. A tall, slender man wearing a cowboy hat and boots offered me a cup of honeyed coffee and a hot tortilla with melted butter. It was David Pratt. He looked tired. He truly believed in sharing what little he and his wife had, but his idealism was costly. His blue eyes flashed

Hanging out and chillin'. Our civil disobedience was to be in the moment. We discussed everything—the practical matters of everyday life as well as the philosophical innuendoes of those practical matters.

Photo by Rich Jamison

angrily around the room. David was telling someone that if this peyote meeting didn't bring the needed peace, he would consider leaving. He was close to burnout.

Part artist, visionary, farmer, philosopher and pioneer recycler, he existed as a cornerstone for this community where people discussed the practical matters of everyday life as well as the philosophical innuendoes of those practical matters. I had no idea that the garbage in and around his room was destined to become a unique form of collage art. Since food stamps could not buy art supplies, he recreated the world around him on giant pallets using found stuff and garbage.

The only women from Morningstar at this meeting were David's wife Penny and Rubria. And only Rubria expressed her opinions. The other women were too busy cooking, baking, gardening and taking care of the children to deal with the threatening issues being discussed today.

I felt welcomed at Morningstar in spite of the chaos. My visits there left me with the impression that the forces of light and dark had been given free rein to run amuck and see which would be the victor. At its heyday, this communal pueblo sprawled across the mesa to include acres of corn, alfalfa and vegetable gardens; outlying suburbs consisted of tipis, hogans, pit houses, cave dwellings or sleeping bags under the stars. Miracles transpired regularly, like the miracle of the midwife who kept mothers and babies healthy under conditions some would call squalor and some would shout, "Let's burn the place down." Despite all the difficulties, the children, pregnant women, animals and shelters gave Morningstar the impression of permanence, the feeling that this community would be fruitful and multiply.

Fountain of Light   April #2

Dearest favorite Third daughter, Vicki "Cinnamon" Hammer, known at times as Betty &/or Mary Russell,

Vicki, come home now, please. It's been so long, honey, and we miss you so very much. Don't you miss us just a little bit by now, too? I'd always figured I was raising you kids to someday fly the nest; and that's the way it should be. I tried to teach you good enough so that in a pinch, even while young, you could manage for yourself, and for me if necessary. And you are all of you, pretty darned good; all 6 of you. Yes, Vicki, you're pretty grown up for fourteen (14) years...but honey, that's still too young. And so soon for us to have to lose you. —At 17 or 18 yrs. I would have been prepared to see you go,—with enough education to get a job and a place of your own, like Phyllis did. Come on honey give us a couple more years, will you? We need you. You help lite up our lives. Didn't you know that? Can't you see how upset we are as a family? You know what worrywarts we are. Your dad can't work regularly, he spends so much time trying to figure out where you're at and sometimes going where he thinks you might be; but of course it never is right. And only rumors have given any comforting clue to the condition of your health or safety.

But your dad and I ache inside constantly. You know how I hate to cry. So I try not to talk too much about you, or look at your pictures, because my throat and eyes get all messed up from lumps and all—you know...Anyway,—did you know Gina's back home now? And we were so disappointed you weren't with her. She said the two of you were planning on being here for X-mas. Please make her be right. You know how it will be here with us without you? You must know! Phyllis is going to try to be home, too.

Come home, "Cin"; no big hassle;...some talk;...some figuring;...but "Cinnamon," don't let our family stay under this depression of needing you here to make it right and as crazily normal as usual.

Your dad and Ray spent a week going to Colorado and back, on a tip, trying to find you. But you had left just two days before he got there—wouldn't you just expect the luck!!? How depressingly disappointing it was when his trip turned out to be a dud. I had your clothes packed for you to use on the way home and everything. But I didn't cry then either. Because if I got started I might not know how to stop. And that's no good, either. They (Red and Ray) did meet a lot of swell kids tho—at Drop City and Boulder and all over the country. They brought back Jim and Gale, and Wendy from A and Lolita from the same. Wendy and Lolita stayed the other nite with us and then went along with Gina and a couple other kids with Ray, to the West Palm Beach Festival for the weekend. Sheila went with Daryl and others.

Shelia has quit "hi" and is working and going to nite school. We hoped you'd be here to start a cashier's course with us in January, (lasts 3 weeks) if we can get the necessary o-k's for you. Then you could have a good job (they find you one at the class) for after school. We can get a tutor meanwhile to get you caught up on the studies you've missed.

Remember, dear daughter, we ALL miss you. Sheila tells me of dreams of you. Steve says he misses you especially when he goes to the 7-to-11; you always went with him...—and Phyllis calls all the time, hoping for good news. And every time the phone rings we silently hope and mentally cross our fingers, that maybe this will be you or the lead to you...Maybe the next ring...?? With Love as much and as ever, Mother and Dad and all of us...

"Mom"

P.S. We hoped and prepared in case you dropped in at last moment—really looked! And we missed you sadly—couldn't you scrape up enough to call direct even? We can't stop looking for you to be ready to come back home.

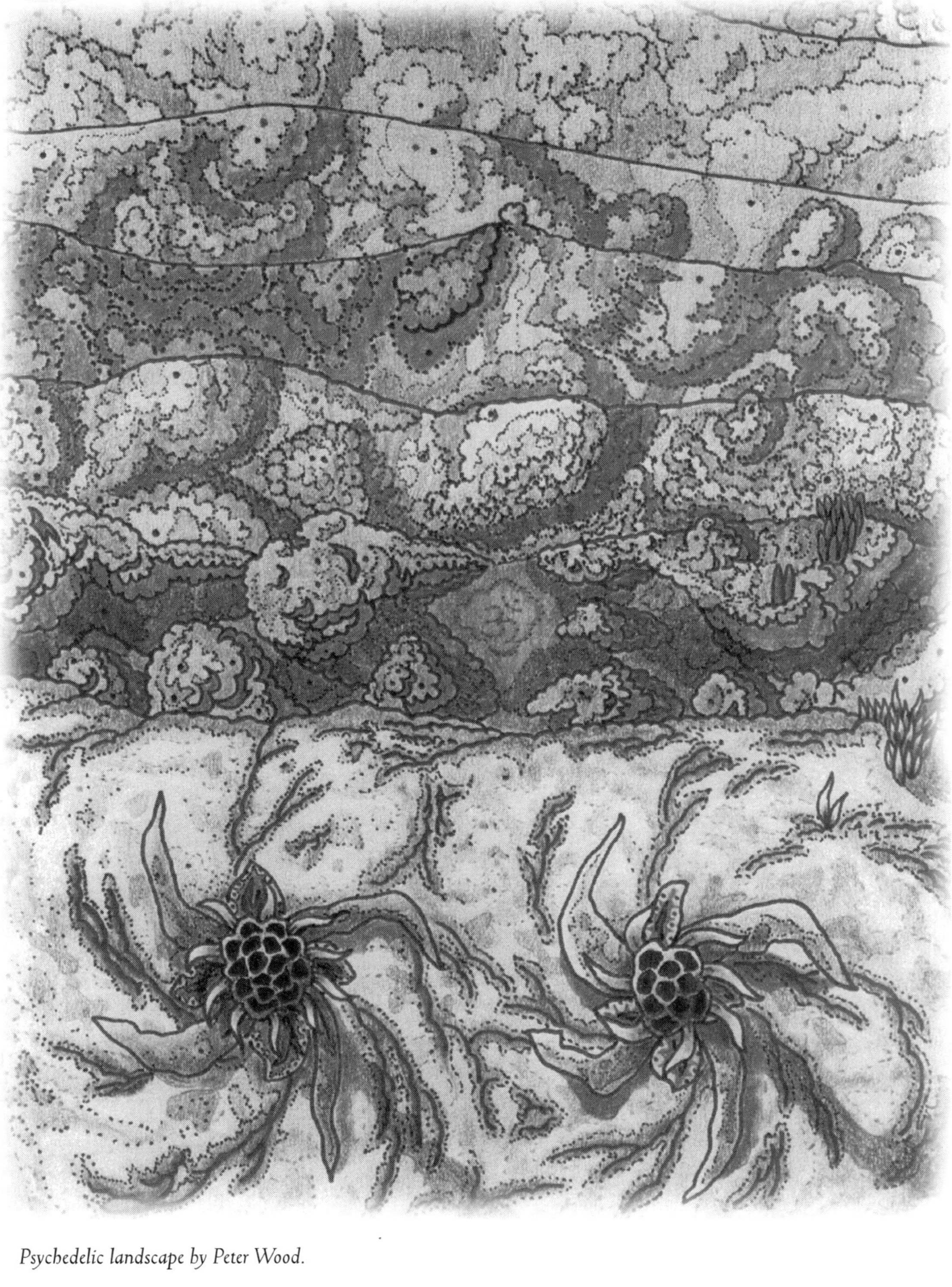

Psychedelic landscape by Peter Wood.

The Peyote Church

by Iris Keltz

In the dust of a summer's evening, people gathered around the tipi on Morningstar mesa, dressed in an interpretation of church clothes. My hand-sewn ankle length skirt—with fuchsia, gold and blue shocks of corn growing in ultraviolet light—rippled around my hips. The cloth came from El Mercado, a popular dry goods store on the plaza, where Indian and Hispanic women purchased fabric for fiesta and ceremonial clothing.

It was the eve of Mother's Day and this meeting was to honor Mother Earth, mothers-to-be, our own mothers, and nurturers in the community. It was also to deal with the problems at Morningstar commune. Michael Duncan, the patron of the mesa, was threatening to kick everyone off his land if the plague of thefts and violence didn't stop.

I helped Little Joe's wife Adrian organize the food for the morning breakfast and she made sure I was aware of the strict protocol.

"Once you go into that tipi, be prepared to stay until morning. No one leaves in the middle of a meeting. People have gotten into bad trouble for doing that, like dying or worse." What's worse than dying, I wondered.

"Not even to pee?" I asked.

"You can go outside with permission, but you better come right back. They're not fooling around in there. They mean business. You'll learn how to pray with your heart and soul."

Dignity and simplicity shone through Little Joe, an old pueblo Indian who was tonight's roadman. He spoke broken English and had the awesome task of making sure the ritual was done right. Every detail had to be taken care of so that everyone made it safely through the night. Little Joe was as diminutive as Adrian was large. He reached her shoulders.

The tipi faced east. I entered it with reverence and a little fear, following the person in front of me around the edge, always moving from east to west like the celestial cycles. I remembered Moe's stories about the power and mystery of the church. A fat peyote button sat on an earthen altar next to the crackling fire in the center. Justin, the fire tender, was the scruffy Davy Crocket-look-alike Faisal and I had met on our first day at New

Buffalo. He welcomed me to the peyote meeting just like he had that day. His job was to make sure the fire burned clean and strong all night.

Justin was respected when respect was associated with rebellion against authority. The mischievous look in his eyes seemed to say, "Here I am, a fire tender for the church, but don't you think I'm not a sinner."

A gourd rattle, a water drum and Little Joe's singing started the nightlong ceremony. The sounds merged like the wind, rain and lightening during a storm and became the heartbeat of the world. Little Joe's attempt to teach transplanted dropouts of an urban materialistic society to pray and to revere the natural world was nothing less than noble.

The Indians called it medicine. They told us to chew slowly and taste the bitter peyote. People were vomiting all around me, but that only made them want more. I gagged on the peyote tea and spit up the dried buttons. The taste was vile.

The drum and rattle passed around the circle. I stared through the flames and got lost in faces. Across the fire was a woman in red. Her rouged cheeks, thickly spread red lipstick, and a red silk Chinese dress made her look as if she were bathing in flames. I'd seen her at the Lama Foundation when I went Sufi dancing. They called her the little nun as she silently walked around in monk's robes, carrying a small chalkboard, smiling to everyone. Tonight the drab browns and grays of her former life vanished. She became a warrior woman on the hunt.

Bapook's wife contentedly suckled her baby, a shawl modestly covering milky breasts. A man across the fire was swaying while he prayed, reminding me of an old Jew praying in synagogue. Wearing his turquoise Navajo wedding shirt, David Pratt stood out, not for his dress but because everyone knew he was the acknowledged non-leader of Morningstar. He was here to make peace between the warring factions.

With his shovel, the fire tender scooped up reddening coals, shaping them into a glowing phoenix that grew until the bird seemed ready to fly. During the night, Justin blessed me at the adobe altar, flapping black eagle feathers around my body and gathering smoke from the dried cedar needles sprinkled on the coal bed.

I felt an urgency to go outside and asked for permission to leave the tipi. Stars glowed in a cobalt sky. A light breeze carried the scent of sage and cedar. I took deep breaths to help with the nausea. Little Joe was vomiting in a nearby arroyo when his wife, who'd been preparing the morning feast, saw him and started running. They moved towards each other as if in slow motion, with the intensity of two worlds about to collide. They met. Fragile and petite, he looked like a child lost in his mother's bulky, hovering embrace. She finally released him.

"Are you all right, honey?" she asked.

"Yeah, yeah," he muttered. The Milky Way lit their silhouettes. He paused for a moment and returned to the tipi, she to the hogan.

The drum and rattle passed around the circle, each singer's song a unique prayer to the universe.

Rubria's voice jolted me to alertness, cutting off the possibility of sleep. One of the only women who sang at peyote meetings, she belted out her songs like Janis Joplin. Most people sang in Tewa; she sang in English.

Meet me, Jesus, meet me,
Meet me in the middle of the air.
And if these wings should fail me,
Meet me with another pair.
Well, well, well, so I can lie easy,
Well, well, well, hold my hand.
Well, well, well, so I can die easy,
Jesus, won't you make me another pair?

Little Joe Gomez was our wise man and our teacher. He was one of the elders from the Taos Pueblo. We knew we were very lucky to have him guiding and helping us. *Photo by Tony Vinella*

Suddenly someone spoke. He was not holding the drum or rattle. The tipi became silent as the man's voice gained momentum from his extravagant confession. "I am telling everyone here of my love for a woman who is married to one of the men sitting in this circle. I am asking for help. The temptation is great. I am a tortured man about to do something I might regret forever."

All eyes turned to the wife in question. She sat with the straight back of a primal animal waiting to be taken away by the victor. The husband in question was blissed out on peyote and missed the confession. His face never wavered from the beatific grin of someone listening to the sound of a different drummer. A person in the group responded. "We hear your struggle, brother, and we forgive you your sinful thoughts. May you find the strength to overcome your temptations." Heads nodded in agreement. The tormented lover smiled humbly and the drumming and singing started again.

The drum and rattle were being passed around the circle for the last time. David Pratt, the non-leader of Morningstar, had waited for this moment to speak. He held the rattle like a scepter. "You all know who I am. I love Morningstar and our life here, but it won't last with all the thievin' and gun shootin'. I've thought and prayed about what to do. We all know who's behind this—Tom Brown and his friends. Let's make him sheriff of Morningstar. Maybe he'll feel so proud of bein' sheriff, he'll get his friends to stop drinkin' and thievin'. Anyway, it's worth a try." This was a desperate plan, and the pain in his voice was palpable.

Anarchy ruled at Morningstar. It was anti-laws, rules or leaders. Everyone knew the violence would destroy it. David's idea was like giving Billy the Kid a badge, but no one had a better idea. The chief signaled the end of talking. When David sang, his prayer floated out the smoke hole into the heavens.

The sky to the east was getting lighter. Morning was close. A pregnant woman with a shawl on her head entered the tipi carrying a bucket of cold water. Her prayer was long and rambling. She spoke in glorious generalities on one hand, and personal desires on the other. We revered her as the Earth Mother bringing the life-sustaining water. She awoke in me a desire to have a child.

During the night, everyone seemed larger than life. Like the patriarchs and matriarchs of old, we needed no last names. The local flora, fauna and animals were especially honored. With names like Feather, Fig, Light, Echo, Sage, Cedar, Chamisa, Willow, Raven, Tahiti, Justin Time and Justin Case, the counterculture simmered away ethnic differences.

A shaft of sunlight came through the smoke hole with a silent thud. The colors lost their intensity and people looked more human, less mythic. The Earth Mother and others who had been sitting up all night brought breakfast into the tipi. They served food from the three kingdoms—roasted blue cornmeal, fruit and cooked meat. After the closing song, peyote fans and gourd rattles were carefully placed in their cedar boxes.

Out the tipi door and into the rising sun we went, greeted by snow-capped mountains, unbroken blue skies, cedar-and-sage scented air. It was like being present at the dawn of creation. I was filled with a longing for my unborn children. We'd made it through the night with help and were hopeful that Morningstar commune would survive for a while longer. People were smiling, embracing, telling jokes, sitting in the shade, lying on blankets, eating, drinking coffee, gossiping and reliving the meeting. A group of us headed to Black Rock hot springs for a luxuriant soak on a divine summer day.

Hippies Blamed For Fiesta's End; Scored in Resolution By Teachers

Mayor Rumaldo Garcia made it official with a "non-announcement" of the Taos fiesta at a regular meeting of the town council Tuesday night.

Noting that it had been the custom that the mayor proclaim three days of fiesta annually, honoring the early Spanish people who established Taos, Garcia said this year he had been asked to announce there will be no summer fiesta, "due to the widespread publicity Taos has received regarding the so-called hippie situation, which has been exaggerated out of all proportion."

He said that "it is felt that as a result of this publicity there might be an influx of undesirables…during fiesta" and that "this could result in serious health and law enforcement problems."

He concluded that "it is hoped that by next year the fiesta will resume and that these young people who remain to make Taos their home will have learned the personal hygiene and sanitation and also to conform to the customs of the community and will have developed an appreciation of the historical traditions of Taos, so that they may take part in the activities."

In another aspect of the hippie situation Tuesday, members of the Taos Municipal Education association by a margin of more than two to one, approved a resolution condemning the hippies and their influence.

Rudy Pacheco, president, said the unofficial count was 81 "for," as drafted, and 21 "against" and 14 for a revised resolution. He said the results are subject to change for a five day period.

The resolution in part echoed one approved earlier by the schools' administrative council. It concludes: "As parents, citizens, and educators, we ask to be included in the fight to crush this cancerous epidemic for all time."

The resolution also states at one point that the hippies' "presence among our people poses a real and verifiable danger to the moral, health and beliefs of our youth, because of their known excesses in drug addiction, sexual, obscene behavior, personal filth and general exhibitionism."

Further exhibiting the community's preoccupation with the hippie situation, the town council, Tuesday night, was advised that one resident had written the state's attorney general for advice on how to eliminate the hippies "without discrimination."

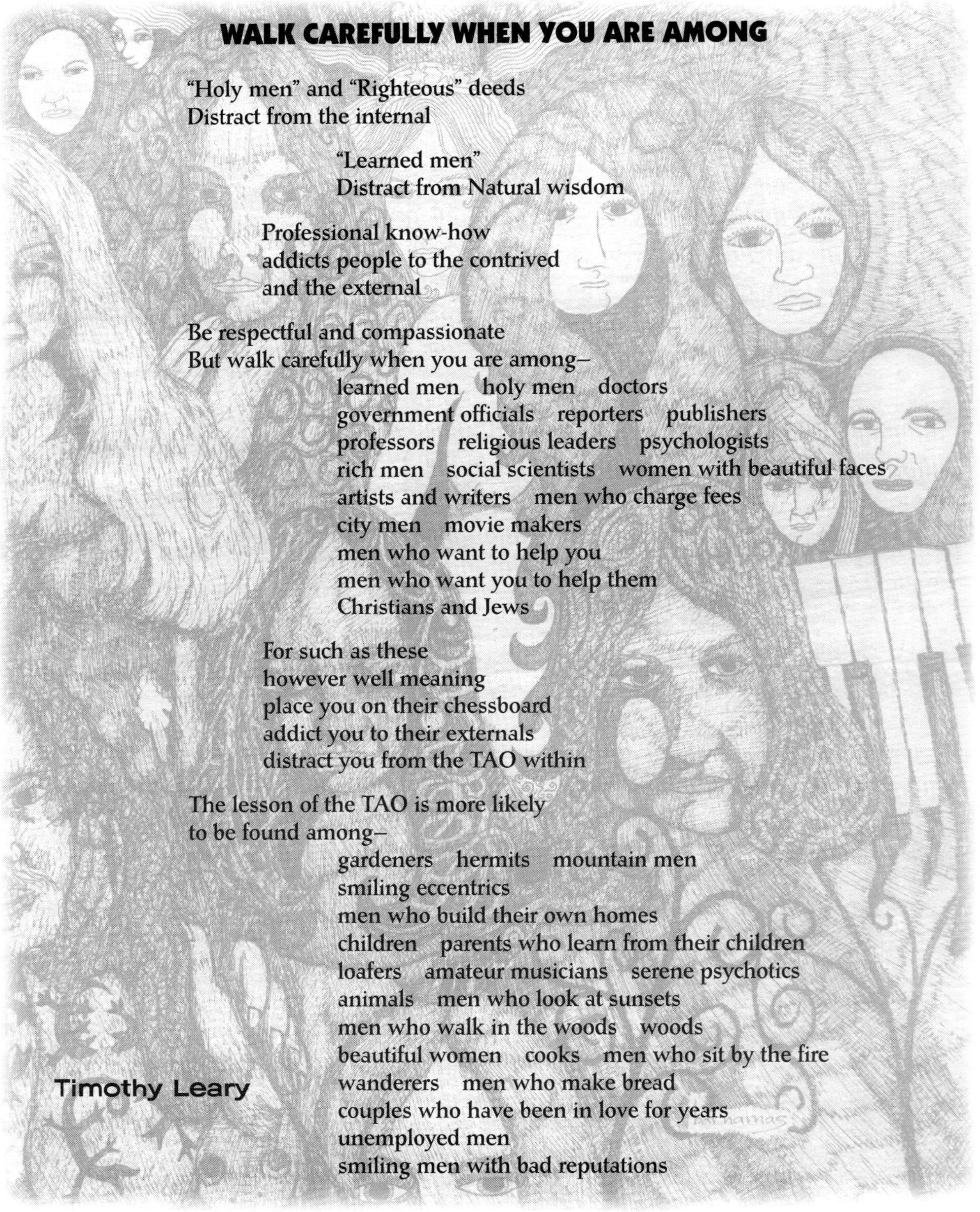

WALK CAREFULLY WHEN YOU ARE AMONG

"Holy men" and "Righteous" deeds
Distract from the internal

"Learned men"
Distract from Natural wisdom

Professional know-how
addicts people to the contrived
and the external

Be respectful and compassionate
But walk carefully when you are among–
learned men   holy men   doctors
government officials   reporters   publishers
professors   religious leaders   psychologists
rich men   social scientists   women with beautiful faces
artists and writers   men who charge fees
city men   movie makers
men who want to help you
men who want you to help them
Christians and Jews

For such as these
however well meaning
place you on their chessboard
addict you to their externals
distract you from the TAO within

The lesson of the TAO is more likely
to be found among–
gardeners   hermits   mountain men
smiling eccentrics
men who build their own homes
children   parents who learn from their children
loafers   amateur musicians   serene psychotics
animals   men who look at sunsets
men who walk in the woods   woods
beautiful women   cooks   men who sit by the fire
wanderers   men who make bread
couples who have been in love for years
unemployed men
smiling men with bad reputations

Timothy Leary

The Eddie Gaudet Story

told by Michael Duncan to Iris Keltz

"Eddie Gaudet was a Creole from south Louisiana. Somehow he passed the test to become a rookie cop in New Orleans. He was illiterate and not too bright, but he had his principles and sense of morality. When the department taught him how to roll drunks and keep their wallets he told them, 'That's not right,' and went to the newspaper. Eddie was immediately fired from the police force. He was tossed out into the streets with his wife and two kids, so he came to Morningstar. We were already being written up in the newspapers by then.

"He came to Morningstar and practiced paramilitary techniques. He was always in top shape and had hiding places all over the mesa. Meanwhile, Watergate had just broken and President Nixon was in deep political trouble, but decided to go on with his parade through the streets of New Orleans. Eddie had just gotten back from New Orleans to visit his parents. Someone, it was never established who, burned a flag by President Nixon's motorcade. In order to try to get sympathy for the president, his people portrayed that incident as an attempt on the president's life. The pharmacist who lived down the street from Eddie's family in the French Quarter allegedly told someone, 'Eddie was in town and said if someone doesn't kill that son of a bitch, someone should.'

"The next thing I know we've got cops, helicopters, the sheriff's posse and the National Guard up here, looking for Eddie Gaudet. I'm driving back home in the old '46 Chevy fire truck loaded with rocks. We were clearing the road that led up to the mesa. Suddenly I see state police all around. Colin and Adela's people—from the Taos Learning Center across the valley—had loaded rocks onto their truck to take to their site. They were building a stone growhole. I said to the police, 'Would you kindly get out of the way?' They pulled over so I could get the truck up the road.

POSSE PREPARES — State policemen and sheriff's deputies, some of the more than 20 armed men who pursued Edwin M. Gaudet for two days in the rugged hills near Arroyo Hondo last week, prepare for their final search party Tuesday. Gaudet surrendered on Wednesday, after being coaxed down from his hiding place by his wife and cousin.

from The Taos News

"When they were trying to apprehend Eddie Gaudet, they'd knock on a door at Morningstar and whoever'd answer would say, 'That's me. I'm Eddie Gaudet.' Of course he wasn't. Meanwhile, the real Eddie grabs his rifle and his bag of ammo, which is tied with a deerskin thong around his neck, and takes off down the canyon. He cuts back. They get close to him. He had one shot in the magazine and the rest of his ammo around his neck. He shot close enough to scare them so he would have a chance to split. They opened up on him and cut the ammo from around his neck with a 45-caliber slug. They came within a few inches of taking his life.

"Eddie takes off and lays in the irrigation ditch all day. The troops are tromping the property here, there and everywhere. Finally, I go up to the FBI guy and say, 'You're on my fuckin' property. Where's your warrant?

"He says, 'We don't need a warrant. A warrant was issued in New Orleans by a federal judge.'

"I said, 'Well, how about a fuckin' copy? You've got 150 armed men on my property and I've got women and children living here.'

"I go down to Harvey Mudd's house, which is the nearest telephone, to call my lawyer John Ramming. 'You better get up here quick. We've got a situation.'

"By this time we've got ABC, NBC, CBS, and the BBC here. Harvey Mudd agrees to let the FBI camp on the edge of his property, which was down the valley near the entrance to the road that comes up here. All the cops were down there. Every day they search the mesa and every evening Eddie slips back home and makes love to his wife at Morningstar. He had an underground tunnel dug into the hillside. Every day he's holed up over there. Meanwhile they've got the sheriff's posse on horseback and there are helicopters from Channel 7 News.

"All this time I'm entertaining the press at my house, feeding them organic salad and tofu sandwiches. Finally I have it tracked down that at the moment of the alleged offense—the burning of the American flag by the motorcade—Eddie Gaudet was in the office of his welfare worker in Taos, New Mexico, applying for food stamps!

"I bring all this evidence to bear. His brother and mother come in from New Orleans. I'm talking to Eddie all this time and finally I convinced him that they don't have a case. He turns himself in. They took him to Albuquerque and let him plead guilty to negligent discharge of a firearm with a totally sus-

IN CUSTODY — Photo above shows Edwin M. Gaudet, front, as he surrenders to Secret Service Agent John Paul Jones (crew cut and tie) at noon Wednesday and newsmen. Below, Gaudet is shown with Taos County Sheriff Arthur Trujillo, right, and deputies in background at Taos County Jail on Monday shortly after his scheduled arraignment on state charges Monday. Federal charges that Gaudet threatened President Nixon were dropped Friday.

from The Taos News

pended sentence. No fine. They went away with their tails between their legs.

"I finally ran everyone from Morningstar off the land. Eddie, who had also been a boxer, confronted me along with the other guys. I had a shovel in my hand and said, 'Don't fuck with me, it's over.' Everyone except Holly, Army Joe, Goat John and Tall Neil left. When Morningstar became an armed camp I said, 'It's over, it's all over.'"

Update:
Michael Duncan divides his time between Taos, Hawaii and Thailand. Part of the year he lives in the adobe house that was built during the days when he shared the mesa with Morningstar and Reality. Since then he married a Thai woman, and has built a home there. He also owns a resort three miles from the border with Laos. His farm on the big island of Hawaii produces avocados and coffee. He is equally at home in Hawaii, Thailand and Taos.

A caravan of buses traveled around the country going—wherever. The Road Hog, the lead bus and the oldest, was followed by the Just Bus, the Lust Bus and the Us Bus. They were at the Chicago convention in '68 supporting their candidate, Pigasus the Pig. When Pigasus lost the bid, he retired to the Hog Farm in Llano. *Photo by John Stearns*

The Hog Farm—1969

by Phaedra Greenwood

The Fountain of Light, April #12

"The Hog Farm! What's that?" I asked Tom Stoney as we lay in a hay stack one summer dawning.

"Oh," he said, "It's about 75 people living on 14 acres of land in New Mexico, all taking care of each other and this one hog and her friend."

And I started laughing—"All those people taking care of just one hog?"

"And each other. And 15 chickens that lay ten eggs a day on methedrine."

"Hmmmm...Now let me see if I've got this straight...Seventy-five people living on 14 acres of land, all taking care of one hog and 15 chickens laying ten eggs a day, and each other?"

"Uh huh," Stoney said, grinning at me. "They're my brothers."

That was my introduction to the Hog Farm at Woodstock, where they had been hired to set up the festival and work as part of the Security Please Force—to keep the peace and get folks spiritually high. They did a tremendous job—everything from setting up a free kitchen and cooking for about 100,000 people, to talking down freakouts and picking up the garbage afterwards. It was primarily the Hog Farm vibes (though there were many other beautiful people involved), that turned the Woodstock "disaster" into a reservoir of strength and hope for a new world in which we might all learn to live together in peace and harmony.

From Woodstock the Hog Farm was hired to go to Dallas and police the pop festival there. Again, they set up a free kitchen, first aid and freakout tents, ran a light show on the free stage, and gave both physical and spiri-

Phaedra sitting on one of the original Hog Farm buses. Photo by Stewart Warren

Wavy Gravy aka Hugh Romney carrying the "Great Bus Race Multi-Dimensional Compass" at Aspen Meadows. Mr. Gravy now runs a camp for kids in California called Camp Winnarainbow. *Photo by John Stearns*

tual nourishment to anyone who needed it. On the last day of the festival, the Police Chief of nearby Lewisville got up on the main stage and congratulated the Please Force, saying that they had policed themselves so well that they didn't need anyone else to help them do it. And he resigned his job.

From Dallas the Hog Farmers came home to New Mexico only to find the house full of strangers, some stranger than others. On waves of publicity, seekers from all over the country who had been turned on by the Hog Farm washed up on the property and pitched their pup tents. When the dinner gong rang, long lines of people stood outside the kitchen with their plates and tin cups, waiting to be fed. Often there wasn't enough to go around.

Overcrowding almost inevitably leads to uptightness. *The Daily Hogtopus*, the Hog Farm paper, ran the following item about a meeting held near the Sea of Krasnakovitch (a small pond). "It was one of those occasions on which everybody got a chance to speak out," (which took almost two hours, going around the circle one at a time), "and even then, some passed that opportunity. It seems that the biggest theme still hovering over us is the 'new people'...and it seems that the 'old time family' is split into two different camps, overlapping in various ways. One side, generalizing, feels that the greatest favor we can do for newcomers is to tell them, although nicely, to split. The other side, again generalizing, feels that whoever comes up the hill is here for a reason and becomes family in such a sense that whether he stays here or not, we should be able to enjoy his presence and either help him on to do his own scene, or to become a Hog Farmer. It all sounded sort of confusing, but somehow a greater feeling of benevolence prevailed.

Meanwhile, Hugh Romney, then the Hog Farm's spiritual leader and spokesman, had gone on to California to set things up for a seven-day starve-in which was supposed to happen on October 11th. With the hogs' double consent, Romney committed them to be there, but the caravan busses were delayed day after day at the farm by mechanical difficulties and sluggish Cosmic Machinery. On the night the busses were finally ready to roll, the Starve-In had already begun. "They'll still let us in if we've been fasting from the beginning," the hogs said and were faithful to that all the way through snow in Nevada and bus breakdowns...and they made it, but too late.

Romney was upset. His word had been violated and he chose to sever all visible connections with the Hog Farm, even to changing his name. He wanted to get together a few people, about 20, who could be responsible for their commitments, and a fast bus that could speed to wherever it was needed. He wanted nothing from the farm, not Pigasus, not even the farm's psychedelic bus, the Road Hog.

The old Road Hog is becoming part of the Llano landscape.

Photo by Phaedra Greenwood

The Starve-In, instead of coming off as planned (thousands of devotees determined to save our Earth, fasting inside a huge plastic dome in Berkeley) ended up in a backyard in Oakland, with a handful of people fasting in the rain, and photographers taking pictures of them through a chain link fence.

After the Starve-In, the hogs were supposed to continue on to Los Angeles for a Halloween festival—another fantasy that fell through. Not feeling welcome back at the farm, tired, hungry and broke, the caravan was escorted from town to town by the police, who were glad to see the last of them.

Some hogs drifted back to the farm, some stayed on in California. Others joined Hugh Romney on his super bus and went on to other things.

Meanwhile, back at the farm…a handful of people decided to stick out the winter, put up an A-frame and tried to make the farm into a real home so that the rest of the family would have something nice to return to. Now, instead of long lines of people waiting outside for dinner, the family sits down together at three long polished tables, holds hands for a few moments in silence, and dines by candlelight.

Alberto has organized the back room of the information house into an arts and crafts workshop, where he is turning out some very attractive jewelry, and Mark Twain is into building adobe ovens. Although a well has been dug on the property, there isn't any indoor plumbing. Meals are cooked and houses heated by wood stove. The farm now has three chickens, five rabbits, some cats and kittens, four goats, too many dogs!—and dear old Pigasus. Come spring, the hogs are planting a vegetable garden.

There are two adobes and a cabin which are capable of housing a maximum of about 25 people. The Hog Farm population is down to about 20 people ("No men, no women—all children,"), and they would kind of like to keep it that way. A three-day visiting limit has been posted. The A-frame, which is intended to be a family meeting room (no crashers), is not yet completed because the Hog Farm is presently in the hole for about $500. Hog Farm light shows are almost inevitably for someone else's benefit, for instance, the one given for the Embudo Hospital.

The hogs have been surviving mainly on welfare, but this week when they came into Taos to collect food stamps, they were told that they must all present valid identification, which means something, preferably a driver's license with photograph. Social security cards and birth certificates are also acceptable. If one member of a certified household can't come up with ID, the whole household is disqualified.

Lately the "children" have been out doing odd jobs around the neighborhood, pulling stumps and transplanting trees to earn enough money to make the land payment every month. Some well-meaning idiots bought the farm a flatbed truck and half a backhoe, hoping that this would make the farm self-sufficient. The flatbed is presently out of action because it will cost $91 to register. The backhoe keeps breaking down and can't even finish paying for itself, much less anything else. But somehow, with faith in the cosmos, themselves and each other, the hogs keep on trucking. They made a deal with a neighbor who fixed the backhoe the first time, and in return, the children dug him a hole for a septic tank. Hog Farmers would really rather trade services than deal in cash.

As for new people, there are still a lot of them coming, some just to visit, and some hoping to stay. "One of the main problems," Jerry said at a recent community-problem meeting in Taos, "is that we don't have enough land to support ourselves by farming. We're trying to get more land. Besides that, we're walking a thin line between the folks leaving the cities and the people who have lived here all their lives."

(However, the Hog Farmers have done a good job of making friends with the neighbors, who visit the farm freely and frequently. The hogs were also invited to drive the Road Hog in Peñasco's St. Valentine's Day Parade.)

"The problem with the new people," Jerry went on to explain, "is that they're leaving the cities because so much has been done for them. They come up here because they want to find a new way of life, to learn to do things for themselves. The first thing they see to do is chop wood, and we've spent more money to replace axe handles and sledgehammer handles. Then they get sick. As soon as they hit the area, they catch everything that moves on the wind, in the water, or in the grass."

Inexperience was the main factor involved in the Hog Farm's latest loss. Some newcomers who were living in a tipi on the land went out to dinner one night, leaving their campfire blazing. The canvas caught on fire and the tipi burned to the ground.

But somehow, in fact and in spirit, and without a leader (for now it's time for us to learn to lead ourselves), the Hog Farm survives, carrying with it a heavy legacy of publicity and tradition. Growing, changing, hurting, crying. Laughing, singing, sharing, trying...in faith and love and peace. The Hog Farm. They're my brothers.

Update:
Phaedra Greenwood lives a quiet life in her adobe home in Arroyo Hondo with her two cats and a horse. She writes for the arts and culture section of The Taos News *and is working on an autobiographical work of fiction called* My Life in the Valley.

NOTICE!

NOTHIN BUT THE TRUTH KIDS
OR
ITS GOTTA START SOME PLACE

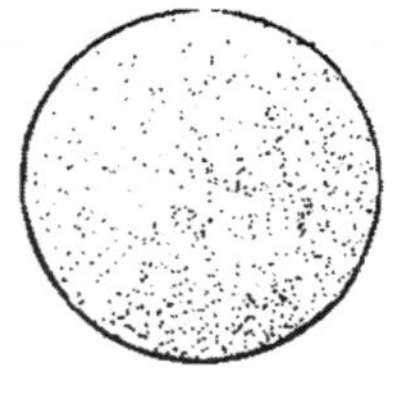

ATTENTION: COMMUNES, EXTENDED FAMILIES, GROUPS, TRIBES, FAMILIES, LONERS

PEOPLE

SUBJECT: HEALTH & SANITATION OR SANITATION & HEALTH

IT IS RAPIDLY BECOMING CLEAR THAT IF WE DO NOT PAY ATTENTION TO SOME BASIC FACTS ABOUT HEALTH & ITS RELATION TO SANITATION WE ARE GOING TO HAVE SOME PROBLEMS. THESE PROBLEMS WILL NOT/CANNOT & WONT GO AWAY. NEITHER CAN WE. THERE IS NO WHERE TO GO. PEOPLE THRU OUT TIME/SPACE HAVE ALL WAYS HAD TO DEAL WITH THESE PROBLEMS.

SO

PEOPLE EAT FOOD WHICH MAINTAINS BODY WHICH REJECTS WHAT IT CANT USE AS WASTE

WHAT TO DO WITH IT OR HOW TO GET RID OF IT

THE EASIEST WAY IS TO LEAVE IT WHERE YOU LAID IT. PROBLEM: SOME ONE ELSE HAS TO COPE. DONT PASS YOUR LOAD ON. WE ARE ALL ONE. WHATS YOURS IS MINE. AN OTHER EASY WAY IS TO PUT IT IN THE RIVER/STREAM/DITCH. YOUR STILL PASSING ON YOUR LOAD. REMEMBER WATER EQUALS LIFE. WHO WANTS TO DRINK WATER WITH YR. LOAD IN IT. THERE IS A GOOD SOLUTION PUT IT IN THE GROUND. GIVE IT BACK TO MOTHER NATURE. SHE CAN USE IT (NITROGEN ETC.)

DIG A HOLE

BUILD A LITTLE HOUSE OVER IT. KEEPS THE RAIN/SNOW OFF. SCREEN IT TO KEEP FLYS OUT (IN?) DONT SHIT WHERE YOU EAT OR EVEN NEAR IT. DONT PUT IT UPWIND OF YR. KITCHEN. FLYS FLY. DONT PUT WHERE IT WILL LEACH INTO GARDEN. PUT IT SOME PLACE WITH A GOOD VIEW. LET GO IN BEAUTY. KEEP A CAN OF LIME INSIDE. (HARDWARE STORE HAS IT) USE IT! SPRINKLE A COVER ON EACH LOAD. COVER HOLE/SEAT. SQUAT OR SIT. WASH YR. HANDS WHEN DONE. HEPATITIS & DYSENTERY ARE SPREAD THRU FECAL MATTER. WHEN YR. PILE GETS TOO BIG. MOVE HOUSE BURY REMAINS OR USE CAUSTIC SODA. KEEP AWAY FROM KIDS IT COULD KILL THEM. GEN'L STORE SELLS IT & DIRECTIONS FOR USE. OTHER SYSTEMS AVAILABLE CHECK C.I.C. OR LIBRARY. THEY COST & WASTE WATER (5 GALS. A FLUSH) BUT! YOU MUST DEAL WITH SHIT. DO IT WELL! DO IT NOW! TOMORROW NEVER GETS HERE.

JUST BECAUSE YOU DEAL WITH DONT ASSUME I DO. OK?

KNOW WHERE YOUR WATER COMES FROM. A DITCH/STREAM/RIVER IS MOST LIKELY POLLUTED. IF THERE IS NO OTHER BOIL WATER OR USE PURIFICATION TABS. CHINESE ADD HERBS CALLED IT TEA. THERE IS NO WAY AROUND CONTAMINATED WATER. IT IS OR IT ISNT. IF POSSIBLE FIND A SPRING. HAUL IT IF YOU HAVE TO. 5 GAL MILK CANS ARE GOOD. IF YOU DRILL OR DIG A WELL CHECK LOCATION FOR NEARBY SEPTIC TANKS, OUT HOUSES ETC.

NEXT

DISHES & UTENSILS – EASY AS 1. 2. 3. WASH, RINSE, STERILIZE. IF SOME ONE IN YR. WHATEVER IT IS IS SICK IF YOU DONT DO THIS YOU MAY BE NEXT. DONT BE PARANOID 1. WASH DISHES. USE BIODEGRADABLE SOAP (CHECK GEN'L STORE FOR INFO. DONT USE DETERGENT. ITS A POLLUTANT. IT GIVES YOU THE RUNS. RINSE OFF EVERY THINK. WASH & RINSE USE HOT WATER. IF YOU DONT HAVE A STOVE BUILD A FIRE. IT CAN BE DONE. AFTER RINSE STERILIZE. THIS IS ESSENTIAL METHODS: BOIL – AT THIS ALTITUDE ADD SALT BOIL 40 MINUTES NO LESS. USE CLOROX. WORKS BUT LOUSY AFTERTASE. USE GERMICIDES SOME OF WHICH ARE BIODEGRADABLE. FOLLOW **ALL** PRINTED INSTRUCTIONS EXACTLY THEY CAN BE DANGEROUS. BY BIODEGRADABLE IS MEANT – IT BREAKS DOWN BIOLOGICALLY. RE-UNITES WITH ORGANIC COMPOUNDS. CHECK RECENT MAGS FOR PICS OF DETERGENTS IN OUR RIVERS. PRETTY!

IF YOU GET SOME "THING"

HEPATITIS, DYSENTERY, VD ETC. GO TO LA CLINICA OR YR. DOC. TAKE YR. MEDICINE TELL THOSE WITH WHOM YOU LIVE/LOVE WHAT YOU HAVE/HAD THEY MAY NOT HAVE TO GET IT TOO! DOCTORS ARE US TOO. ALLOW THEM TO SERVE THE PEOPLE. HELP THEM.

FINALLY

KNOW & UNDERSTAND

THESE FACTS ARE NOT UNIQUE TO ANY GROUP. THESE ARE REALITIES WE ALL MUST FACE

NOTHING WRITTEN HERE HAS TO DO WITH GOOD OR BAD. ITS COMMONSENSE IT HAS MOST SIMPLY TO DO WITH YOU & ME & HOW WE ARE GOING TO LIVE

TOGETHER
WITH EACH OTHER & OUR PLANET.
IN BEAUTY/PEACE/LOVE/CO-OPERATION.

REPRINTS AVAILABLE – COMMUNITY INFORMATION CENTER 758-4299 OR RAINBOW PUBLICATIONS. POST FOR THE PEOPLE TO SEE/READ/DO

Communes Face 'Red Tag' Threat

Six Taos communes face the possibility of being closed down by New Mexico's General Construction Board for not conforming with New Mexico's uniform building code.

Lila, Lorien Retreat, Morning Star, Reality Construction Co., New Buffalo, and Lama are the communes under question according to Minor Van Arsdale, community organization specialist with the Health and Social Service Department (HSS). Van Arsdale accompanied Robert H. Berntsen, assistant administrator of general construction, on a tour of the communes recently.

Van Arsdale said New Buffalo and Lama appear to be off the hook. Definite action, however, will not be taken by the construction board until their next meeting for which the date has not yet been determined.

Aspects of the building code violated by the communes pertain, for the most part, to be the fire hazard because of lack of a concrete cap on the adobe walls, and fire resistant building materials. An inadequate foundation is also of concern to the board, and the lack of indoor plumbing (which McNeill insinuated should be of concern to the HSS as well.)

Tensions between Van Arsdale and members of the board run high. Van Arsdale said all efforts at compromise with the board have been to no avail. "My position is pretty hardnosed," he said. "I have tried to talk to them and work with them. They tried to go into the communes last fall, but I stopped them. In the spring this year it came into the open again. I went up there with them and an environmental specialist (Lewis Gray, sanitation engineer, Environmental Services) to talk about what the communes could do to improve and what they couldn't do. It is ridiculous to insist they have a flushing toilet in every house. They listened to everything and then turned right around and pulled something like this."

Van Arsdale further claims the code is being differentially enforced. "They simply can't go around and force everyone to drill a well and have a flushing toilet, they can't tell everyone in the Tules to do that just because of that silly code, it's absurd."

(Excerpt from longer article.)

Government Liason to the Hippies: 1969-70

told by Minor Van Arsdale to Iris Keltz

"In '67, I was living in Berkeley and hanging out with the Meher Baba people. We believed that California was going to fall into the ocean, so we left and came to New Mexico.

"I'd been coming to New Mexico since the '50s, having spent two years at the New Mexico Military Institute down in Roswell. I knew Barbara and Steve Dirkey who were living at the Hawk Ranch in San Cristobal. They had already bought the land in Lama and were planning their community.

"Every day we took the back road up to Lama to work. Until the summer of '68, there was no place to stay. That summer we built the big dome room where they do the Sufi dancing and the room to the north that became the bathroom. We built all those temporary little A-frames that turned out to be more permanent than we thought. They lasted until the recent Lama fire a few years ago in 1996.

"One day I got this idea to build an eight-sided kitchen. The second story would be the dining room and the food would come up on a dumbwaiter, through the center of a table. After lunch we staked it out and started building. It was one of the buildings that survived the fire. In those days we'd get some eight-by-eights from Abe Cordova down at the sawmill, stick them in creosote and put them in the ground. Years later they were rotten and had to be dug out and replaced. I lived there for six months and went to India because Meher Baba called people to the last Darshan before he died.

"When I came back, at first I did construction work in Albuquerque. Then I heard about a job from a guy who had government money to hire someone to assess what was going on in the communes from the point of view of social service concerns. Every state has an obligation to provide health and social services to people. We're talking community development as well as basic health concerns, like putting screens on your outhouse and looking to your water supply. We needed to make it clear to people that there were health services available to them at no cost.

"One of the things we set up was La Clinica. It provided health care at no cost, primarily to the hippie population. Dr. Rosen and Dr. Kilgore helped with this project. It's still going on. We used medical students as interns.

"I traveled around the whole state, made some reports and did some statistical analysis. The hippie culture was an oral culture and that's how you found out about everything. There were at least 35 communes all over the state, with probably15,000 to 20,000 hippies. There was a lot of public flack against them. I got into a lot of trouble because I pointed out this was a free country and that elections in Taos County were won by only a couple hundred votes. With a little organizing, the hippies could put whoever they wanted in office. This statement created an outrage in the press. There were reporters from NBC news interviewing me. I had a meeting with Governor Cargo for almost an hour.

"Primarily I went around to different communes and visited with hippies and saw what they really needed. I had shoulder-length hair and a beard down to my belly button. I looked like one of them but I had a state car. Hippies who didn't know me would head for the hills. One time at Morningstar, they all ran away when they saw me coming. They had hallucinated the flashing red lights of a cop thing on top of the car.

"I knew the people from New Buffalo from the time when I lived at the Lama Foundation. It took a lot of negotiating to get New Buffalo to screen the outhouse, which was much too close to the kitchen. The hippies that came out of the cities simply did not have a knowledge of basic health issues. Most of the people at New Buffalo were friends, so I'd go there to visit. Sometimes I'd stay for dinner. One time they took a squash from their garden that must have been four feet long and about twenty inches around. They cut it in half and filled it with other vegetables and stuff. It was delicious. I used to drop in there regularly. I kept a record of where I went for my boss, but other than that I went where and when I pleased.

"I remember dealings with a commune in Placitas. Someone had given them permission to live on their land. The kids were living out in the fields with the prairie dogs when bubonic plague was discovered in the area. The State said, 'We've got to come in and gas those prairie dogs.' Ulysses S. Grant, also known as Thor, who may have been a sociopath, met them at the gate with four sticks of dynamite and a cigarette lighter. So the State calls me. 'You're the liaison guy. Go down there and negotiate something.'

"I'd met Ulysses S. Grant before. He used to take out his hunting knife and cut the Bible and say, 'See, this is what it all means, this is the prophecy.' We sat down together and came up with an agreement. Since the commune didn't want to kill the prairie dogs, they agreed to voluntarily quarantine themselves and stay in the community so they couldn't infect outsiders. Everyone at the commune thought that was a good idea, but of course they never abided by it. That very night after the agreement was negotiated, a couple of guys slipped out through one of the side fences and went down to the bar in Placitas. Maybe two months after that incident, Ulysses S. Grant had a disagreement with some local Hispanic men and murdered them with a thirty-thirty. He fled with his wife and nine-month-old baby, got on the FBI's most wanted list and just disappeared. The FBI never found him.

Many of the structures at Lorien were built out of slab-cuts from the sawmill. They were cheap. Photo by Rich Jamison

About five years ago there was a report that a cabin in northern Montana had burned down with a couple of people in it. When they examined the remains, they believed it was Ulysses S. Grant. He was able to evade capture for twenty-something years. With anarchy, there's an opening up of possibilities. Anarchy attracts all kinds of people including sociopaths and delusionals.

"There was a lot of paranoia among the hippies. They thought they were excluded from a lot of the social services. The major part of my job was to convince people that if they needed services, they could go and get them, including food stamps. No one suggested that a hippie living on a commune should go and get a job.

"One time I went to Guadalupita, north of Mora. It was late on a Friday afternoon when the fan belt broke on the state car. I couldn't drive ten feet without blowing the engine so I pulled off the road and hitchhiked down to Taos. I called the State Motor Pool on Monday morning but they were upset with me and acted like I had done something wrong. There were people in the government that didn't like me telling the hippies that they were entitled to government services. The head of the Transportation Department tried to bar me from having state cars, although the car hadn't been vandalized and nothing happened. That went on for a couple of years and then things got bad—lots of violence, rapes and beatings. The State tried to get rid of me before the funding ended, but I kept my job for two years. By then there were established lines of communication.

"Lama was the only commune I would have lived at. All the others were pretty drug-based like The Hog Farm, where everybody was stoned out all the time. When I'd lived at Lama we used to say, 'If you do pot off the premises that's your business, but we don't want drugs brought into the community.' I'd been off drugs since '68. Not being part of the drug culture was the only way I could legitimately be a government liaison. I'd tried pot and hash and had taken LSD in 1966. That was it. By January of '68, I stopped doing all drugs. That's when I got into Meher Baba.

"Today Taos has building codes, but in those days you could dig yourself an outhouse and the state and county had no say. Now you can't even use gray water. If you started a commune in Taos County today, there'd be an inspector all over you. Things have changed a lot in 30 years."

Update:

Minor Van Arsdale currently lives with his wife of 28 years, Diana, in a community north of Questa, New Mexico. The community tries to blend Eastern and Western meditation concepts based on the teachings of Herman Rednick. There is a lovely white stupa in the wilderness near their home, which is a memorial to Herman Rednick. The stupa is a quiet place to meditate and practice Buddha Dharma. The Van Arsdales teach meditation and work with couples who want to develop the spiritual aspect of their relationship. They are also working on a manuscript based on their work with couples.

Standing under the portal of their house in Valdez Valley, Ian and Susie welcomed you in for a hot shower and a fun afternoon in trade for guacamole, chips and a bottle of wine. They were also the parents of one of my first-grade students at DaNahazli. When asked how their family ended up in Taos, Ian once said, "I was driving on the Long Island Expressway, got into a wreck,and woke up in Taos." *Photo by Paul Dembski*

A page from Be Here Now, *an amazing book and a publishing phenomenon. First printed in 1971, Year of the Earth Monkey, and made in love for Love "to ring the bell of dharma." Its opening pages explain the right livelihood mission of Lama—"We incorporated in the spring of 1968 as a non-profit foundation with the sole purpose of serving as an instrument for the awakening of consciousness. Guided by the premise that 'the essence of spirituality is practicality on all levels,' we are attempting to develop bodies, minds, and hearts in an integrative way. We don't fully understand the relationship between the energy formed here and the green energy that flows through us. Practicality suggests that we here should work toward economic self-sufficiency by means of publishing and of cottage industries such as woodworking, pottery, printing, and textiles. Toward this we are working."*

Mama Lama:
told by Barbara Durkee to Iris Keltz

"I was attending Stanford University when I became friends with Richard Alpert who was teaching psychology there. Later on he became known as Ram Dass. We'd have Friday night parties and discuss things like: Do you have to be neurotic to be creative? At that point he was selling 'psychology as the way.' Then it became 'acid as the way.' Beatniks were the way then. Later he turned to God and became one of God's best salesmen.

"While en route home from Europe, I met Steven Durkee at the Cedar Bar in New York City, a place well known by artists in the '60s. He was a painter living in a downtown loft. A year later—on the fourth of July, Independence Day—we got married in San Francisco. We bought an old Methodist Church thirty-five miles north of New York City. This became a workspace for Steven's art. We took acid there for the first time, and used the church to give the psychedelic experience to people who had never taken any. Many people came through the church including The Jefferson Airplane. Like many of those who started taking acid in the '60s, we believed it was the way to open doors to altered states of consciousness.

"There was an interconnected group of people doing acid. Our group, USCO, stood for 'the company of us.' We were the first people to use technology to put on a light show. We toured colleges putting on psychedelic light shows and backed up a show for Timothy Leary once. But the church became too commercial for us. When Scott Paper wanted to hire us to do a Tampon ad for television, Steven and I left. We eventually donated the church to friends of ours from USCO. The Church of the Living God is still in existence. The people managing it now are Zen Buddhists.

"Steven and I lived with Richard Alpert (Ram Dass) in Menlo Park for a year, taking acid weekly. Every week,

The Lama dome roof before it was enclosed.

Photo courtesy of Rick and Terry Klein

Alpert lectured somewhere on how to take acid safely. To become more conscious when you took acid, he told us to have a set intention. Acid was a sacrament and should be used in an environment that was pleasant, clean and safe. Never take acid with people you didn't trust. Always have someone straight around, so if things get weird there's someone who could help you. Actually every time it got wobbly during an acid trip, Steven and I would meditate on a picture of Meher Baba and things would fall into focus.

"Acid started off as an experimental drug that was being tested by psychologists around the country. Ken Kesey was one of the early subjects at Stanford—that's where he got the idea for *One Flew Over the Cuckoo's Nest.*

"Several fantasies were born then—spiritual dude ranches, centers for dying, and liberty ships. When the Mafia got into acid, the whole vibe changed. Acid was becoming illegal so we got the idea of "liberty ships" that would go three miles off shore so paranoia would not take over.

"Our other fantasy was to build a spiritual dude ranch called Solux. Designed and dreamed up by Steven Durkee, it would be a huge community complex, with space for 12 tribes. Like a pueblo—only bigger—it would be built in a place with lots of psychic space and no police. On entering the building you would see all the major arcana of the tarot deck on the walls. A ladder would lead you to a huge meditation hall like the meditation sphere at Aribindo Ashram in India. Pie-shaped apartments would go out from the center to accommodate different lifestyles—like the macrobiotics or those wanting sexual freedom or more conservative family types like us. We didn't know how to make all the different types get along with one another so we decided to separate them and give each one a piece of the pie. It was an inspired and naive idea—a community in New Mexico that would welcome and take care of us, like the great ship that would take us to peace and happiness forever.

"Richard Alpert took off for India to get enlightened while we went to New Mexico to look for land. Steven and I spent a year living in a rented house at the Nambe Pueblo. Steve painted OM symbols all over the house. Almost every day he took off to look for land while I was home taking care of babies. One day Steve met a guy on the streets of Santa Fe selling pictures of Shiva and Krishna and the Blue Gods. That was Chris West. We became friends with Chris and his wife, Cynthia, who later started a community at Pilar Hill.

"When Meher Baba, our teacher, went into seclusion and stayed there for a year, Herman Rednick became our advisor. Rednick was our elder and an artist on a spiritual path. We had questions about how to structure a community. He said he wouldn't help us if we used drugs. We told him about Solux. He told us to start small. He wanted us to be a spiritual, rather than a utopian community. Meher Baba had already advised us to give up drugs so that by this time Steven and I had given up acid and marijuana. When we told the others 'no drugs at Solux,' our numbers went from around 250 to 3 leaving my husband, one friend, and me. Many people who went on to build New Buffalo and Morningstar were involved with Lama until we said no drugs.

"I was pregnant with my second daughter Shanti the day we drove up the road that had a sign that said "La Lama." We went to the closest neighbor and asked if there was any land for sale and he said José Rael was selling 100 acres for $40,000. Someone had pledged to give us $20,000 dollars for the land. We got earnest money to put down, but when Herman looked at it he said, 'This is not the land you should get.' All the wheels were in motion, but we stopped and listened to him. We returned to our house at the Nambe Pueblo and sat twiddling our thumbs waiting to hear from Herman. He called a few days later, 'I have something to show you.' He had found 100 acres for $20,000 with a spring, three ecologies and the foundation of a 40-foot house. We bought it and moved onto the land that summer and started building. It was 1968. We put $7,000 down and saved the rest for fencing to keep the cows out. Any new per-

Lama was blessed with many skilled craftspeople.

Photo by Rich Jamison

son who came to live in Lama was introduced to Herman Rednick.

"We hired Henry Gomez who brought in a crew of Pueblo Indians. Henry, his wife Susie, and Henry's father Grandpa Joe became our elders along with Herman Rednick. Different groups of people volunteered to help with the building during the summer. Some black guys who'd offered to help build tried to talk the young Indian boys out of volunteering for Vietnam. They pointed out that dark-skinned men were more likely to be sent to dangerous fronts, that they had a greater chance of getting killed. But they could not crack the Indian's connection to the Marines. Little Joe Gomez lost seven of his sons in WW II. Henry was the only one of his sons who survived.

"We decided to build the community buildings first because Steven felt that people might lose momentum if they got too comfortable. When there was no place to live, there was nothing to do but build. We built some temporary A-frames that lasted almost thirty years, until the recent fire at Lama.

"Building the great dome was a totally magical event. Steven was fixated on the number eight so we cut off the corners on the original foundation—that gave the dome eight sides. Then we built a wing on each side of the dome. One wing became the library and prayer room, the other the bathhouse. All doors had to face east. Steve Baer came up with the design for the dome which is basically diamonds that fit into each other, creating a helix pattern. They called it a zome, short for zonal polyhedron and Steve Baer's business became known as Zomeworks.

"The Vietnam War and the civil rights movement were going on, but somehow we had sidestepped much of that into this other world. We were forced to ask ourselves what kind of a world we wanted to create. What did we really need? I had babies, so I needed hot water to have some way to clean the diapers. It was a time before plastic diapers. I wanted a bathtub and found an old six-foot bathtub in Española. I wanted to look out on a view when I was in the tub.

"Even before we moved onto the land, before the dome and the prayer room were built, we started sitting for half-an-hour a day. Herman advised us to have a half-hour of silence and a half-hour discussion every day. We spoke about community things a lot more than spiritual stuff and it got awful. We weren't kind to one another. At that time, not too many people talked about God or love. We weren't brought up to do that.

"People would come and go, but there was usually a core community. It started out as a family monastery, but sometimes there were no families or kids other than my own four daughters and their friends. It was important to have kids there although I thought the number should never be more than 25% of the entire group's population, one child to four adults. I also felt there should be equal numbers of men and women. And that there should only be one or two refugees for every 25 people—a refugee being a person who couldn't contribute work or integrate into the community.

"Decisions were made by consensus. I was able to influence the consensus decision by letting people know what I thought. A lot of people didn't have any idea of what we were trying to do. The policy of consensus helped to balance the place and educate the people living there.

"We were still making adobe bricks for the prayer room when a couple showed up who had seen Murshid Sam Lewis in Golden Gate Park and thought he might be someone we'd like to have for a teacher at Lama. Steven wrote a letter inviting him to come visit. Murshid Sam sent a lieutenant to check us out. He showed us a couple of Sufi dances.

Baba Ram Dass, one of our great teachers, held retreats at Lama. This photo could have been taken anytime in the late '60s or throughout the '70s. *Photo by Paul Dembski*

Original Lama kitchen with an approaching, much-needed rainshower.

Photo courtesy of Rick and Terry Klein

There we were in the great dome, five Marine-type men, including my husband and Van Arsdale—Sufi dancing! We had a great time and started doing it regularly.

"When Sam Lewis came to New Mexico, I went to pick him up at the Albuquerque Airport, which was much smaller then. When I entered the building, this little guy with stringy hair looked up at me and said, 'I'm Sam Lewis, I'm the one you came to get. I've seen all the starry skies and I've met all the holy people and I know the secrets of the universe.' He looked a little like E.T. and a little like Yoda. He kept on talking all the way from the airport through dinner and during the three-hour drive to Lama. He had everyone at Lama rolling on the floor with laughter with his wonderful stories. Later on, I found out he was the black sheep of the Rothschild family.

"The next day he wanted me to take him to see the local communes. Before popping into the car, he sprayed the Lama garden with fish emulsion to help everything grow.

"First we drove to Morningstar, which I had never been to before. As we drove up their road, we saw a big green velvet couch sitting outside in the sun. On it were two nude very pregnant women with a fire crackling in front of them and chickens walking all over. Murshid Sam had insisted that I wear a long skirt. We got out of the car and walked towards them. They didn't move. They didn't even greet us. I said, 'Hello, my name is Barbara Durkee and I'm from the Lama Foundation and I've just brought Murshid Sam for a visit.' Two heavy-lidded sort of guys drifted onto the scene. We all stood there. Murshid Sam, who was a perky guy, asked questions, but only got grunts back.

"'A little dense there,' commented Sam as we drove off to New Buffalo. He had a great time with the people there. He just talked and told his funny wonderful stories.

"He was both a Zen and a Sufi master. One day he had this incredible inspiration to combine square dancing with saying the names of God. He had seen dervish dances in Turkey and knew the power of chanting. It got people's bodies and voices engaged. Those dances are now called the Dances of Universal Peace.

"When Richard Alpert came back from India, he wanted to share his experiences in a book. About seven of us helped him with this project. The book was written, illustrated and designed at Lama. It took a couple of months to complete this project, which became the well-known *Be Here Now*. Alpert changed his name to Ram Dass while in India. While living at Lama, he recreated his experience at the ashram in India. People took turns doing three-day meditation retreats. Most of us had never been in seclusion for that long. His book and the seminars he has given over the years are Lama's most lucrative endowment.

"Murshid Sam died around then and his black coffin came into the middle of the dome while the *Be Here Now* books were being put in boxes and mailed out all over the country. The mood in the dome was somber, but also magical. Stacks of boxes lined the walls showing the words *From Bindu to Ojas*. We buried Sam up the hill in the middle of winter, in a grave dug five feet into the frozen ground.

"Over time Lama has became a universal college for ongoing experiential classes in world religions. There is a strong spiritual hunger in our culture that is not being fed. Lama is a place where people can meditate, practice Tai-Chi and yoga, Sufi dance, fast for Ramadan, welcome Shabbat or praise the Lord in any way they want. It is a community for people with a non-traditional bent and a place where people can discover what community is about."

Update:

Barbara Durkee lives in Batesville, Virginia, where she is an artist. In her free time, she works as a registered nurse in a local hospital. She is still a practitioner of the Japanese tea ceremony and enjoys serving her guests.

A close up of the Lama kitchen. Hanging from the logs are bomb casings from Los Alamos, which were used as a gong to announce meals. The sound echoed over the mountainside.

Photo by Rich Jamison

Gersh

Bill Gersh, 1968.
Photo courtesy of Renée Gregorio

Bill Gersh was an artist who migrated from the East Coast to the Bay Area and then came to Taos. His first studio was in Talpa, but he ended up at Reality Construction Company near Arroyo Hondo, becoming adept at building with adobe and living an on-the-edge existence with creative flair. In 1970, Gersh joined others at Magic Tortoise. He built a home and studio and became well-known as painter, sculptor, printmaker, poet, raconteur, teacher, and lecturer. He acquired the label "outlaw modernist" and was much-loved in the New Mexico art scene. He could really talk the walk. After suffering from liver cancer, Gersh passed on in 1994.

Georgia Gersh: *born in 1975 on Lama Mountain, the daughter of artist Bill Gersh and Annie Degan.* "I was born on Lama Mountain in the middle of winter during a huge snowstorm. There was no midwife. My dad was there and our neighbor Beverly delivered me. The story goes that my father held me in one hand and a five-pound jar of honey in the other to find out how much I weighed. They didn't have a midwife set up and I don't think they were planning on a home birth. The ambulance from Questa got there too late. I have a brother Marley (from a different father). Marley's 17 years older than me. He went to the Taos Learning Center when he was in high school and moved to California shortly after, so I never got to grow up with him. My half-sister is from another mother. My parents were together for about five years, until I was two years old. It was very primitive living on Lama Mountain. We didn't have indoor plumbing or electricity. We used kerosene lamps and an outhouse and heated up water to bathe with in the winter. And there was no phone! In the summer, we just laid the hose out in the sun to heat up the water and took a solar shower. I had a great crew of kids to run around the mountain with. There was my sister Willow, and the neighbor kids—Lyra and her older brother Orion, Sonya H., Joaquin, Mateo, Leona, Jordon and his sister Rochelle. Along with five other kids, I was home-schooled on the mountain for kindergarten, first and second grades by Annie. Then I went to the public school in Arroyo Hondo. After that I hopped around to different private schools. In junior high I realized that I didn't have the privileges the other kids had but when I was younger I never missed having a television.

Bill Gersh standing outside the home/studio he built with several of his assemblage/sculptures. Photo by Renée Gregorio

"I realized in junior high school that I was different from the other kids. I didn't conform to the popular fashion. My parents gave me a lot of freedom, so I dressed however I wanted to. My most infamous outfit was when I borrowed a pair of my dad's boxers—white with red hearts on them, one white jelly shoe and one red jelly shoe. This was seventh grade. I got a lot of flack in the cafeteria from the other kids for being so unique.

"My dad got a color TV when I was in junior high which is when we also got electricity and indoor plumbing. I didn't mind living primitive partly because I didn't know anything else."

Magic Tortoise

by Iris Keltz

Beverly and Rollo dreamed of living in community. They bought 46 acres of land on Lama Mountain from Rick Klein who owned the property next door. The private property was converted into a non-profit New Mexico corporation, which was governed by a board of directors, similar to New Buffalo. There were no shareholders.

The corporation got its name—The Magic Tortoise Trust—this way: in the '60s, it was common to refer to the *I Ching*, the Chinese Book of Changes, as an oracle for higher wisdom. Most everyone had a copy of this book. Seeking guidance, Beverly and Rollo threw the coins and got the 27th hexagram—"Providing Nourishment." One of the changing lines in this hexagram referred to a magic tortoise, a creature possessing the supernatural powers to live on air without needing earthly nourishment. As explained in the *I Ching*, this cryptic message is also a prophetic warning—the person who was in a position to live freely and independently instead looks with envy and discontent at those who appear to be in better outward circumstances. This brings serious misfortune.

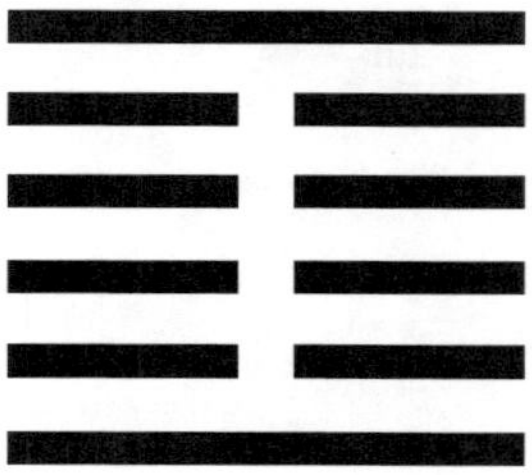

THE CORNERS
OF THE MOUTH
(Providing Nourishment)
above:
KÊN :: **keeping still, mountain**
below:
CHÊN :: **the arousing, thunder**

THE JUDGMENT
The Corners of the Mouth.
Perseverance brings good fortune.
Pay heed to the
providing of nourishment
and to what a person seeks
to fill one's own mouth with.

There were eight original members in the Magic Tortoise. After a one-year residence, you could put in an application to become a permanent member.Most of the time it worked, although some of the core members felt they never really discussed difficult and complex issues surrounding private and community property existing side by side.

Community meetings were held once a week, rotating from house to house.Visitors helped to build in exchange for a place to camp out. At its heyday everyone ate and gardened together, shared a cistern and helped each other build homes as well as a community root cellar, chicken coop and barn.

Homes were built on faith that the community would survive since no individual held the deed to the land his house was built on. The Magic Tortoise lasted for about 20 years. Sadly, Beverly and Rollo lost their home and Gersh his studio in the devastating fire of '96 that ripped through the mountain and burnt 7,200 acres in the Carson National Forest. However, even before the fire, legal disputes were going on between people who once thought they were friends and neighbors forever.

Hippie rake *Photo by Matt Tinker*

Origins of Pilar Hill

told by Chris West to Iris Keltz

Strategically located at the southern end of Taos Valley, Pilar Hill has spectacularly uninterrupted views of the Rio Grande gorge to the west with the Sangre de Cristo Mountains on its eastern shoulder. It was an earthy, raunchy, accessible community where counterculture type people lived, got married, had babies, built houses and died on land privately owned by Chris and Cynthia West.

"My wife Cynthia, two stepdaughters, and myself moved out to Santa Fe, New Mexico from California in 1965. We'd been going to peyote meetings at Pyramid Lake in Nevada for some time. My wife was into the Peyote Church and I liked to eat peyote. We ended up renting a little house in Tesuque on 500 acres for $60 a month and having a bunch of peyote meetings there.

"We started looking for property to buy in '67 and on the first of July in '68 we closed on this land on Pilar Hill. Beartrack Law, an Anglo cowboy, sold us the land. When I met him, his oldest son had just gone to Vietnam while the Tet offensive was going on to be a helicopter pilot. Before the deal was consummated, we walked the 7 miles of fence that bordered the land with a six-pack of beer. When I bought the land there was an old adobe and a shed, built by Beartrack. That was it.

"Actually I had been looking for 5 acres of irrigated land in Ranchos but got a deal on land in Pilar—205 acres including our own ditch and water rights for 40 acres and 2,800 acres leased from the Bureau of Land Management on the north side of the horseshoe curve. I'd seen people shooting each other over water rights in Ranchos and figured that was a great advantage.

"Cynthia and I wanted a community, not a commune. People could own their house but not the land and if you wanted out, you could sell the house back to us for what it

View of the Rio Grande Gorge from Pilar Hill. *Photo by Bill Davis*

cost. The one thing you couldn't do was speculate, sell your house for profit. One time someone wanted more money than I was willing to pay. He told me, 'This house has a great view, so it's worth a lot.' I said 'I never promised you any kind of land appreciation, just the original cost of the house.' We got into a fist fight and people had to pull us apart. The next day he came to me and agreed to the cash amount I had offered. We've been good friends ever since.

"That first summer Cynthia and I lived in a tipi. Within weeks we started building a house a mile below where the ditch started coming out of the mountain. Cynthia became pregnant that winter and when our daughter Pilar was born in November, we had a room built, with two-foot thick adobe walls. We had bought 20,000 adobes for 10 cents a piece and hired the Suazo family and the hippies to help us build. On Cynthia's inspiration, we built the house in the shape of a cross. We drilled a well by the house but it went dry, pumped only three quarters of a gallon per minute into the cistern.

"I went up to Alamosa where they were tearing down the narrow gauge railroad and bought all these boxcars for $175 each. Two of the boxcars became my stepdaughters'—Mona and Sybil—bedrooms.

"The following year, we had to fix the ditch. There were huge arroyos cut in it because it had been allowed to overflow. We ran a pipeline from the top of the mountain down to the bunkhouse on the western side of the highway. I paid the people living at

Pilar to help lay the pipe. They earned more money than they could in town.

"All that we asked in return for living on the land was help in cleaning the ditch. I've been cleaning and maintaining the ditch for twenty-five years. Every spring we have at least two days of ditch cleaning. Some years it's just me and two or three people and some years we've had over twenty five. Sometimes people who have lived here in past years show up to help. In the old days we'd clean the ditch and have a feast.

"We planted 20 acres of alfalfa to feed our herd of cows. We'd slaughter a cow every year and distribute the meat. I'd get help bucking the hay and everyone would get 80 pounds of meat in exchange.

"Pilar Hill has been a sanctuary for many people. Asha came and stayed in the big house with her 4 daughters after she got divorced. Marilyn came up here after a failed relationship. She wanted to build a growhole and planned on living here and growing her own food. Since I had just bought a bulldozer up in Colorado, I helped her excavate the ground. After about ten years, she wanted out and traded a box car and a kitchen cookstove for the growhole. With another couple who left, I bought them out with cash. They signed a quitclaim deed and it was over without a problem. Joe took over crazy Janey's house and kept it alive. If he had money, he'd buy the tar paper and we would both fix the house. There was never any real money exchange.

"In the last 25 years over 100 people have lived here. They've found their way to the hill through an elaborate network. Sometimes a friend of a friend directed them here. Sometimes they just wanted to stay a while and sometimes they wanted to build a house. Cynthia and I had the right to turn anyone away but it didn't come up very often. No one was allowed to build on the top of the hill so no house could dominate over everything. You can't even see the big house that Cynthia and I built till you get there. It's kind of tucked into the hillside. Most of the houses are near the ditch. We built a cabin without electricity or water for Aunt Elizabeth. Soon after our son Abel was born in '74, Cynthia and I got divorced. She moved to Santa Fe.

"In its heyday there must have been at least 50 people living here—everyone with their own reasons and story. Buffalo Bob lived in his boxcar near the ranchhouse until he died. No, I never stocked the place with my lovers. There was no unifying idea or religious belief except for the fact that we were friends who wanted to live on this land and not have anybody bother us.

"The community lasted for 10 years through voluntary cooperation. When the folks who had built the houses left, I had to go on a rent basis to keep things balanced but I never made a profit. The rent money was eaten up maintaining the house and land. The idea was to base this community on the stewardship of the land, not ownership. The land is in trust for our four children. Someday I'm gonna get out of here and recycle. I don't know whether I'm coming back to this planet or not."

Update:
Chris West still owns all the land at Pilar Hill. He says it will never be subdivided, a concept he inherently disagrees with. "Land is our mother," Chris says, "and we don't have a right to own it, only the right to use it. I'm not a capitalist in the sense of owning the land. My covenant with the land was: You take care of me and I'll take care of you."

Some of the best conversations happened in the kitchen. The cook stove was the center of life and women often bonded beside it. Keep talking, keep feeding that woodbox… *Photo by Rich Jamison*

Life at Pilar Hill

as told by Jean Kenin to Iris Keltz

"I was teaching at DaNahazli School when I met a man who lived part-time in a railroad box car at a place called Pilar Hill. He came to a fund raiser I had organized for the school. Twenty-five pieces of artwork in varying degrees of beauty and accomplishment had been donated by local artists. My brother loaned me his gallery on the plaza to show the work. At the end of the month we hoped lots of people would come and buy the art.

"At the time, Asha and her four daughters, who attended the school, were living at Pilar Hill. They came to the gallery on opening night and brought a friend who lived in Santa Fe but on weekends stayed at Pilar in his boxcar making stained glass lamps. I thought Stephen was a fascinating guy and as our relationship deepened, I got to know more of the people who lived on the hill.

"By the time I moved up to live on the hill with Stephen, I was pregnant. We stayed in Chris and Cynthia's big house. They had since gotten divorced. I thought Stephen would be a great father and somebody interesting to spend time with. I had an image of bungling along in a pickup truck with a sweet child in between us.

"People seemed willing to contribute to the community but were able to have a private life. Lots of amazing projects were going on— like a huge terraced garden just below the big house. Everybody helped with the work and could pick from the abundant garden filled with lettuce, corn, beans, peas, squash and other vegetables. I remember harvesting carrots in the spring that had been in the ground all winter. The garden master was a young man from the East Coast we called Peter Person to distinguish him from a dog by the same name. He lived in a refurbished chicken coop. Marilyn came around this time with a dream to build a growhole and grew seedlings for the garden.

"I learned about irrigation and helped out on ditch days which were always a major event. Folks who lived on the hill were joined by friends and former residents. People grabbed their tools and went trekking up the canyon. To make sure that the water had clear passage into the pipe, we started cleaning at the natural spring, way up the canyon. Then we'd walk the pipeline, about a quarter of a mile long, to make sure there were no leaks. The water ended up in a cistern on the hill where people could siphon off water as they needed it.

"Farther down the hill, a huge pond had been dug and lined with plastic so no water would be lost into the ground. This water was used to irrigate the alfalfa fields on the other side of the highway. By this time Chris had been there for eight years and knew what to do. At the end of these long, hot days there would be riotous times, jubilation at finishing the work on the ditch. By this time, the light around us was becoming incandescent reds, golds and violets. I remember people putting down their shovels, guzzling lots of cold beer and an amazing mud bath scene with everyone jumping into the pond. Then Chris would heat up rocks in a fire pit for a sweat which was always brutally hot. There was always a discussion about which rocks to use since certain rocks could explode when cold water was poured on them in the sweat lodge.

"For drinking water we drove a few miles down to the Rio Grande and got fresh water from a spring that fed the river. There was never enough water on Pilar Hill. We would watch thunderheads in the distance move across Taos and dump on the town while we were waiting, waiting, waiting and not a drop would come to us. When the rain finally came it was cause for celebration. One evening when Joe Cota, a local musician, was visiting there was a long awaited downpour. Everyone was so grateful for the water. Joe played the piano while everyone danced in and out of the rain.

"At one point we got a milk cow. Buffalo Bob, who worked hard for the community, surprised everyone by telling us he knew how to milk a cow, something he may have learned when he lived at the Hog Farm in Peñasco. It was a huge commitment and he didn't want to be the only person responsible for milking every morning and every night. So Marilyn learned how to milk the cow and helped him. Buffalo Bob lived alone in his boxcar which was near the ranchhouse on the west side of the highway by the cattle. Once a week he'd go to town and stock up. He was a huge, scruffy looking guy but one of the gentlest, most caring people I ever met, happiest when he could retire to his boxcar for a 6-pack and TV. He lived out his days on the hill quite peacefully and happily. Until Buffalo died a few years ago, he and Chris were the two permanent figures on the hill.

"People were clever at figuring out ways to survive. Stephen made yogurt from the milk and sold it to the co-op under a pet food label. Marilyn and her boyfriend that summer sold burritos from a wagon parked in the parking lot at the crest of Pilar Hill, where many people stopped to take pictures of that huge fissure in the earth

"Branding day, when they gathered up the herd and slaughtered a steer, was also a day of celebrating. Chris was proud of the quality of the meat, which was tender, organic, off the land meat. Everyone gathered at the big house for a feast. Chris cooked up huge, thick steaks. Our usual diet was beans, rice and vegetables from the garden because we didn't have much money. But on those days everyone gorged on meat.

"Once, with their parent's permission, we brought a group of kids from DaNahazli school to witness the

One of the original box cars from Pilar Hill is planted in Jean's garden and serves as a guest house and quick getaway.
Photo by Iris Keltz

slaughtering of a steer because we felt it was important for them to learn where their food came from. They watched Jerry the cowboy isolate a steer from the herd before shooting it. A huge tractor lifted the dead cow off the ground so it could be hung and butchered. They saw the heart continue to beat after it was cut out of the body and watched in fascination at the removal of the entrails. Some kids were horrified and vowed never to eat meat again.

"Before the baby was born, I started feeling that this little person should know who it belonged to. Stephen and I got married one rainy January morning in the local hardware store owned and run by one of the local magistrates. It was the kind of store that was poorly stocked, with dusty shelves and very few customers. When the magistrate asked us for our witness, we had none. There was a drunk in the store who we invited to witness our marriage for five dollars which he gladly accepted. There I was, huge with child, standing next to Stephen in front of the magistrate and a drunken witness. I took the lapis ring Stephen had given me a year before off one finger and put it on the ring finger and married we were.

"Then we went for a ride in the mountains in Stephen's truck. I cried because there was no celebration. Neither one of us had wanted to make a big deal out of getting married. The commitments was between us and we didn't need lots of people. We had both been married before and felt that this was a

Jean and Stephen and baby Noah, early '70s in the orchard.

Courtesy of Jean Kenin

mature and clear step but as we were driving around the mountains, it struck me, what a lonely step we had taken without the support of friends. I dried my tears and went back to my folk dancing class at DaNahazli school.

"I always planned on having the baby at home. and when I got rumblings of this imminent delivery somebody drove up to Lama for the midwife, Sharida, a beautiful serene woman with silver hair. We had a friend, a medical student who had also agreed to come. The labor lasted 26 hours. Sharida sat in the corner of the room the entire time and breathed with me, just letting nature take its course. She was perfect. At the point when I was ready to push the baby out, I looked over at the door and saw five heads peeking in—our Pilar Hill family. When you live in community, you have to be ready to share your life.

"Our baby was born on February 23rd at 11:30 p.m. Stephen was there to catch him. The midwife and the intern were standing by. We didn't know what to call the baby. He was quite large and for three months we tried different names. Maybe because he was a Pisces and water was lifegiving and especially precious at Pilar Hill—his name became Noah.

"Exactly one month after Noah was born there was a tragedy on the hill. Another baby had also been born there several months before Noah. The mom was a far-out hippie who smoked a lot of pot. She asked me to babysit one night while she went to a boogie at ol' Martinez Hall. The baby was a beautiful 6-month-old little girl with round rosy cheeks. Her mom would always do her up in tight-fitting swaddling clothes. That night the two children fell asleep side by side. The mom came home from the dance and took her baby home. The next morning the baby was found dead. The doctors from Los Alamos diagnosed it as acute viral pneumonia also known as sudden crib death, an unexplainable, mysterious illness. It was the most terrifying time of my life. The two babies had been sleeping next to each other and I was frightened beyond belief. At that moment I realized that there were things in life beyond my control.

Bringing in the sheaves to decorate a wedding feast. Imagine an intense, turquoise blue sky and shimmering grasses.

Photo by Seth Roffman

"Wintertime on Pilar Hill. There was a great pit fireplace in the big house which you could sit around with your feet near the fire. We kept the toilet seat closeby and when anybody needed the outhouse they took the warmed toilet seat with them. On those long winter evenings, a joint would be passed around accompanied by the most amazing storytelling and camaraderie. Chris would get into his fantasies for making money. One of them was around Bernice's amazing hats. Older than most of us, Bernice had ended up living in a boxcar through a serendipitous chain of connections. She was an anchor, an island of stability. She also crocheted one of a kind, amazing, imaginative hats for everyone on the hill. One night Chris went on about the thousands of hats Bernice would make for our cottage industry. He even had national distribution plans. Needless to say, Bernice had no intention of mass-producing her special hats.

"Although I treasure the experience of being part of Pilar Hill, I didn't want to raise my children in a hippie life style, meaning the dope, the rugged individualists, the transients and the rough language. It was a time of folks finding their home. And Pilar Hill would always be Chris' scene. He was the lord of the manor, the one who called the shots, made the rules and created the atmosphere of the place. He was one of the greatest storytellers in the valley and had a great appreciation of women. But he was also the kind of guy who'd come out with a rifle if a stranger drove up. It was fine living by his rules most of the time but when you're raising a family you get this strong nesting instinct to have your own home. Taos was fierce enough without living with the wild frontiersmen."

Update:

Twenty-five years later, with two strapping grown sons, Stephen and Jean are considering celebrating their marriage—something they never got around to while living at Pilar Hill. Their adobe house overlooks the Taos Valley with extraordinary views in all directions. Planted near their garden is one of the fabled Pilar boxcars which became the home for Bernice who lived in it for 7 years while being the grandma-in-residence for their boys. Jean now teaches a teen-issues class in the local high school and is the Director of the New Mexico Community Education Association. She sings in a madrigal group and dances whenever she can.

People would come and meditate in front of this stone carving of Hanuman who has a temple in Taos. Photo by Iris Keltz

How Hanuman Came to Taos

told by Karen Pettit to Iris Keltz

"I was 18 years old in 1970 when I got my hands on the book *Be Here Now* by Baba Ram Das. He was also known as Richard Alpert. Ram Das' version of Hinduism became a bible to me. I was living with my brother, working as an artist's model at Washington University, and hanging out with all kinds of avant-garde poets, writers and artists—that's how I met Charlie. He was an artist and very interested in the dark side of eastern philosophy—the path of tantric and kundalini yoga that burns through your destructive nature. He became my first teacher. We had gotten together through our interest in *Be Here Now* and did yoga and mediation together. He planned to go to India and offered to buy me a ticket so I could go with him. We got our shots and took off.

"Having never been far from home, this felt like jumping out of the Empire State Building. Our planned itinerary included Bhutan, Sikkim and Mustang, all the northern countries that had just opened up to Westerners. Tibet hadn't been opened up. We were going to live in caves and eat berries and nuts, like yogis and yoginis.

"We stayed in an ashram outside of Bombay, near where our plane landed. We wanted to meet Neem Karoli Baba who was Ram Das' guru, so we took a bus to Nanital in northern India. That took us a day and a half.

"It was easy to find out about ashrams. You could spot someone on the 'white light circuit' a mile away. Usually they were Americans or Europeans who carried a certain type of bag for their prayer beads, although Maharaji—that's what we called Neem Karoli Baba—had plenty of Indian devotees.

"When we got to the ashram in Nanital, Charlie immediately wanted to continue further north in search of

This beatific madonna is Kausalya (aka Karen Pettit) as she looked when she lived in India, late '60s. Photo courtesy of Karen Pettit

yogis. There were twelve Westerners at the ashram and I wanted to stay there a while so Charlie gave me $300 in traveler's checks and took off. By cashing them at the black market, they lasted ten months. Charlie only lasted in India three weeks.

"When I first got to this ashram in a small hill village, everyone knew each other and appeared to be very close to Maharaji. He had given Hindu names to all the Westerners and was flowering them with attention. He didn't give me a Hindu name until I was starving for one. I love the name Kausalya that he eventually gave me. Life in the ashram was peaceful and unstructured. People cooked, talked, wrote in their journals, meditated, went for walks, read the Upanishads and the Ramayana, or sat by the river. Although he ran the ashram, Maharaji was not into directing. Of all the gurus Westerners were attracted to, he was the simplest and most down-to-earth.

"We tried to surrender to the guru in a very Christ-like way. I did the best I could for a wild 19-year-old from the States. Maharaji touched me greatly. Day in and day out he'd be there for us. There was a scary quality about him as well as great compassion. I heard him chew people out in Hindi, of which I didn't speak a word. He always wore a shirt underneath a blanket and walked around barefoot. I spent ten months in India following Maharaji from villages in the mountains to villages in the plains. I got to know some of his Indian followers who were the most generous people I've ever known. When they say, 'Guest is God,' they're not fooling. You could walk into a home where they had nothing in their cupboards to feed their family, hear this scampering going on with the children and before your eyes would be a metal tray filled with sweets and chai. They'd drop everything to serve you and welcome you into their home.

"The Indian devotees paid money to keep the ashram going. I never had to pay a penny. The small ashram in the hills did not have enough lodging for all of us, so we stayed in homes or in the hotel run by one of the devotees. It cost practically nothing. We paid by the week for our lodging, meals and a bucket of hot water in the morning.

"Towards the end of my stay, Maharaji was marrying off restless Westerners who were trying to be celibate. Whenever a man and woman started spending time together, Maharaji would proclaim them man and wife and a marriage would take place. I started spending time with Vishuambar, an American with a Hindu name. Everyone called him Vishu. We'd take walks to the bazaar or spend time down by the river.

"One night Vishu took some acid. It was windy and the chiffon curtains were flowing in the breeze. At about three o'clock in the morning, Vishu ascends to my room, and stands at the foot of my bed. Zipped up in my mummy sleeping bag, I sat up with my arms still stuck inside the bag. He bowed saying, 'Maharaji has come to me. You're to be my wife.'

"I told him to stay calm and see how he felt in the morning. I didn't want to startle or upset him because he was tripping. He told me that he was sitting in his room and a trillion Maharajis were floating around in tiny bubbles, when all of a sudden the Maharajis turned into me! The room was filled with floating Kausalyas. That vision meant that Maharaji and I were one and I was to be his bride. We stayed up all night and decided that maybe I better take some acid, but all I got was doubt.

"'I can't get married now. I'm too young.'

"But Vishu was still convinced that I was meant to be his wife. Maharaji was down in the plains when this happened. We wanted to talk with him about this and another couple that had decided to get married came with us on the long bus ride. When Maharaji saw us he started yelling from his porch, 'Vishu's got a wife! Vishu's got a wife. Laxman too, he's got a wife.'

"I went up to Maharaji with tears in my eyes and asked, 'Would you please give me the message here? I'm not getting it.'

"Maharaji kept getting us mixed up saying, 'Vishu and Sunanda, Lakshman and Kausalya.'

"We'd say, 'No, it's Vishu and Kausalya, Loxman and Sunanda.'

"He looked at me and started laughing, 'So, you're to be a new bride.' He smiled.

"Vishu and I stayed together for about two weeks when I freaked out and decided I was too young and this was a big mistake and I wasn't getting married.

"I went back to the States and stayed with my parents in Winnetka, Illinois, where I grew up. After a while I became homesick for my life in India. I was working in a nursing home and started thinking that maybe Maharaji was right, maybe I am supposed to marry this man. I wrote to Vishu who was now living in California and told him we should get married. He drove out to Chicago and we got married by a Presbyterian minister in my parents' living room. I wore a sari. He wore a lungi, a long skirt-like garment. My liberal parents went along with everything, but thought I had gone off my rocker.

"Vishu's family owned a ranch in Tijeras Canyon outside of Albuquerque. He used to visit there as a child. While in India, he dreamed of returning to the mountains in Northern New Mexico. We rented a place in Tres Piedras, 25 miles west of Taos. It had been vacant for some time and was infiltrated with huge rats that would take over at night. Every weekend guys from the Forest Service would come to the arroyo near the house for target practice. In the barn we discovered animal heads, torn apart. When I became pregnant with my first child, we broke our lease and moved to Taos.

"For $125 a month, we rented a great house on the Valdez rim with three bedrooms and a sauna. It backed up to Morningstar commune. We'd take long walks to the edge of the mesa and got to know Gay and Michael Duncan, who owned the entire mesa but lived separately from Morningstar.

"Jed was born at home on May 22 with the help of Sharada, the midwife from the Lama Foundation. We lived in the house two weeks before moving into a tipi on land we'd just bought in Arroyo Seco. The tipi was set in the middle of some cottonwoods, next to a running ditch. We built an outdoor kitchen. It was exquisite, although it was hard with an infant. Once a week, I bathed the baby and myself at the

Kausalya with her husband Vishu and their two children, Jed and Aaron, and a friend outside their tipi in Arroyo Seco, late '70s.

Photo courtesy of Karen Pettit

Hacienda de San Roberto where the managers were my friends. My hair was long then, past my ass. We were still living in the tipi when the first snow came. Vishu had been building our house but it was not quite done. We moved in and put plastic on the windows with plywood doors. The house was freezing. I got pneumonia and went to stay with my parents in Illinois for about a month.

"Through Baba Ram Das, we heard about Joya, a Jewish housewife from Forest Hills, New York, who supposedly had visions of Maharaji after his death. Since Ram Das had gotten me to India in the first place and he was now following Joya, we figured she must really be something. So we moved to Queens, New York. We spent eight months with Joya, Ram Das, and their followers. About 18 people rented a house together. At one point we lived in the boiler room with Jed who was almost a year old. There was a series of rented houses in Forest Hills and Brooklyn. They were highly organized. Everyone got up at the crack of dawn to meditate. We were required to be celibate—even the married couples. Vishu and I made out in the car once or twice. I began to see Joya as an egomaniac. When Vishu and I became disillusioned, we returned to our home in New Mexico and I became pregnant with my second child Aaron who was born at home on July 22, 1977. Our home in Seco was beautiful, but I felt isolated.

"Ram Das had also gotten disillusioned with Joya. In the Ramayana, Hanuman saves Sita, captured on the island of Sri Lanka, by taking the land mass in his hand and flying over the ocean. Ram Das decided to have a marble mortie carved into Hanuman, flying. A mortie is something that's been given life, like an idol. It weighed over a ton, was gold-leaved and beautifully painted. It sat in a crate on the dock in San Diego for over a year. Nobody knew what to do with Hanuman. Someone suggested to Ram Das that Hanuman should be brought out to Vishu and Kausalya's land in New Mexico. It sat in the crate on our property for another year. Once a mortie is unveiled, it's given life and you just don't crate it back up. You have to take care of it. Hanuman is bathed, clothed and fed. He's always being fussed over. Sometimes he wears a crown. It's an old tradition from the temples of India.

"That summer we held a bandara on our land. A bandara is a gathering on the full moon in September to celebrate the passing of Maharaji. We had an incredible feast. A bunch of people tried to jump into Hanuman's crate, but there was a hidden beehive and they got stung like crazy. Hanuman was unveiled for the first time that weekend. At first it was a glorious day and then it started raining. It rained and rained. People were wallowing in mud. At first my house was off limits because I didn't want a thousand people traipsing through. The day ended with at least 50 people in the house.

"Hanuman was crated back up after the weekend. We couldn't leave him exposed to the elements and there was no place to protect him. He sat in our driveway for about a year, until Vishu and I moved to the property on Geronimo Lane in town. There was a barn near the house that got fixed up by Hanuman devotees. At first it was just a room where Hanuman sat and people came to meditate. Then a group of people built a kitchen, then a bathroom and a second story for retreats. Finally, Vishu sold the house and the land to the Hanuman devotees. It has became a full-fledged temple with a board of directors.

"In Hinduism, faith is called bakti, which means intoxicated with love for the Divine. I once visited this town in India, where Krishna was suppose to have been born and raised. I almost got caught in a riot there. People were stampeding through the streets to get to the temple that was unveiling a mortie of Krishna. Many of them were little old ladies who thought of nothing but divine love.

"Taking Hinduism across the world from India to Taos, New Mexico, religious fervor looks different. When I tell people that I was in India with Maharaji and know Ram Das personally, they bow and say, 'Namaste. It's so beautiful here.' They're starry-eyed with religion. Sometimes, someone at the temple who doesn't know me will say, 'Oh God, this is just so blissful. Have you ever been here before?'

"I smile sweetly and think to myself, 'Honey, you're looking at Ms. Hanuman!' In the end, Hinduism, like other religions, is about faith, about surrendering yourself to the belief that there's a power greater than ourselves."

Update:

Since those days Karen Pettit has worked with severely disabled children in an elementary school in Oakpark, Illinois, where she lived for 4 years with her second husband. When she returned to Taos, she opened an art gallery, which lasted for 8 years. She has also been a youth worker in a residential home for disturbed teenage girls. Currently she is working towards becoming a certified yoga instructor, specializing in working with people with disabilities and the aged. She lives in a lovely two-story solar house in the foothills of Taos. The most exciting thing in her life is her brand new grandson!

TAOS GENERAL STORE

Here on
S. Sante Fe Road

SPRING
SOUTH

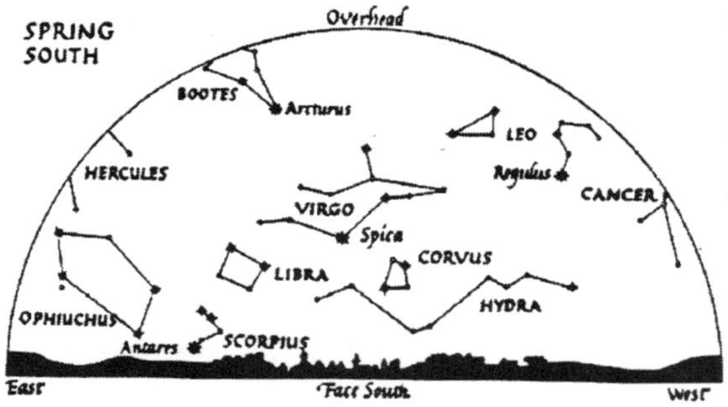

OAT FLOUR	.20 lb
OATS, ROLLED	.22 lb
OATS, STEEL CUT	.30 lb
BLUE CORN MEAL	.35 lb
WHOLE WHEAT	.06 lb
WHEAT GRITS	.25 lb
RYE FLOUR	.20 lb
WHEAT BRAN	.50 lb
BLACK EYED PEAS	.30 lb
LENTILS	.30 lb
SPLIT PEAS	.20 lb
AZUKI BEANS	.30 lb (4 lb for $1.00)
NAVY BEANS	.30 lb
KIDNEY BEANS	.35 lb
LIMA BEANS	.35 lb
MILLET	.35 lb

CHIA SEED	1.45 lb
FLAX SEED	.45 lb
ALFALFA SEED	1.30 lb
SUNFLOWER SEED	.90 lb
SESAME SEED	.75 lb
GINSENG (KOREAN)	4.00 oz
AVOCADOS	.45 ea.
PEANUTS	.40 lb.
ALMONDS	.75 (8 oz)
CASHEWS	.95 (8 oz)

ORGANIC AND TREATED SEEDS

FRESH PRODUCE DELIVERED ON TUES. AND FRI. MORNINGS - COME IN AND PLACE YOUR ORDER.

SPRING
NORTH

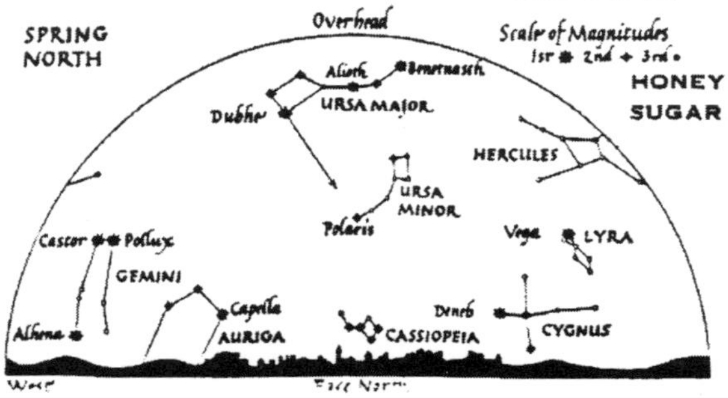

HONEY	13.00/60 lbs
SUGAR - RAW	.30 lb

From Capitalist to Communist and Back

told by Chick Lonsdale to Iris Keltz

"In the late sixties, I was living in the Haight Ashbury of San Francisco. I had dreams and visions that there would be cataclysmic change—earthquakes, social disruptions and violence—and felt that it was time to move inland. About ten of us traveled across the desert in a caravan of painted VW vans, old cars and a pickup truck, looking for a new place to live. Except for brief stops in Flagstaff, Santa Fe and Madrid, we practically drove straight through to Taos. My first wife was from Taos, so I was familiar with the town. I figured we could stay with my ex-in-laws for a day or two and get showers.

"I bought a Taos newspaper and found a church with a parish house for rent right in the center of town for $80 dollars a month. We turned the church into a coffeehouse and lived in the parish house in the back. The coffeehouse was a sanctuary for people coming into Taos. Rick, the manager, provided sleeping bags for the first night's visit. There were always Indians that needed a place to stay and hang out. We felt they were checking us out. Pretty much every night, people played guitars, smoked dope and talked about things.

"The parish house was so busy, I only stayed one month, then rented a rundown 18-room, rambling adobe in Talpa with four to six thousand square feet. It became known as 'the palace' and rented for $200 a month. About 50 people lived there through the winter of '68. Most of them were people I knew from San Francisco or their friends.

"That winter I purchased 50 acres in the foothills above Sunshine Valley, 35 miles north of Taos. In the spring some of us moved out to the land. We built shelters and

The Taos General Store was an information center, a bookstore and probably one of the first bulk health food stores in the country.

Photo by Bill Davis

started our farming community that came to be known as Lorien. Back in the '30s there had been 300 or 400 people living in the valley doing farming. During the depression years, it dried up and people moved elsewhere. There was an abandoned farmhouse on the property and nine houses in the area. Six of them were empty, only three were occupied.

"Some people chose to stay in town and became involved in various business activities in Taos. We'd already started the coffeehouse. Next we started Lorien Construction Company. Its purpose was to build structures for whoever needed housing. The idea of money was totally changed. Things were done out of the desire and joy of improving everyone's life, not for profit or gain.

"Our society was communal in its orientation. The construction company purchased a warehouse where we stored building supplies. We converted it into a grocery known as The General Store, a bookstore and an information center. The General Store was the first health food store in Northern New Mexico, the only bulk health food store for 200 miles. We got our supplies from organic farms in California. Every two weeks or a month, we'd send a truck there.

"I funded projects with my inheritance money for two years. When my money ran out most of the projects stopped. I helped start the hippie newspaper, *The Fountain of Light*, and bought the medical supplies to help La Clinica get started. It was a cooperative venture with Drs. Kilgore and Rosen. Everything started out of need. Holy Cross Hospital refused to admit hippies, so when someone was stabbed in a fight because they were sleeping out in the street and the nuns at the Holy Cross Hospital refused to admit them, there was an emergency need that was not being fulfilled by the community. Hippies were suspected of carrying a variety of diseases and were considered 'unclean.' The hospital was reluctant to allow them in the door for fear they might contaminate the place. Doctors Kilgore and Rosen arranged for student interns in their final year of medical school to come and take care of the routine problems like birth control, venereal disease, hepatitis, and minor inju-

The General Store was also a place to bump into old friends and hang for a while.

Photo by Rich Jamison

ries. Anything else would be referred to one of the medical doctors.

"Along with the businesses, there were three communes that I was directly involved with. The Family Commune was on Ranchitos Road in a large house down the road from *The Taos News* office. I was not a member of their commune, but was supportive of their activities. I purchased the house they lived in. They provided the volunteer assistance for a variety of activities from auto repair to selling *The Fountain of Light* around town. They worked as receptionists at La Clinica, opened up the grocery story every day and worked at the bookstore.

"These guys were a self-appointed security patrol who worked day and night to protect homes and property belonging to hippies. There were break-ins, shootings, people torching cars and harassing people at the hot springs. They were quite a focused group and quite promiscuous compared to Lorien. They had what they called a group marriage. The 35 or so people who lived in that commune shared each other sexually. It was a different moral system. They believed it was okay for any man and woman to get together in that community, but it was not okay for someone to get sexual partners outside of the commune. They voiced a great belief in their communal marriage.

"Lorien was home to 30 to 50 people including myself. The name comes from the Tolkien Trilogy. Frodo, the hero, is charged with the responsibility for taking this magic ring that has evil in it and throwing it into the volcano so it would be melted down and neutralized, but the possession of this ring corrupts a person. As he is traveling, Frodo is corrupted by the evil emanations from the ring and becomes weary from his struggles to maintain his higher focus. He stumbles into Lothlorien, a tree forest community of elves in the process of evacuating from the Middle Earth—it was becoming too corrupt for their higher energies. We chose the name Lorien after that elfdom. Lorien had hundreds of cottonwoods and so we were a forest community and a sanctuary for peace from the mundane and corrupt energies of the outer world.

Some people built a geodesic dome to live in. Invented by R. Buckminster Fuller, the geodesic dome is a structure shaped like a piece of a sphere or a ball. It's made of a complex network of triangles that form a roughly spherical surface. This one was at either Lorien or Lila.

Photo by Rich Jamison

"The commune's primary focus was back-to-the-land like New Buffalo, but Lorien was also a place to meditate and hang out. We plowed the land using an old horse-drawn plow. We planted by hand and irrigated from the stream that ran through the farm. Everything was done without the help of machinery. One summer we grew three acres of beans and a little corn. People lived in tents, tipis and wooden shacks in the winter. We bought some bark-side lumber from the mills. You could buy a bundle of 200 two-by-four slabs for $5, so we bought 10 bundles and people built houses from these slabs.

"At first I lived in a tipi and then built a shack, 10 feet by 10. I considered my family to include hundreds of people. People hung out in the central kitchen built from the bark-side lumber. It was 16 feet wide and 20 feet long, with a pitched roof and a tarp thrown over the top to keep the rain out. I provided the basic foodstuff like oatmeal, rice and beans. Anything extra like beer and potato chips came from individuals. We ate a lot of beans and rice and oatmeal.

"There were two groups that lived there. The yoga-meditation group, about 15 to 20 people, would get up before light and greet the sun with yoga exercises. They'd do their gardening in the cool part of the day and were into healthy foods, smoking grass and a quiet lifestyle. Once in a while some peyote or LSD would show up, but it was mostly grass.

"There was another group of about 15 to 20 people that would get up at noon and stagger into the kitchen, grab a cup of coffee and roll some tobacco. They were truckers and bikers and horse people, and liked to go riding in the mountains. Afternoon was their time to work on the communal farm. As it got dark they'd light a big bonfire and drink wine and beer and beat on drums and whoop to the moon, when there was one. The two groups had very little social interaction. One lived in the morning and the other lived at night and had very different personalities. That split the commune. Eventually there were feuds and fights between the two groups, and that's what caused the termination of the community. We had community meetings fairly often, something like once a week. But people just couldn't get along.

"Whether I liked it or not there was a psychological separation between me and the rest of the community because I owned the land. New Buffalo was more egalitarian because Rick Klein didn't live at the commune. As much as I tried to say we were one family, it still came down to the fact that I was the one who bought the rice and beans, the one who owned the land. I was the landlord. Very autocratically, I made a clear command that we weren't going to overpopulate the commune and that not more than 50 people could live there—50 acres, 50 people. On several occasions I moved to another commune for a month so they could explore their relationships without me.

"Sexual freedom at Lorien meant the freedom to have sex or to not have sex. There was some partner swapping, but that was not typical. It wasn't a big orgy. People tended to get into relationships and stay in them for a period of time. Some came with a partner and stayed with them the whole time. My partner and I met at the commune and had two daughters during the 15 years we lived together. In the summer of '69, 10,000 hippies visited Taos. Many of them came to Lorien. After that, the whole movement lost momentum. Lorien lasted for two years.

"My first daughter was born in Embudo in1970, at the time the commune was dissolving. I ran out of money and could no longer support the community activities. I'd started out with about $250,000 and was broke at the end of two years, but it was a time to live and be a part of, not a time to count shekels. The newspaper folded, the grocery store folded, the bookstore was sold. The clinic was taken over by other charitable sponsors. The house on Ranchitos Road was sold. Maria, my companion, and I rented a small house in Talpa. I got a job chopping firewood with Van Arsdale. We chopped 400 cords of wood in three months.

Kerosene lamps gave a soft light to get stoned and dream by, but they were a lousy way to read. Nevertheless, many of us still use them! *Photo by Rich Jamison*

"Lorien is still a farming cooperative today for an enterprise called Roots and Herbs, which is an organic farming educational center. People come from the University of New Mexico to study with them. They are my tenants. I am no longer a communist.

"Philosophically, I felt that there was a wave at the latter end of the '60s—an opportunity to transform our culture that required a lot of sharing and cooperation—but the wave receded into our establish-

Medical care was very affordable at La Clinica—free or on a donation basis. Patients were seen first-come, first-serve. For awhile it was staffed by Drs. Dale Cogrove, William Kilgore, and Albert Rosen. A registered nurse and volunteers completed the staff. It was in Taos for many years, often shifting locations.

Photo by John Nichols

ment culture. We were given an opportunity to reexperience and grow back through cultural roots that were thousands of years old. The communistic ideas didn't have deep enough roots so I abandoned those philosophies for a more capitalistic approach. I own property. I'm a merchant. The projects I worked on in the '60s took all of my resources. But then I started over. I had three farming properties in different parts of the county that I owed mortgages on. I sold the properties to pay the mortgages—that created home sites. That's how I got into real estate.

"Hippie culture across the country was colorful. People were free to assume new personalities and that was part of the wonder of it all. People got a chance to explore parts of themselves that had been prohibited by our culture. Some of it was beautiful, some ugly. Everybody was transformed in some way. Two or three times a year for the past 30 years somebody comes to visit me from those commune days. I got a note from this guy who wrote, 'I came by to see who's here and heard that you were still in town. God bless you. This was such an important part of my life.' The hippie movement in Taos—and across the country—was a birthing place for thousands of people."

Update:
Charles Lonsdale is at a place of completion in many parts of his life. He has just celebrated the 18th birthday of his youngest daughter. Also, he has successfully completed a ten-year career in real estate which was a survival job for him. His current interests are world travel, art, meditation, contemplative writing, going on a vision quest and celebrating the wonderful changes coming to our country.

Don't Worry

TAOS FREE CLINIC

Taos now has a free clinic. At the present time it is open on Monday and Wednesday from 10:00 AM and Friday 2:00 PM.

In the near future a Medical student will arrive and the clinic will be open every day. Also on the agenda is a dentist to work in the clinic for the summer.

The clinic has it's own Pharmacy and small lab.

The Church of Macrobiotics is sponsering the free clinic and hopes to turn it into a community program as soon as it gets more under way.

A bus service is also being set up to haul people to and from the clinic on a regular schedule from nearby towns.

The clinic can use funds in addition to sheets, blankets, towels, furniture, etc. Donations are tax deductible. They should be sent to CHURCH OF MACROBIOTICS, RANCHOS DE TAOS, NEW MEXICO. For more information, call Joe Sage at: 758-4294.

Coffee house now offering 'switchboard'

A new community service was opened this week with the beginning of something called the Taos Switchboard.

Joseph Sage, a former resident of Taos, began the service, located at the Dawn Coffee House, as a "liason information service" for anyone and everyone who calls the phone numbers 758-4295 or 758-4294.

Sage is a minister of the newly chartered "Church of Microbiotics" in Taos. The Switchboard is operated 24 hours a day to assist people in any number of desired services.

"We provide information like finding babysitters, clothes, housing, jobs, and we also are available if someone needs to talk to someone about anything. If some cases, we may even act as a suicide prevention center," Sage said.

He said that many of the people involved with the service were ready and willing to give their time and talents free. "We have a lot of people interested in working — and working hard —who have experience in many fields."

The service will provide any needed assistance to all who call, including answering questions of "frustrated people with questions about services available in the community or matters which might require professional help."

Sage emphasized that the service would be a "relay service" between those who need something and those who might be

The Mabel Dodge Luhan house. The original house was a three-room adobe, purchased in 1918 for $1,500 by Mabel Dodge Luhan. It was renovated and expanded to its present state by a crew from the Taos Pueblo. This is a view of the courtyard looking up to the solarium. Throughout the 1920s and '30s, Mabel and her husband Tony Luhan invited a variety of artists and writers to be guests in their home. These included Georgia O'Keeffe, D. H. Lawrence, Willa Cather, Carl Sandburg, Spud Johnson and many others. The house is still a bustling cultural center.

Photo by Iris Keltz

The Silversmiths at the Mabel Dodge Luhan House

told by Lorelei Brown, Seth Brown and Jennifer Sibvonen to Iris Keltz

I am talking to three of the jewelers who lived in the Mabel Dodge Luhan House during the mid-'70s. Their average age at the time was 21. Dennis Hopper, a well-known Hollywood actor who co-starred with Peter Fonda in the movie Easy Rider, *was their landlord. All three have become well-known jewelers. Jennifer is a lifelong friend of Seth and Lorelei who are brother and sister. The jewelry-making commune started at the Brown House, which was the family home of Lorelei, Seth and Kinlock Brown. To those of us who watched them wander through town draped in turquoise and silver earrings, necklaces and concha belts, they appeared to be having a grand time while being surprisingly focused on their craft. This oral history is a weaving together of our conversation.*

S*eth Brown*: "For seven years, from 1972 to 1979, a core group of us lived communally, making jewelry and sharing our lives. We were called the Sterling Smiths. When friends live and work together, there's a renaissance in any kind of art and that's what happened with us.

Lorelei and Seth Brown and Jennifer Sibvonen. Photo by Iris Keltz

"My brother Kinlock and I started making jewelry when we were about eight and ten years old with an old anvil out in the barn. When I went to Navajo country with my parents, my mom bought me this lovely turquoise ring. It cost $6 and was diamond shaped with five or six pieces of turquoise. I fell in love with it. When it washed off my hand into an open septic tank, I was determined to have another ring just like it and spent years trying to figure out how to make one.

"My brother and I began selling silver overlay rings in my mother's weaving gallery, The Craft House, which opened in '64 in Arroyo Seco. They were $15 each and sold like hotcakes. From that point on, except for some odd jobs, I've made my living by selling jewelry.

"Russell Green moved into a house down the road and started teaching us what he knew. He was older and made beautiful sawed-out brass buckles. He taught us how to melt a glob of silver and pound it into a round disk and make conchos. My brother Kinlock and I had stumps out on the patio. We'd be sitting out there, naked in February, stamping away on our jewelry. I slept under the porch that winter.

"One of Russell's mountain-man friends had an idea to polish these belts with ashes, bury them in the ground and sell them as old authentic Indian belts. We were interested in making a living at selling jewelry so a friend and I went to work for him. We made 600 silver buttons out of mercury dimes, soldered copper loops on the back and were to be paid ten cents a button.

"It's important to remember that most of the people who ended up living at the Mabel Dodge Luhan House had grown up together in Taos. We were homegrown local Anglos who had been living together since we were teenagers. My grandma first moved to Taos in 1945. When we lived at the Brown House—our family home—we'd hitchhike to the co-op in El Prado to buy groceries until our neighbor let us use a beautiful white horse named Lightening. We put these huge pack bags on the horse and filled them with groceries. One time, walking the eight miles home, the horse got spooked, took off running and tore the baskets on a barbed wire fence, scattering our groceries everywhere. After that Kinlock got an old Plymouth Valiant for $300. When our family home sold, we found another house to rent.

"The idea of making money as silversmiths traveled to New Buffalo because of Pepé, one of the guys who lived there. He had been a machinist and wanted to get New Buffalo into jewelry-making. Sequoia, Bill, and Pepé started working with us. They were totally inspired.

"Pepé grew up in rural Wisconsin and knew how to chop wood and grow food. Most of the hippies who lived at New Buffalo came from the cities and weren't prepared to survive in New Mexico.

"Dennis Hopper's brother David and his wife Charlotte lived in the Mabel Dodge Luhan House with a group of individuals including Pepé who left New Buffalo and moved into the Log Cabin Room. Pepé believed in communal living. When his housemates decided to move on, he got the idea of turning the place into a jeweler's commune. He was about 15 years older than most of us."

Lorelei: "There were 13 bedrooms and a fairly stable group of 15 people living there, not including the freeloaders. Pepé and Kinlock were driving forces in organizing the place. We would meet after dinner once a week on Sunday to say our complaints and pay our $90 a month rent, which included food. Kinlock acted as the group's accountant. He'd take out the book and say, 'So and so's behind in his payments and needs to pay up.' We'd make up a menu and a cooking and cleaning schedule for the coming week. You only had to cook two meals a week with a partner. Everyone decided what he or she wanted to cook.

"We ate in the huge dining room. Whoever was making breakfast would go around to all the rooms and knock at the doors at seven saying, 'The pancakes—or whatever—are ready. If you want 'em, get up.' There were gorgeous dinners every night at

The core group of jewelers who lived communally at the Mabel Dodge Luhan House. Jennifer is in the middle next to Pepé Rochan with daughter Kachina on his lap. Lorelei is standing up on the far left. Seth's not there, but his brother Kinlock is the man standing on the far right with long hair and a silver necklace. *Photo courtesy of Jennifer Sihvonen*

seven o'clock. It was like living in a castle and eating at a banquet table. Once a week we'd stock up on groceries from Safeway and the Co-op. We'd get fresh meat from the butcher in El Prado. Every week New Buffalo delivered milk. We had a few communal cars—a Volvo and a Valiant.

"The Mabel Dodge House was huge. We had to work hard to keep it clean—that was where a lot of our arguments came from. Pepé was captain of the ship and he wanted the house kept spotless. When cleaning and mopping had to be done, certain people would split, leaving others to clean."

Seth: "We restored the house. We painted the entire interior, fixed the roof that was in bad shape. The volcanic flagstone patio that you see outside was under six to eight inches of dirt and leaves that had accumulated over the years. Someone with a shovel hit a rock and realized it was embedded. Pepé and Kinlock dug out nine loads of dirt and hauled it away in a flatbed truck. We talked Dennis into letting us put part of our rent money into buying materials to fix the house. We did the work.

"Come fall, the guys would bring home huge truckloads of firewood. We probably burned 40 cords of wood that first winter. The guys gathered and chopped the wood. The ladies would can salsa, green chile, applesauce and jam. We had freezers full of food."

Jennifer: "The second winter we bought wood but the women still did the canning. Friends would visit and think this was totally cool and want to move in. Sometimes people would show up at dinner. If that happened for a few days, Pepé and the other guys would take them into the yard and give them a talking to and you wouldn't see them anymore. Sometimes we'd band together at a meeting and say, 'This person's got to go.' It was difficult to ask someone to leave without hurting his or her feelings. Occasionally new people would join us but we were incredibly stable, partly because there were several families living there, brothers and sisters as well as friends who had grown up together. Sometimes a new personality moving into the house could disrupt the core group.

"My father, Oli Sihvonen, lived with us for a while. He stayed out in the Gate House. He would saunter around discreetly, painting all the time. It was like having an artist-in-residence. He sat in on the family meetings and told us how democratic we were. Seth and Lorelai's mother, Rachel Brown, came for a short stay when she was writing her weaving book. We charged them rent. They were not parental authority figures. They were family and needed a place to stay."

Lorelei: "After breakfast and cleaning we'd go to the shop in the Log Cabin Room. There were five setups of everything because everyone put all their jewelry-making tools together. There would be shifts of four or five people working all day long. The early birds would get the fire going and be out there working at five in the morning. By midday they'd be pooped and the next crew would come in. The guys busted a hole through the adobe wall of the Log Cabin Room, which had another room behind it, and made a foundry so we could do casting, polishing and the dirtier stuff."

Jennifer: "Sometimes we collaborated on a piece of jewelry, like the centennial concha belt. We were known for reviving the old techniques of traditional silversmithing, which blossomed into a huge thing in New Mexico."

Lorelei: "None of us were on welfare or food stamps. We had a way to make a living. Sherry was good at selling jewelry. She'd make the round of the bars and shops in town drenched in gorgeous jewelry. Sometimes a few people would take everyone's jewelry down to Albuquerque and Santa Fe. They'd come back and say, 'I sold one of your bracelets—here's your money.'"

Jennifer: "There were several occasions when Dennis Hopper would show up out of the blue with his L.A. friends. They'd be totally messed up and want us to give them a tour of his house. He lived next door at the house that had been Tony Luhan's. Dennis and a friend rented it from the pueblo. The roof is caved in now and the place is a ruin. One time he brought the Japanese Playboy people to the house and wanted us to belly dance for them, which we did. Dennis was into this Wild West game and when he was around there were guns and alcohol."

Seth: "He was a great landlord though. He never harassed us. He was this crazy guy who lived next door and we were friends. He lived off the $750-a-month rent we paid him.

"Kinlock traded a beautiful concha belt that we would normally sell for $300 for one of the motorcycles that had been in the movie 'Easy Rider.' It was the famous one with the flag-painted gas tank. We'd discovered the four 'Easy Rider' bikes in the pump room and drooled over them. Dennis came over one

Easy Rider *montage from the* Fountain of Light *1970*

day and Kinlock went out to the car and asked, 'Dennis, would you be interested in trading that motorcycle for this belt?' He said, 'Sure. No problem.' Kinlock gave him the belt, wrote up the papers, and the bike was his. He used to drive his girlfriend Maya to high school on the 'Easy Rider' Bike. Three of the girls living at the house still went to high school."

Jennifer: "People talked about us having orgies and lots of drugs, but other than marijuana there were none. Either you had a girlfriend or boyfriend living at the house or friends would come over. No one had to drive around looking for parties because the social scene was at our house. Surprisingly, there was little partner-swapping."

Seth: "I still remember the great Halloween party—I wore a filthy trench coat and a wig made from salt and pepper handspun wool held on with an old hat. I looked like the dirtiest funkiest street hippie you could imagine. Only my mom knew who I was. I'd start talking to people I'd known my whole life and they would ignore me. Even my brother tried to kick me out of the party."

Lorelei: "Some nights we'd play games like backgammon or the guys would play music. We had a collective tab at the Airport Bar if we felt like going out. I hated to be left alone in the house; when everyone was gone, it felt very spooky."

Jennifer: "Pepé and I had a daughter, Rochelle, while I was living there. Everybody took care of me. I was relieved of all household responsibilities. We planned a home birth with a midwife in Mabel Dodge's room, in her bed, but ended up having to go to the hospital."

Seth: "We'd all heard rumors that Dennis was going back to Hollywood, back to the movies. He was destitute and had to sell the house. He tried to make it possible for us to buy it. We thought about it seriously, even tried to get a loan and a down payment. Hopper went back to Hollywood and became incredibly successful. We never saw him again. I'm glad it ended when it did because most of my memories are good. Towards the end, we were all thinking it would be nice to have our own scene. A core group of us moved into Grace Parr's house

Artisans from the Mabel Dodge Luhan House and the Taos community gather prior to a group exhibition. *Photo by Seth Roffman*

and set up another jewelry shop and continued our work."

Jennifer: "Over the years there had been members of the group that didn't contribute and some of us felt used by them. Others worked really hard to make this scene happen and those people looked forward to having their own place. Some couples just wanted to live alone."

Seth: "At the time, I believed this would be our way of life forever, but we needed to survive. We each inherited or bought a piece of land and built houses, but I think we've slaved far harder being alone. Of course it's a lot easier living together when you're younger."

Lorelei: "I would love to live that way again, if we could pick the people. I miss working with people. It's much harder working all alone in my little shop. When communal living works, it's like a village. I think that's how the human race is happiest. We treasure those times."

Update:

Lorelei, Seth and Jennifer are still making their living as jewelers. Lorelei is married to a contractor who built them a lovely adobe home on El Salto Mountain. They have two children—Theresa and Tyler.

Seth lives alone in a self-built adobe house up the road from where he grew up. He is proud of the fact that he hauled the vigas for his roof from the mountains by himself and made his own adobe bricks.

Jennifer lives in Arroyo Seco in an adobe house built by Lorelei's husband, who is also her step-brother. Her 20-year-old daughter Rochelle is a Latin dancer and a personal trainer.

by Susie

The splendid Sons of Thunder have some miscellaneous winter advice for newcomers: Don't put the high octane fuel used for Coleman lanterns in a kerosene lantern or it will blow up. . . and if you round off the wick in your lantern, the glass won't blacken. Don't leave your axe outside, the cold will make it brittle and breakable. If your axe handle should break and you're holding it over a fire to burn it out, pack the sharpened edge in mud. Frozen wood is easier to cut or chop than dry wood. Avoid trying to cut green wood with a chain saw or you will break the chain. A cast iron stove is superior to a tin stove, but if yours is tin fill the bottom with about 2 inches of sand until the ashes build up or you will burn up the bottom. Save your wood ashes for the outhouse in place of lye, or the chicken house where the chickens will dust themselves and eliminate feather mites. You can also feed your chickens egg shells so the eggs will lay with harder shells. Cut up inner tubes make great kindling and tires give off tremendous heat. Hot ginger tea or a couple of garlic cloves will cure dysentery within a few hours.

The winter survival expert with the most successful method of keeping feet warm will be rewarded with a wonderful pizza at House of Taos where, so far, sitting by the fireplace is the only way I've found to keep my feet warm.

Looking forward to the Institute of Applied Creativity that George Bacon plans to begin towards the end of the month. Classes such as sculpting, painting, drawing, photography, creative writing, etc. will be taught with a zen-like approach which you will learn more about when the pamphlet for the school is circulated.

If it's repairable, Clarence can fix it. Specializes in autos. Look for a garage on Hiway 3 in El Prado with his name on it.

Those bright lights at the wonderful Seco Rock Benefit weren't the Hog Farm's Light Show. Lorien and The Family are making a movie: *Peace, Love, Two Hours, Taos 1970*. Being made by and about the community... a spontaneous film ... with plans for showing segments of the movie as it flows along to the community for reaction and involvement. Intended for distribution by Easter.

Michael and Lynn are cutting and polishing deer and elk antlers into fine buttons for earth clothing, as well as pipes and necklaces. Samples can be viewed at the General Store and we invite you to leave word with the Store folks if you want any of the items.

The Taos Switchboard and Information Center has recently moved to the Lorien Building which also houses the General Store, this newspaper, and the Clinic on S. Santa Fe Trail.

There has been an enthusiastic response to the class Tom Law is instructing in Kundalini Yoga. Classes are at 4:00 Monday and Thursday at the Taos Band's house in El Valle Escondido.

Communes that need welding done should write: WEIRD WELDING, P.O. Box 4165, Albuquerque, 87106 ... "we have tanks in a truck and may be able to trip it out" ...

The One Loose Eye Gallery now has a varied selection of used books for sale ... and desires more if you've some you'd like to sell.

The Community Information Center is now equipped with a research library. A list of some of the books available include: *How To Grow Vegetables and Fruits; Zen Macrobiotic Cooking; The Wilderness Cabin; The Indian Tipi; The Natural Foods Cookbook; Machinery Handbook; The Way Things Work; Light Weight Camping Equipment; Whole Earth Catalogue; Back To Eden; Modern Utopia Magazine; Organic Farming Magazine; Complete UNESCO Book of Sun Energy*. The books must stay in the Center, they only have one copy of each. This is so people who need them can get them.

DONT TREAD ON ME

The Bicentennial Belt

told by Ed Morgan to Iris Keltz

"Before coming to Taos, I lived in Kansas City, Missouri, and got trained by Hallmark Cards as an engraver. I had never worked with jewelry. I was also an Eagle Scout in charge of an Explorer post that dealt with authentic Indian lore and taught quillwork and tanning hides to the Boy Scouts. I'd gotten a call from the Philmont Scout Ranch in Cimmaron to pick up several frozen buffalo that I planned to skin and use in a ceremony. When I skinned the buffalo in the street outside my house, the neighbors reported me to the police.

"When I first drove into Taos in 1967, it had only one paved street and one stop light. I'd never been anyplace in this country that still looked like it did in 1840. I quit my job as an engraver and moved there. For the first year I worked in construction.

"I lived out on the mesa, down the road from the Millicent Rogers Museum, at a place we named Badger Mountain. About five or six guys, including Pepé, Tahiti, Greg, Kevin, Bob and myself rented the house from a guy who owned the friendly bar in El Prado. It was like a commune. We added women as we went along which was basically our downfall.

Ed Morgan at home in his studio, summer of '99.

"Pepé had been making jewelry for a while. I learned by watching, using my experience as an engraver to learn sculpting jewelry in silver. We did several craft shows when we lived at Badger Mountain—one at the Millicent Rogers and one in Santa Barbara at a craft institute. We were making silver jewelry, porcupine quill embroidery, woodcarvings and wooden inlay belt buckles. Kevin did leatherwork and made saddles.

"Word about the work we were doing just spread. We made buckles for the Grateful Dead. Greg's brother had been the equipment manager for them. Tahiti had been the bus driver for the Merry Pranksters and knew Owsley, the guy who made the best acid.

"The first belt we did had a Hopi man engraved on each concha, based on a photograph taken in the early 1900's we'd seen in a book. The second belt we did was about the major tribes from the Southwest. Each concha had a scene, like the Navajos crossing Canyon de Chelly, Apaches drinking from a stream, a Hopi man standing with an eagle behind him, and a Pueblo man drilling hishi for a necklace. Pepé did the stamping work and cast the ingots. I did the engraving. Jeffrey did the inlay in the background. We sold that belt for pretty cheap. Since then, I have bought it back at a cost of $22,000.

"When we moved out of Badger Mountain, I rented the upstairs of the Mabel Dodge House and Pepé rented the downstairs. We worked hard to fix up the place—we stripped the latillas in the kitchen that had been painted and redid the old wooden gate that was in pieces. I still have one of the big buffalo skulls that were on either side of the gate. We uncovered the flagstone patio that was covered with dirt. We loved the place.

"Transient people came through all the time. At one point the Rolling Stones came through. So did Mr. Clean, the guy from the advertisement. Even Bob Dylan and his wife showed up. They were all friends of Dennis Hopper. This was the Wild West for these guys. Sometimes there'd be crazy parties going on all around—at the Victor Higgins House next door, the Mabel Dodge House where we lived and the Tony Lujan house where Hopper lived.

"Dennis would be playing downtown with Jerry Jeff Walker and tell all these guys to go over and stay at our house even though it was rented. People would wander in and crash all over the place. Dennis would have dinners at the main dining room of our house. The most memorable dinner I've ever been to in my life was with the guy who played the mole in El Topo and the famous psychic who had found the Boston strangler. He was flying over Taos looking for some doctor who had crashed in a plane around here. John Nichols, our local celebrity writer, was at that dinner.

"I remember early one morning looking out the window and seeing this beautiful young woman dancing naked through the poppies in the backyard. This memory is burned into my mind.

"We lived communally, shared the kitchen and set up a jewelry workshop in the Log Cabin Room. Pepé and I were older than the others but it didn't matter—we were age blind. Pepé, Jeffrey and I would sit around and talk. Ideas would come and we'd build on it. We were like musicians playing together. In fact, I started off as a musician, playing drums at 11 years old. For the bicentennial belt, we used what we'd learned from the first two belts. We threw in our individual stashes of lapis, turquoise, serpentine, coral, ivory and silver. Someone got the idea of doing flags that represented major social changes in this country. We were patriotic but mainly we were trying to make a bunch of money. No one kept track of time or materials. We figured, when the time came to sell it, we would deal with it. We were caught up in the creation of the belt and didn't really think about money. Our concept of making money was immediate—enough to buy a running car, or pay the rent and get groceries.

"We would get up at 6 o'clock and fire up the forge in the Log Cabin Room to melt the silver. I did my engraving upstairs in the glass observatory. Rumor has it that Mabel built this room to watch the Penitentes' Easter ritual in the nearby morada. The room had high windows all around with a glass bathroom a few steps below. Her bedroom was below the observatory.

"In designing and making the belt we got into the mysticism of the founding of this country. The number 13 appears in everything. There's 13 olives in the olive branch. There's 13 letters in *E Pluribus Unum*, 13 feathers in the eagle's tail. The number of bricks in the pyramid is a multiple of 13. Thirteen is a magic number among the Masons and all the founding fathers were Masons. The Masonic Order is an old secret society that came from Europe.

"Each concha had 13 stars around the edge. The stripes were coral with lapis behind ivory stars. The social changes represented were for the Civil War, the Revolutionary War and the two World Wars. An engraved rattlesnake stood for the Revolutionary War. The concha that fits in the small of your back was engraved with the great pyramid with the eye over it, the one that appears on the dollar bill. The front buckle was an eagle with red, white and blue in the background. When I was engraving the eagle, I almost went through, which I never do. If you make a mistake engraving metal, you can't put it back. When I turned it over and looked at the place where I almost went through, it made a mouse that was in the eagle's mouth on the other side. Everybody went, 'Oh, isn't that cool!' I designed all kinds of stuff around the mouse.

"A lot of the inlay techniques we used were Japanese—like bezzling the stones without solder. The Japanese engrave the back of a box or the underneath of a table. So the backside of the buckle and the conchas are engraved with olive leaves and scroll work that are hidden by leather backing. You could show them to other people if you wanted, but if someone didn't look they'd never know it was there.

"Jeffrey and Pepé made sand-cast ingots. An ingot is an oval-shaped piece of silver that the concha is pounded out of. It's important to get a certain thickness before you start to saw, hammer, trim, stamp, cut and engrave. Sherry was great at cutting stones, so we contracted her to cut all the turquoise stars that went around each flag. It was a difficult job, but she cut them perfectly. Jennifer helped with the inlay. Someone else cut the coral, ivory and lapis. Kevin did the leatherwork behind the conchas, using red leather to match the American flags.

"I don't have much of my jewelry left. In those days you wore it and sold it off your body. I sold my first belt when I was standing on a street corner at the plaza. A guy asked me if I made it and how much I'd want for it. I told him. He called that night and asked, 'Would you take this much and a trip to San Francisco?' I said, 'You bet!'

"We finished working on the bicentennial belt early in the spring of '76 after working on it for about one year. People were surprised that we'd made the belt without a commission. But if we sat around and waited for that it would never have happened. Nobody would have commissioned us to do a project like that. Locally, it was on display at the First State Bank. It also went on display at the Chase Manhattan Bank in New York and the Anchorage Best Western Hotel in Alaska.

"Creamy, a blond dude from California who played congas, was the guy who offered to take it on tour to try and promote it. Creamy offered us a sum of money, something around $10,000, to rent the belt and promised to pay us more when he sold it. He flew Pepé, Jeffrey and me to Anchorage, Alaska, with the belt, all expenses paid. David Von Riper came with us to take photographs.

"Creamy ended up disappearing with the belt. He sold it and made a lot of money. Some of us had been against letting Creamy take the belt, but in the end it was the cash in the suitcase, the $10,000 dollars that attracted the people to do it. All that's left of the belt are the metal plates that David Van Riper photo-etched of each of the conchas. The inlaid box with the pyramid top, especially designed to hold the bicentennial belt, is at El Rincon, the original trading post in Taos where it's being used to display antique beaded peyote fans.

"When Creamy disappeared we thought about hiring a private detective to find him. The word came back that they found the belt. A guy in California had it. He'd broken into someone's house, stolen it and said that he'd destroy the belt rather than let it go. Like the Hope diamond, the belt drew people out of the woodwork. I thought, 'Hell with it, I'll do another one.' Even if I got it back it would have to be exorcised by a priest or a peyote guy.

"The Return Gallery, built behind the plaza, was inspired by all the unbelievable jewelry that was being created at the time by a whole group of us. The gallery is gone and nobody is doing jewelry like that now. The jewelry at Zales and Tiffany's is mass-produced. The jewelry we did was all one-of-a-kind. The people who bought our jewelry were high rollers—like drug dealers and famous rock musicians. It was a unique era that lasted about four years at the most. It was at the time when New Buffalo, Morningstar, Badger Mountain and the Mabel Dodge House were all happening.

"The bicentennial belt is legendary. Grace Slick of the Jefferson Airplane wore the belt at a concert in Denver and sang 'Up The Revolution.' Some guy has it and when he dies it will surface again. We thought the belt should become a national treasure and dreamed of getting it into the Smithsonian, but had no idea how to go about getting it there.

"The belt was signed by Pepé, Jeffrey, myself and others. We worked well together. Pepé is still doing jewelry. If I ever did jewelry again it would be for fun and not for sale. I have this idea for a pectoral necklace like the Egyptians made with engraved scenes. Someday."

Update:

Ed Morgan has returned to his engraving work as a master printmaker. The fluctuation in the gold and silver market was too great. When he met his wife he was sleeping in his car because he lost everything in the silver market when it went from $10 to $50 an ounce. People wouldn't pay the higher price. When he left jewelry making, he got work designing the background for expensive jewelry catalogues.

Morgan and his wife Virginia live in Taos and have a successful gallery on Bent Street. His engravings are in demand by people from all over the world. And he has made another belt. Someone once wanted to buy it for a quarter of a million dollars but he told them, "I'll never make another one." He gave it to his wife for Christmas and it will go to his kids when he's gone. Each concha is a gold engraved animal—antelopes with ivory horns, elk in front of serpentine mountains and wolves under a lapis sky and a gold moon. Their tracks are engraved on the reverse side. When Ed speaks of his creations, his eyes light up and it becomes a little like listening to Sheherazade spin stories about the Arabian nights.

Three artists in search of America

By MERILEE DANNEMANN

Three Taos artists set out to make a piece for the Bicentennial.

What they produced is a work of art magnificent in concept and execution: a statement of America, of the Southwest, and of the very special culture alive in Taos, 1976.

What they discovered in the process is a deeper meaning for the American Revolution, and for America.

The artists are Daniel "Pepe" Rochan, 35, "Little Jeff" Morris, 23, and Ed Morgan, 32, and the work they created is a Bicentennial concha belt.

The belt contains seven conchas and a buckle. The buckle and the center concha depict the Great Seal of the United States of America, and the remaining conchas show six of the flags that have flown over America.

The piece is of silver, stamped, tooled, and engraved. The multicolored flags are inlaid pieces of ivory, coral, lapis, and jet. Surrounding stars—13 on each concha—are of turquoise, the most pure in tone and matrix-free its creators could find.

Gold was used for the pyramid symbol on the Great Seal.

Gold also appears on the reverse side of each concha, where it was used for little stars. The backs of the conchas are fully finished, also containing stone inlay, with the identification and date of the flag engraved in the silver.

The leather belt and concha pads were made by leathersmith Kevin Cannon. A display box was produced by Jim and Linda Rannefeld of The Box Company and inlaid by Rochan, and a flag of the group's own design was crafted by Jennifer Savonin.

The group are marketing the piece with the assistance of John and Dixie Yaple of the Millicent Rogers Museum. They hope their creation will find a place in the Bicentennial Show at the Smithsonian Institution.

The project came out of a cooperative artistic effort that these men have been practicing for several years, and whose current center in Taos is the Mabel Dodge Luhan House, now owned by Dennis Hopper and used as home and workshop by a group of silversmiths.

It began light-heartedly, with the idea of making an artistic statement about American commercialism and the "Buy-centennial."

As research progressed, it became something quite different: an occupation of total dedication for more than three months, consuming most of the artists' time and virtually all their money.

"We put everything we had into this belt," said Morris.

They gambled on making the piece without a prior commission or a potential buyer, preferring the greater creative freedom of being responsible only to themselves.

And the belt evolved idea by idea, with no blueprint to check the flow of its development.

"We don't feel like it was made BY us," said Morgan. "It's more like it was made THROUGH us."

"Our investigation changed our minds about the meaning of the Bicentennial," said Rochan. "The people who founded this country were looking for harmony with nature, spiritual freedom, an investigation of the truth...

"We found that it is the responsibility of each individual American to find for himself a lifestyle that comes parallel to the Declaration of Independence...The Americans who put these things together were revolutionaries more than we could ever be."

The Bicentennial Concha Belt is on display for the public Thursday and Friday, March 11-12, at the Plaza office of First State Bank of Taos.

The bank is open from 9 a.m. to 2 p.m. on Thursday, and from 9 a.m. to 2 p.m. and 4-6 p.m. on Friday. One of the artists will be present with the belt during the display.

ED MORGAN

from The Taos News *(Thursday March 11, 1976)*

"We looked at that symbol in the Great Seal, the symbol that nobody notices on the dollar bill," reflected Morgan. "That's a pyramid with the third eye on top, a Masonic symbol that goes back to the Egyptians. The people who founded this country and started this whole trip were heavy guys."

Many of America's founding fathers, the artists discovered, were Masons, guardians of ancient, esoteric teachings such as the power and meaning of the pyramid.

The third eye atop the pyramid represents an inner vision of the future, which, they believe may be retained and revealed through the power of the pyramid.

The eagle is also a symbol of vision.

An eagle design is on the reverse side of the Great Seal. The eagle is placed on the belt such that, if it were worn, it would be opposite the seal concha on the body of the wearer.

The eagle design for the buckle is not a replica of the Great Seal eagle, but Morgan's own design, in which he tried to emphasize the bird as a visionary being rather than a militaristic predator—which is the way he sees the eagle on the dollar bill.

As if by magic, the symbols manipulated themselves during the creation of the eagle.

As Morgan worked on the fine details of the eagle's mouth, a shape appeared through the silver on the reverse side.

The shape was that of a mouse.

In the symbolism of the Plains Indians, the characteristics of the mouse are opposite to those of the eagle: the latter is the great high soarer who sees the earth in broad perspective, while the tiny, scurrying mouse is ever busy with the immediate moment right in front of him, and lives in fear of the shadow of the bird above.

The group chose to embellish the engraving of the mouse, and to use that space on the reverse of the buckle for their signatures.

"That mouse is us," Morgan said. "It's the mouse in the mouth of the eagle, and it's also the mouse becoming the eagle—humanity achieving vision."

The belt itself, worn as a closed circle, repeats the theme of unity without end, expressed in the circular arrangement of the 13 stars in the first American flag.

The artists believe that the number 13 has its own esoteric significance, based on numerology and astrology.

"If they founded the country based on those numbers, it would succeed," Morgan commented. He believes this was a factor in the American Revolution occurring at a time where there were 13 colonies.

Rochan agrees that these symbols contain power and meaning on the psychic level.

He believes further—as an artist—that it is necessary to understand the symbols he uses on every possible level, so that his work will make a true statement.

The group researched the history of the American flag, and chose to depict six flags that represented periods of great social change.

Historically, the first is the British colonial flag, showing the Union Jack of Great Britain at the upper left, with the stripes of the 13 colonies.

Second is the revolutionary "Don't tread on me" flag of the Continental Navy. Before the revolution, navy ships flew this emblem as they fought to stop British revenue ships.

The "reverse" flag—dark stars on white background—was a personal emblem designed by John Hancock, they said.

The artists describe it as an example of the making and adoption use of flags as a folk art.

Flags have been made, throughout history, from any available material, frequently old uniforms, they said. A flag may be adopted informally by a person or group and flown without becoming an official national symbol.

The belt represents the Civil War through a flag of the Confederacy: three stripes and a circle of seven stars.

This flag, according to Rochan, was the official Confederate flag, although most Americans are more familiar with the "stars and bars" emblem. That, he said, was the Confederacy's battle flag, adopted for military use because the stars and stripes in the official flag bore a confusing resemblance to the flag of the Union—and the soldiers needed to keep track of which side they were fighting for.

The artists chose to include the Bicentennial flag, rather than the 50-star American flag, to represent the present.

The 50-star symbol is simply an evolution of the older design, Morgan observed, whereas the Bicentennial symbol is a new concept, using a current graphic style — and developed by the modern technique of computer graphics.

Its position on the belt, between the symbols of colonialism and revolution, is the artists' statement of the Bicentennial as another new birth: a revolution in consciousness for the next century of America.

As much as it is American, the belt is also Southwestern. The concha belt form is itself a Southwestern art form. The inlay technique is also a regional tradition, especially in the use of turquoise, "the diamond of the Southwest."

The edges are stamped with arrows; along with the eagle symbol, a reminder of the Indian origin of the American nation.

The making of art as a group process is not new to these men, who also attempt to conduct their daily lives as part of a conscious community.

"The belt was in the tradition of the Mabel Dodge House, with the artisans collectively coming together and no individual ego," said Rochan.

Rochan adopted a communal way of living about 12 years ago, in San Francisco, in rural California, and in Taos. A native of Wisconsin, he worked for several years as a machinist before "dropping out" to join the hippie movement.

Ed Morgan practiced his art in the professional world for 10 years, as an engraver for Hallmark Cards and American Greeting Cards.

He lost interest in the craft of engraving, he remembers, and stopped working for some time before discovering how to use the techniques he knew as a vehicle of personal creative expression.

Now he specializes in the engraving work on the pieces stamped and inlaid by his friends.

Jeff Morris, the youngest of this group, has spent most of his life in Arkansas but learned his craft here, in association with the younger members of the Brown family.

Each of these three men has, in some personal sense, thought of himself as a revolutionary; where revolution is understood to mean ongoing non-violent change and the discarding of outworn social habits.

What they learned from making the belt, the three agreed, is that being a revolutionary is the same thing as being an American.

A Family House

We came to communal life with a desire for a tribe, to belong to a village, or to form new family structures. What mattered was sharing for the good of each other. Many communes were only a shared house which became your family. We pledged allegiance to our own culture—not to the State. 'Live and let live' was our motto. This was the counter-culture in a nutshell, even when it made us nuts! Living with other people wasn't easy. One day someone would visit and a week later they were living on the couch or had built themselves a lean-to out back. Yet all of us came up the road at some point and who were we to say that the gate was closed? We were experiments of our own making. We invented conflict resolution as we went. There were struggle meetings over cheese and chores, over who's pulling their weight or wielding a power trip. Creating consensus could be tiresomely difficult. But everyone who participated with even a tiny bit of love and cooperation couldn't help but feel a sense of belonging. To finally be part of something sincere and unique, outside of the military/industrial complex that brought us the Vietnam War, affected you with a hope that lingers even after everything falls apart.

A walking advertisement for Rosie's Italian night bragioli dinner at Joe's Restaurant: flattened steak with hard boiled eggs, parmesan cheese, garlic, onions and oregano—rolled, baked and sliced for $5.50. Sometime in the early to mid-'70s. *Photo courtesy Rosie Pappaianni*

Joe's Restaurant—More Than An Eating Establishment

by Iris Keltz

Joe's was more than a restaurant. It was a watering hole for wayfaring hippies, it was a place to find a long-lost friend and—for many of us—it was a stepping stone back into a society we had dropped out of and hoped never to be part of again. But never is a long time and a person cannot live on food stamps alone. No matter how we tried to cut needs to a bare minimum, my half of the rent was $25, and the landlord expected to be paid in cash—not barter or food stamps—and so did the gas stations and the hippie-wizard mechanic, Monkey, who kept our old cars running for as long as humanly possible.

A knitting needle holding the gearshift to the steering wheel was makeshift at best. At a red light one day, the needle broke in half and I was unable to get out of neutral. A friend towed me to Monkey's garage in El Prado. He looked at my '56 Chevy station wagon, shook his head, clicked his tongue and said "This is a big job." He mumbled something about rebuilding the engine and transmission. "But then the car will be like new," he added optimistically. Monkey wasn't interested in silver jewelry, weavings, paintings or anything else I had to offer. Like it or not, I needed cash.

Tony cooking in the kitchen at Joe's. Cooks rotated, but Tony and Rex were the two who created the menu and the concept of the restaurant.
Photo by Paul Dembski

So I got a job waitressing and cooking at Joe's Restaurant on Bent Street. My salary varied from week to week. Sometimes the pay was great, sometimes lousy and

Painting of Joe's Restaurant and patio on the Bent St. Boardwalk by Peter Wood. *Photo by Paul Dembski*

sometimes it was a mixture of cash and food stamps. There was a confusing formula that only the accountant could figure out.

After getting over the shock of being on a schedule, I realized that Joe's Restaurant was the center of local hippie life and I was hostess at the greatest gathering around. There was a subtle but visible shift away from the communes as the epicenter of life towards alternative businesses and communities. Coworkers became close friends, some elevated to the status of extended family.

Joe's was started by a spiritual-seeking, wealthy dropout—the same person who donated money to start the Lama Foundation. With these two generous gifts, many lives were enriched, but back then we didn't appreciate Jonathan's generosity—after all, he could have invested in the stock market. It was a common belief that those who lived marginally on the edge of a bloated, capitalistic society deserved the drippings, the leftovers from so much excess. Our benefactors were merely making the necessary adjustments in the distribution of wealth.

The building that housed the restaurant had once been a stable belonging to the notorious John Dunn—a gunfighter, gambler, bronc rider, stagecoach driver, saloonkeeper, outlaw, businessman, and developer of Taos in the early 1900's. He dabbled in anything that could make money—including building a toll bridge across the Rio Grande in Hondo, which was the only access into town from the west mesa short of fording the river. His home, once the site of an illegal gambling operation, had been converted into tourist shops, one of which was the Wilderness Bookstore, another popular hangout with the locals. A wooden boardwalk ran between the shops and the restaurant. Jonathan hired hippie

Sherrie the Hostess. *Photo by Paul Dembski*

craftsmen to refurbish the old stable and build heavy wooden tables and chairs for the restaurant and willow shade awnings for the outdoor patio.

Taos' first alternative restaurant lasted from 1973 to 1977 and had the best hamburgers in town for $1.50. We tried to serve healthful tasty food. Innovative soups, Irish soda bread and rich chocolate cake were baked regularly and only fresh turkey was used for the avocado melts—no packaged turkey roll for us. Our sesame tamari dressing was legendary. Local commune dwellers on town trips would stop by for lunch. So did artists, tourists, Pueblo Indians, and an assortment of locals.

Two gentlemen from Boston—Rex and Tony—were the creators of the first menu and the unique ambiance. Before Taos, they had worked in restaurants on Cape Cod and had met Jonathan while living at the Lama Foundation. Both men were slender, clean and genteel—a contrast to the wild-haired funky tribal types. Rex and Tony would have cringed had they known how many of us climbed into the giant kitchen sinks at the restaurant for our daily bath.

Sherrie, the maitre d', completed this troika of stability. She stood at the entrance booth, guarding or welcoming—depending on who you were—in tight black jeans cinched in at the waist with a silver concha belt, a fitted western shirt, a cowgirl hat and dark red lipstick. She had a certain *savoir-faire* and would get all aquiver when famous local artists showed up. "Oh, God, Dorothy Brett just walked in. You know, she was one of D.H. Lawrence's women." Or "Hurry, go seat Andrew Dasburg by the window." Most of us were ignorant about the art world, but we did recognize Dennis Hopper or Baba Ram Das when they came in. Sherrie's mission in life was to find a rich rancher and become a real cowgirl—she went as far as placing personal ads in rancher and cowboy magazines.

Quality control went out the door with Rex, Tony and Sherrie. Every day they faced a group of hippies trying to lampoon their efforts at efficiency, decorum and sensible business. Tension was born of the fact that Joe's was a business and was supposed to make a profit.

They rightfully got upset at our shenanigans, like the night Carl and Freddie cooked dinner on LSD and drank all the cooking wine. Freddie was blasting a tape of Country Joe and the Fish live at Woodstock when some tourists showed up in time for Country Joe's cheer, "Give me an F! Give me a U! Give me a C!" And before the word was spelled, they were out the door without ever having read the menu.

Meanwhile, Betty the waitress had taken an order from a table of eight. Naturally, she was high, since the acid was her gift to the staff in the first place. Carl looked at the order and wondered how he could cook crêpes, omelets and chicken and get them to the

The first of many ethnic night dinners at Joe's started when I got a couscous craving and cooked a Middle Eastern feast—complete with baklava and belly dancers imported from Santa Fe, dancing in the courtyard with live drumming and clarinet. *Photo by Paul Dembski*

table at the same time. He stood by the stove, ready to flip the omelet, when the sight of eggs flying as if in slow motion mesmerized him. He watched in fascination as the yellow blob twirled through the air and headed back to earth. It seemed futile to interfere in its elliptical orbit. And then, splat, the eggs were on the floor, but in a lovely mandala design. Sherrie, who had been watching him from the hostess booth, shouted helplessly, "Carl, you've done some dangerous drug!"

Freddie, his co-cook, was most likely in the walk-in refrigerator room, checking out the burgers, which was code talk for a marijuana break. Sometimes romances broke out between staff members and the walk-in served as a rendezvous spot. Asha occasionally dropped into the restaurant on town trips from Lama and used the walk-in as her private prayer place.

I was a short-order cook at first, but Rex wanted me out of the kitchen although he loved to cook with Cynthia, my housemate. When they cooked beef bourguignon, they would polish off a bottle of burgundy, but somehow this never affected their ability to catch an omelet or get out an order in a timely fashion. It could be 100 degrees in the kitchen, but their avocado and turkey slices were cut with the precision of a surgeon's knife. Cynthia once told me that cooking with someone was an intimate act.

But waitressing was more aerobic and social. In the outdoor patio, I got to hobnob with guests and banter with passersby on the boardwalk. Cruising between tables in the early morning with a pot of hot coffee was empowering. Once the breakfast cook was unexpectedly greeted by the police with a stack of parking tickets and a warrant. "I can't go," she told them politely. "I have bread to bake, food to cook and people to serve." They politely sat down and were offered coffee with a fresh Danish and waited until the lunch cook showed up before carting the breakfast cook off to the police station.

When hippies drinking their umpteenth cup of coffee were asked to make room for customers buying food, they would move to the grassy sanctuary outside the patio where elm trees and shrubs offered shade and privacy. Newly arrived hippies had the opportunity to make important contacts in the plum thicket, since Joe's staffers smoked their coffee-break joints here. This was how some newcomers wove their way into the community. Myth has it that a person searching for a long-lost friend once tacked a note to a tree by the patio and found a response on the tree a few days later. From this, there was a blissful reunion.

Every day Teddy the Juggler, Phil the Flautist, Guiseppi the accordion player, and a tight rope walker came to practice their crafts next to the patio. An audacious, colorful medieval circus filled with troubadours delighted the tourists sipping their cold hibiscus tea.

Hotsy Totsy, the hot dog vendor, wheeled his cart around the plaza, along the boardwalk and turned around at Bent Street. At one time he was a waiter at Joe's, but selling hot dogs proved more lucrative. Before coming to Taos, he had been a pilot for corporate America. He was older than most of us and had stories about everything. In fact most of the staff at Joe's had been something quite different in their previous lives. The dishwasher had been an architect, the cook had been a monk, the baker a photographer and I had been a teacher. But we didn't focus on our past—the present was much too alive.

A woman returning from Central America once set up her wares at one of the outdoor tables. By the end of the day most of her Guatemalan huipils were sold. I bought two, which cost me a week's work, but it was worth it. A good huipil lasts forever.

The TV show "Sesame Street" once came to Taos to videotape a segment of the show at the pueblo. Buffy St. Marie and the crew came to Joe's for lunch every day, along with Jim Henson. When the filming was over, the restaurant held a bash for them. Someone lifted up the flagstones on the patio, dug a hole in the earth, built a fire and roasted a goat.

Little Joe, a Taos Pueblo Indian, ate for free whenever he came in with his wife. He was the namesake of the restaurant, our holy man and our shaman who taught us important spiritual lessons.

The first of many ethnic night dinners at Joe's started when I got a couscous craving and cooked a Middle Eastern feast complete with baklava and belly dancers imported from Santa Fe. The sellout dinner ended up being a "Zorba the Greek" experience, but since the building was still intact, the kitchen cleaned for the breakfast shift, and money was made, nobody complained. This triggered a series of ethnic nights, like Rosie's Italian bragioli dinner: flattened steak with hard boiled eggs, parmesan cheese, garlic, onions and oregano—rolled, baked and sliced for $5.50. Guiseppi did the publicity, walking up and down the boardwalk and around the plaza carrying a shoulder sign while playing his accordion. He pretended he was from Afghanistan and couldn't speak English. All the ethnic dinners were cultural delights and were always sold out.

By day, Guiseppi hung out on the boardwalk and in the plum thicket, fed royally by friends from the restaurant. One night, hunger drove him to break into the restaurant. He didn't get caught, but the next day confessed to one of the cooks during a coffee break because he thought the security should be improved.

When Rex, Tony and Sherrie decided to leave the restaurant there was a vacuum in leadership and the staff decided who should take over. It was the ultimate town hall: a democratic, majority-rules meeting with not an owner or stockholder in sight—simply the workers. The result was a decision to divide the responsibilities and create a general manager, a business manager, a kitchen manager and two personnel managers. When Carl and Freddy became the personnel managers, they unashamedly hired friends and women with large breasts.

Rex, Tony and Sherrie had created a modicum of stability. Without them, there were no grownups at the helm—we were biding our time until the people's revolution ushered in the Aquarian Age. They were there to run a restaurant, one that hopefully made a profit. It was a daring experiment in social economics. For those of us who worked there, Joe's enriched our lives in ways far beyond our unpredictable paychecks.

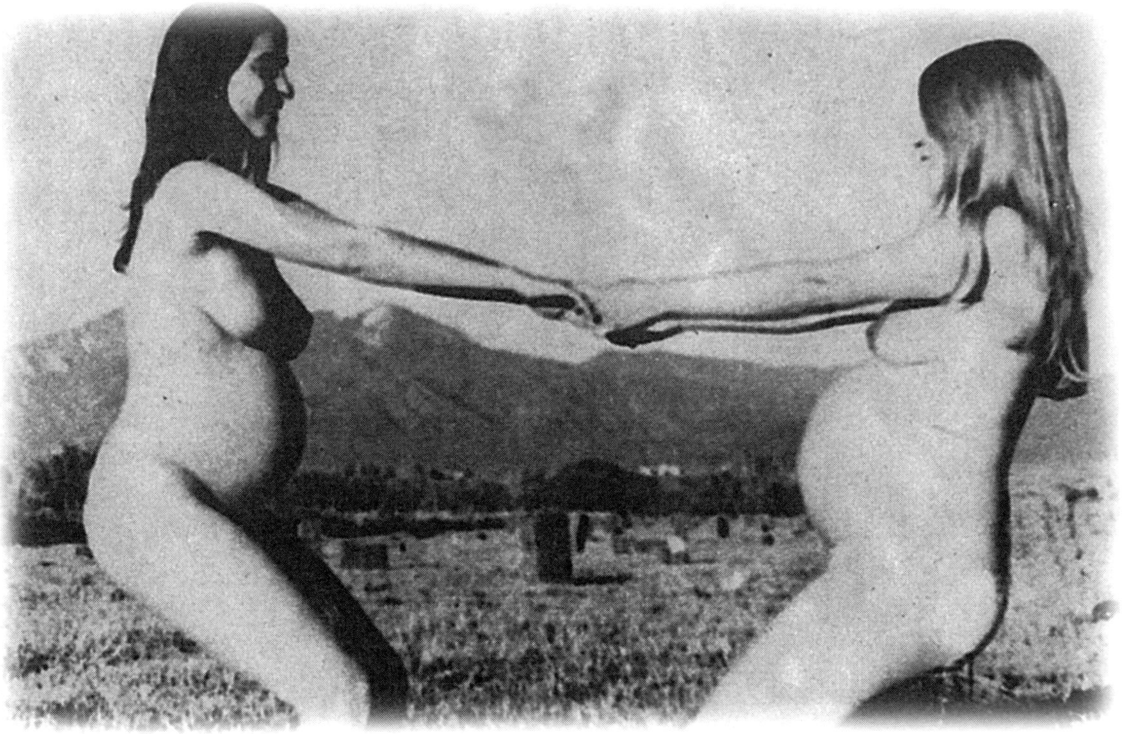

Birthing was a celebration. Taking control of our lives was important to us. Herbal remedies and midwives were rediscovered as healthy and viable alternative to 'buying into' the medical establishment. "Old way, good way" was one of our mantras. Pam Read Hanna, a midwife who lived at Morningstar, estimated that she delivered 43 babies while living there. Tish Demming was the midwife who delivered my daughter Minka in a beautiful home birth in the mid-'70s. A woman usually had a medical doctor willing to be an emergency backup if the pregnancy and birthing warranted it. Now there is an official birthing center in Taos that can trace its roots to those days.
Photo and artwork from the Fountain of Light *(circa 1970).*

MOTHER.... MISTRESS VICTORIA
SON.........JOSHUA
HOME....... FAMILY HOUSE OF TAOS
BORN........OCT. 27, 1969
7:27 AM EMBUDO

Birthing Day Party
by Iris Keltz

Sadie ran up to me at Joe's Restaurant wearing the same embroidered Guatemalan huipil she'd worn for the last six months. It was the only thing that still fit over her ripening belly. A smile of glory lit her face. "I've just seen the doctor. The baby's head is engaged and my water broke an hour ago. Tonight's the night. Don't forget you promised to make falafel. See ya later. Got people to invite."

I was waitressing on the patio. The tourists drinking their hibiscus iced tea smiled politely at this pregnant Madonna who looked like she'd just escaped from a Third World country. I got off work early to go shopping with Melinda, my housemate and unofficial midwife for this birth. She bought birthing necessities and I bought chickpeas, tahini and pita bread, the fixings for falafel.

Home was Dogtown, a seedy part of Arroyo Seco named for its ever-roving packs of hungry flea-ridden mongrels. Melissa and I paid $25 a month for a two-bedroom wooden shack with an indoor cold-water spigot and an outhouse five feet from the front door. When Sadie offered us hot showers in exchange for irrigating and weeding her garden, we accepted.

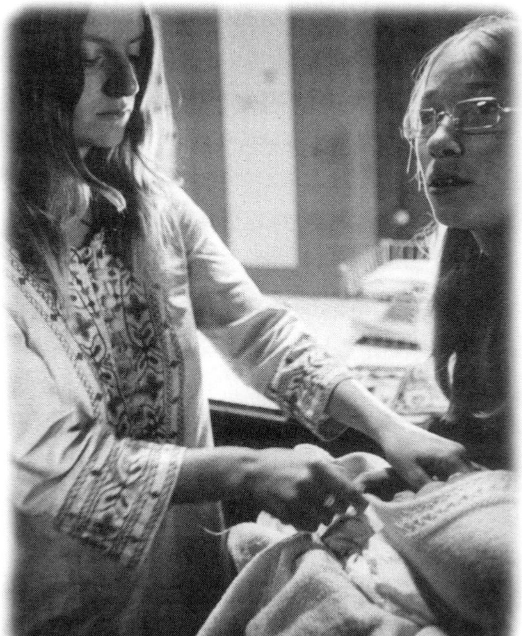

Mother looks worried while baby gets a check-up from the mid-wife. *Photo by Rich Jamison*

Although Sadie went to the doctor for check-ups, she didn't have a midwife for most of her pregnancy. One day over guacamole and chips, Melissa recounted the fascinating details of her three children's births. They sounded so easy and natural that Sadie asked her to be the midwife. She was about five months pregnant.

Melissa—a self-proclaimed expert on mountain climbing, iridology, astrology, art and now midwifery—was confident, as always. Secretly I had spoken to the young intern at the Free Clinic in Ranchos. Dr. Hippy, as we affectionately called him, had his feet in the medical establishment, but his heart was in the counterculture. His shoulder-length hair and India import cotton

Childbirth: Some Questions

by Dr. Virginia Bush, Taos Free Clinic

Fountain of Light

There is a controversy in our communities now on the subject of the good and proper way to have babies. Most people have definite opinions for or against childbirth at home.

As a woman, I can respect and admire the desire to allow a beautiful and meaningful experience to take place at home, with maximal sharing of the joy of the ultimate fulfillment of womanhood. As a physician, it scares me shitless.

Let me ask each one of you who wants to have a child at home these things:

Will someone attend your "confinement" who can recognize conditions that may lead to fatal bleeding during or after labor?

Will someone be there who can prevent stretching or tearing of the birth canal? Some complications of tears can lead to "fistula formation" or abnormal passages between the rectum or bladder and the vagina. The result is not aesthetically pleasing.

Can someone there recognize "fetal anoxia," or lack of oxygen being delivered to the baby? This could require very rapid delivery to prevent retardation. Can anyone there treat shock resulting from excessive blood loss? Or, for that matter, will anyone know how much bleeding is normal? Can someone there revive and breathe for a baby if he is unable to start breathing on his own? Can someone there recognize potentially life-threatening disorders in the child, and will they know treatments for them?

Do you have the proper drugs to prevent blindness in the baby due to often-unrecognized Gonococcal infection in the mother?

Are you in good physical condition and have you had adequate nutrition during your pregnancy?

Is the size of your pelvis adequate to allow a normal delivery?

Is the baby in normal head-down position or is he a breech baby?

Okay. There's more, but my case rests. Granted, many hospital deliveries are conducted in an overly sterile environment. Granted, any institution, especially a medical one, is difficult to change. But any woman who firmly states her desires about her own delivery and who cultivates the mind of her physician during her pregnancy is making a definite move to humanize medicine.

One unnecessary death of a mother or child due to inadequate care is unforgivable.

shirts identified him as one of us. Most of his free time was spent meditating at the Hanuman Temple.

He was somewhat ashamed of being a throwback hippie who needed an official piece of paper to legitimize a claim to practice medicine. When I went to see him, Doctor Hippy showed me a face that was more doctor than hippy. He warned me that he'd never even delivered a baby at the hospital, let alone in someone's house. Driving home I remembered snatches of our conversation. "Tell your friend to come see me at the clinic. Who is she?"

"Sadie from Seco."

"But she's 40 and this is her first baby. Tell her to go to the hospital."

"I can't. And don't tell her I was here. I'll be accused of bad-vibing the birth."

Melissa organized the herbs, lotions, suction syringes, towels and receiving blankets. She was composed and in charge. Nobody seemed worried. Sadie folded and refolded baby clothes, occasionally groaning deeply and bending over the satin-lined dresser drawer filled with a tiny mattress and hand-made quilt.

"Sadie, is there anything I can do for you?" I asked. "What about the baby's father? Do you want to call him?"

It was hard to get a sense of someone on the other end of the phone. Sadie and the baby's father didn't have much to say to one another. Her relationship with him was the casual casting of a seed that miraculously took root.

Sunset was symphonic. Brilliant purples, pinks and oranges strung across the western sky as if to defy the coming darkness. I felt a secret twinge of fear so I stayed in the kitchen frying falafel and welcoming friends. Dennis and Sylvia showed up with their two kids. Dennis impishly handed over a loaf of Sylvia's zucchini bread. He rarely put in a public appearance,

SueAnne showing off her pregnant belly to the waitresses at Joe's restaurant. Photo by Paul Dembski

preferring to remain a naked hermit on the mountain. Ronnie brought her daughters, Lizzie and Denise, who danced around the living room with Ellie. Bottles of wine and beer stood on the countertop. No one came empty-handed. This was the mother of potlucks.

Sadie had taken to her bed, but held court between contractions. A circle of friends formed around her, everybody giving her "good vibes" and "positive energy." As the blood curdling screams escaped from the bedroom, I snuck glances at the serenely composed and very pregnant Ripple who lived in a shack across the road from me in Dogtown.

I'd only known Sadie a few months, but proximity and necessity had caused us to become immediate friends. We'd met at a peyote meeting with the firelight dancing around her face. During morning breakfast, we sat together eating handfuls of blue cornmeal mush. It turned out she lived in an old adobe, two driveways east of me in Dogtown. Her voice was gravely, like an unpaved road, her accent, New York. In the morning light she looked older and confessed to being 40. This was her first child.

Sadie's cries ran through me like an electric current. "Is this normal?" I asked Sylvia for reassurance. "Seems like it's been going on forever."

"Oh, yeah, I howled like a banshee with the birth of my Siddhartha." Both of her children had been born at home under conditions more primitive than this.

Eyewitness reports and hand-carried joints reached me in the kitchen. "Melissa's massaging Sadie's crotch with olive oil so she won't tear, and Ivory is doing a belly dance to help with contractions. Everyone else is standing around giving her good energy."

Empty bottles of beer and wine littered the living room. The banana and zucchini breads were finished, the falafel gone. People were falling asleep on chairs, on the couch. Some had brought sleeping bags and settled down on the rug. Exhausted cries intermittently broke the quiet. Telling no one, I called the hippie doctor.

"Hello? Thank God you're home. We need you. I don't know what's going on except that it's been going on for a long time."

He entered the kitchen, carrying a black satchel, smiled enigmatically and strode into Sadie's room with false bravado. His timely appearance was accepted as a matter of course and no one asked if he had ever delivered a baby. The collective belief was that if you need it, it'll be there and if it's not there, chances are you don't need it.

He looked in amazement at the people gathered around Sadie's bed, didn't say much, just rolled up his shirtsleeves and asked for boiling water, just like Doc from "Gunsmoke." Sweat stained his cotton shirt and drenched his brow. People held hands and stopped breathing. Sadie begged the doctor to end her pain. Dr. Hippie took a moment to check his medical book. I prayed for him: *Follow your hands—trust them. They'll know what to do. It's not in your books.*

He sterilized his hands and took a deep breath before examining inside Sadie's womb. His hands emerged full of mucous and blood. He said nothing. All eyes were glued to the space between Sadie's legs when the black gunk started to ooze. Someone thought the baby's brains were being squeezed out by the intense contractions. Once again hands and wrists up to the elbows disappeared inside of Sadie. This time he pulled out a baby, butt first. The black gunk was the first tar poop. No one knew the baby was breech or we would have had Sadie stand on her head. Tears and sweat ran like rivers down Dr. Hippie's face. From the wriggling creature, came a raucous scream. A beautiful baby boy! Strangely, when Melissa cleaned the baby, she noticed that the penis was really swollen labia. It was a girl!

Sadie smiled at the miracle suckling at her breast. Toes and fingers counted, we left the mother to rest and the baby to nurse. Sofia Willow was born at 5:19, Scorpio with Virgo rising. Someone did her astrological chart. Outside the cold night gave way to hints of dawn. I drank the miraculous events of that night with my mint tea. Sadie was hospitalized two days later with childbed fever. With the help of antibiotics she was fine. Sofia Willow prospered immediately.

Gail and Jimmy's wedding day. Taos Mountain is in the background. *Photo by Paul Dembski*

DaNahazli: Returning Spring

by Iris Keltz

When I left Harlem, New York, I'd sworn off teaching forever, hoping something crafty and creative would come along—like jewelry making, weaving or pottery—something to do with my hands. And something that didn't require a time card or a strict schedule.

Three or four years later, it was Ron who enticed me back to a profession I had given up. We met at the Rexall Drugstore on the plaza—drinking bitter coffee and twirling on uncomfortable stools lining the formica counter. He smoked cigarettes the color of adobe. I probably bummed one. With each conversation, I felt myself being drawn in. "DaNahazli is a community school. You already know half the kids there. Families pay what they can afford or they trade. You might be offered a free massage, an invitation to a sweat lodge, a painting, or God knows what. Lama has just taken over the school and only the Divine knows who'll show up."

I had 15 students, one of whom was my fairy goddaughter Kyra, a girl I had known in New York when she was a baby. This was taken in the mid '70s.
Photo by Paul Dembski

Every hippie in the valley knew about the famous gurus, masters and seekers who found their way to the Lama Foundation. Hand-made prayer flags hung like signposts all over town. *Be Here Now*, recently published by Lama, was the hippie bible, more popular than any of the world's renowned sacred books.

Jeff and Naomi Tatarsky started DaNahazli—Navajo for "the returning spring"—in 1968. They had moved to Taos from California and wanted to give their son and daughter an education strong in the arts. When they tired of running the school, the Lama Foundation took over. When Lama pulled out, the school was left to the vagaries of the current headmaster and board. The binding thread over the years has

Playing in the schoolyard. *Photos by Rich Jamison*

been the belief in the importance of nurturing individual creativity.

Ron caught me at a vulnerable moment. Laying adobe bricks and mixing mud had lost its luster. Cooking and waitressing at Joe's Restaurant had ceased to feel like a daily happening, and it became glaringly apparent I was not about to become a Taos artist. When Ron told me the school needed a second-grade teacher, I was ready. After all, these were the children of my friends. I knew their family histories, who had begotten whom, who was their current family, and who might be their next family. When I told Ron I believed children should know how to tell time, he dragged me over to the school to meet Asha Durkee, the current headmistress.

Incense burned somewhere in the book-lined room that served as her office—an oasis of calm amidst chaos. We sat cross-legged on a flowered rug during the interview. She looked me in the eyes as though fielding my aura. I was a little worried since I didn't subscribe to most of the spiritual smorgasbord practices floating around, but even in this hidden corner of America, religion was separate from education.

Asha was studying the Japanese tea ceremony and offered me a cup of green tea. "I believe in healthy nervous systems. Other than that, I don't know a damn thing about running a school. Are you certified and do you know how to build adobe walls?" she asked as if it were one question.

"I'm a certified English teacher in the State of New York and have just finished helping a friend build an adobe house." Asha never asked to see a resume, or hear about my ideas on teaching or anything about my past. It seemed a foregone conclusion that the job was mine.

"You and Ron are going to share the central room which needs a dividing wall built. Lama has donated hundreds of adobe bricks, so go for it." We walked around the school, housed in a U-shaped adobe hacienda built in the 1930s by the WPA. The building had been a school for furniture making and carpentry. The original vigas and latillas spanned the ceiling.

Learning was hands on or feet first. *Photo by Rich Jamison*

A three-kids-wide slide perched in the arms of an old elm tree at the edge of the schoolyard. A platform without side railings and a giant hump about mid-way down the slide made it dangerously exciting from a kid's perspective.

Chaos belied the fact that school was starting in a few weeks. The front courtyard bustled with people and stuff everywhere—construction material, adobe bricks, couches, chairs, tables, shelves, paper, and a free box filled with clothes. They promised to pay me $400 a month, which took me off food stamps and into the ranks of moneyed hippies.

"I'd like to see the curriculum. And where are the textbooks and supplies?" I naively asked.

"We believe in healthy nervous systems in the school of life," Asha repeated like a sacred mantra. That was a rather broad-based and non-specific curriculum. Feeling overwhelmed, I looked to Ron for reassurance and found him pulling rusty nails out of weathered barn wood.

"Don't worry. We'll create our own curriculum. It's as easy as building an adobe wall," Ron said, smiling. "Lama people have offered to mix mud on Saturday. They've already donated hundreds of bricks. Don't you think an opening in the wall between our classrooms would be great? Oh, and next week a group of us are going to the State Book Repository in Santa Fe. They have shelves of freebies."

"Sounds great," I offered, feeling somewhat relieved. I got to know the other teachers. A sparkling and very pregnant Jean taught social studies and folk dancing. She told me about an inspired teacher from last year.

"Every Thursday at lunch recess, Deirdre would reverently put down a rug, light a candle and incense, and children of all ages would gather to listen to her read about the life of Chögyam Trungpa Rinpoche, a spiritual leader from Tibet. When they found out that he was coming to visit Lama, the students decided to make him special gifts and cards. They were rewarded with a rare invitation to have a personal audience.

"It was snowing when we took the kids up the mountain," Jean continued. "Our vehicle began skidding. We had little traction so we parked and walked the last few miles. Deirdre told them that walking together with someone is like a meeting of old souls. The kids were freezing when they arrived at Lama. Other people were waiting to have a private meeting with this world-renowned man who sat on cushions like a king. The kids sat on the floor. Their gifts were personal, things they knew he would use, like a cigarette case and a whiskey flask. Their audience with Rimpoche was something they'll never forget."

Ellie, the dance teacher who made us laugh, was our own Isadora Duncan. She never walked. She floated over the ground like a fountain in motion, her clothes barely keeping up. *Photo by Paul Dembski*

Deirdre has since been ordained as a Buddhist nun in the lineage of Rinpoche. Known as Pema Chödrön, she is the director of the first Tibetan monastery for Westerners in North America.

Sometime during the year Ron and I raised money from a bake sale to buy an aquarium for the opening in the adobe wall between our classrooms. After that we talked or watched each other's class through bubbles and exotic fish swimming near a plastic treasure chest.

Our classroom was built from weathered barn wood. The orange, silver and rust patinas became a loft and bulletin boards. An old rug nailed to the platform of the loft created a cozy place to curl up with a book. Sometimes it became a stage. Underneath the loft was a great place for solitude or intimate visits with a friend.

I had 15 students, one of whom was my fairy goddaughter, a girl I had known in New York when she was a baby. The children were as fascinating as the families from which they came. Before me evolved future artists, writers, dancers, actors, carpenters, musicians and a gangster. I tried to teach them to tell time, but time turned out to be a very abstract concept. We ate pomegranates while reading the Greek myth of Persephone and Demeter and cried when Orpheus lost Eurydice. One of my students drew compulsively, always holding two pencils in his hand. His pirate ships catching a wind in full sail were amazing for their intricate detail. Drawing with two pencils gave everything an aura—this during a time when everyone was worried about balancing their auras. I guiltlessly excused him from math and learning how to tell time. He was noticeably happier and calmer when drawing and at this school we believed in creativity and healthy nervous systems.

Natalie's slow-paced, nasal voice with a rich New York accent caught me as I passed by her classroom one afternoon. It was a poetry lesson and she was reading from her journal to the 11, 12 and 13-year-olds. "I remember touching my first penis." Not a student moved. Even the attention-deficit hyperactive kids sat perfectly still as she offered a string of metaphors and similes describing how a penis felt to a novice toucher. I'm not sure the students ever learned the object of her lesson, but they were certainly interested in the content.

It was the only time in my teaching career that I looked forward to staff meetings. Asha served green tea on the flowered rug and incense filled the air. After tuning ourselves with a group OM, our main agenda was to check each other's nervous systems to make sure they were still intact. Even in a hippie alternative school, teaching was stressful. Asha sat straight-backed on her meditation pillow, inserting a pearl of wisdom every now and then. Her uncritical and expansive approach at meetings helped people speak their minds openly.

Those of us not used to sitting up straight on meditation pillows squirmed around the rug searching for a comfort zone, using the wall or found objects to prop us up. Large and friendly like a teddy bear, Rick sat in the only chair. He taught the older kids in the art barn, which was a funky outbuilding in the schoolyard. Jean rubbed her pregnant belly as if already comforting a baby. Judith, the drama teacher, told us her plans to have the students present original plays during open school night. Naomi, the kindergarten teacher and original founder of the school, fought to calm her nervous system while chain smoking, unlike Ron who smoked like a lanky Buddha puffing out his quiet opinions with certainty. Our discussions were metaphysical ramblings that somehow worked towards greater bonding among the staff.

One day Asha announced that Charlie's mother had offered to give dance classes in exchange for tuition. Ellie was our own Isadora Duncan. She never walked. She floated over the ground like a fountain in motion, her clothes barely keeping up. When teaching in Harlem, I had felt the need to bring expansive creativity to the bleak institutional setting. At DaNahazli, I invoked gravity to help everyone stay on earth. The afternoon Ellie floated into my class for dance lessons, I smilingly gathered my 15 darlings and officially turned them over to her. Although I was given ample warning, I didn't realize that her philosophy of life was inseparable from her dancing. Slipping back into the classroom after a brief break, the only person left dancing in the room was Ellie. This was the dance of freedom and the kids had danced their way right on out of the room and into the light of the schoolyard not to be seen until their parents came to get them. There was a euphoric smile on Ellie's face as if she were thanking an invisible drummer. I put on some music, so I could hear the drummer too, and we danced, hoping some of the kids might find their way back into the room.

By mid-year, I realized that the students were never going to learn how to tell time in increments of hours, minutes and seconds. We decided that o'clock and half past were enough. Cosmic time was far more relevant and everyone knew their birth sign, what sign of the zodiac the sun was traveling through and the influences of the next full moon.

To wrap up the year, I took my class camping. I was delighted when two sets of parents volunteered to come with us. Someone knew someone who owned a remote ranch, miles away from civilization with acres of virgin land, open meadows and woods with a stream and a small cabin. When we arrived, one of the mothers took off her clothes and started doing yoga next to the stream. She was obviously communing with nature and cleansing herself from the long car ride, but all the kids saw was a naked woman standing on her head. The rest of the weekend was uneventful, almost relaxing.

That was our last formal gathering in a year of teaching that ended as auspiciously as it had began, a year in the life of a hippie alternative school.

Update:
DaNahazli became Taos Valley School and it flourished until sometime in the late '90s.

Names to Remember Us By

These are not made up!

Tinka ☼ Ghost the Dog ☼ Priscilla the goat ☼ Ripple ☼ Pilgrim
The Electric Tomato ☼ The Twittering Clit ☼ Sunday Peaches ☼ Tahiti
Bill Me Later *(name used for magazine subscriptions)* ☼ Army Joe
Cave Dave ☼ Silent Dave ☼ Daddy Dave ☼ The Little Nun ☼ Kiva
Suzie Creamcheese ☼ Sparkle Plenty ☼ Philip the Flute ☼ Guisseppi
Melchizedek ☼ Blue ☼ 9-Fingered Marc ☼ Underwater Peter
Dan the Jan *aka* Peanut Butter and Jelly Dan ☼ Pepe from Greenbay
Strider ☼ Spider ☼ Karim ☼ Dulcimer Dan ☼ Ortejo Goodsky
Justin Case ☼ Justin Time ☼ Wavy Gravy ☼ Monsieur Noodles
Asa Hearts ☼ Morningstar Rose ☼ Heaven ☼ Midnight ☼ Silk
Kachina ☼ Wolfstar ☼ Kahoutek ☼ Heaven ☼ Vulcan ☼ Sassafras
Preacher from the Pleides ☼ Light ☼ Chamisa ☼ Sage ☼ Willow
Brook ☼ Meadow ☼ Sequoia ☼ Dandelion ☼ Yarrow ☼ Sparrow
Raven ☼ Bear ☼ Mouse ☼ Crow and Ivory *(husband & wife)*
Feather and Fig *(sisters)* ☼ Huckleberry ☼ Ram ☼ Spirit ☼ Rio
Peter Rabbit ☼ Goat John ☼ Monkey the Mechanic ☼ Rainbow
Ben Eagle ☼ Vishu ☼ Subra ☼ Amu ☼ Shambu ☼ Sadik
Ravi Dass ☼ Satya ☼ Siddhartha ☼ Shanti ☼ Aurora ☼ Dakota
Savitri ☼ Alabama ☼ Peter Person ☼ Seco Sally ☼ Spring
Buffalo Bob ☼ Jumper ☼ Kabir ☼ Orion ☼ Bear ☼ Cedar

An Evening at the Gay '90s

by Marco Perella

It's the early '70s and I'm playing in a rock-n-roll band around Northern New Mexico. Our group features guitar, vibes and an electric dulcimer. One Friday night, we've got a gig playing in the village of Arroyo Seco, which has a post office, a grocery store, a Mexican restaurant, a weaving gallery and two bars. One of the bars has the unlikely name of The Gay '90s.

There are about 30 people in the bar that night—the largest crowd we've ever played for. About 20 hippies are throbbing to our happening sounds. Only five women are in the bar: hippie nature mamas—unshaved, unashamed and all spoken for by various long-haired squires with whom they do the hippie stomp with braless abandon. Sitting around the edge of the dance floor watching the display are a dozen Chicano miners from the nearby molybdenum mine. We called them the Moly Boys and they are purging their workweek with tequila and beer chasers. The hippies are drinking orange juice with LSD.

This situation is as unstable as a nuclear pile approaching critical mass. Orlando the Dwarf enters the bar. He is very drunk and wants to dance. Orlando starts careening around the dance floor like an inebriated pinball, bumping into dancers and hollering, "Ay! Ay! Ay!" He isn't totally out of control though because he manages to bump into the women a lot more often than the men. Being three feet tall and leading with his face, he is making frequent and intimate contact with these women and generally having a wonderful time.

One of the dancing hippie ladies, Jumper, is half-Indian, but a definite member of the love generation. She was hitchhiking one day and got picked up by a movie star filming a Western. Going back to his motel with him, she discovered his sexual tastes were more than she was prepared for. In spurning his advances, she resorted

Taos had musicans from folk guitarists to psychedelic bands to Middle Eastern to classical and everything in between. Here are real country pickers in the real country doing it off the road.

Photo courtesy of Joe and Sandy Trumm

to jumping out the second-story window of the motel. She busted her hip, but earned the nickname "Jumper."

Orlando the Dwarf is charging around the dance floor and plows into Jumper. He gives her an affectionate nuzzle and she gives him an energetic right hook which leaves him flat on the floor. The Moly Boys take this as a personal affront and send a volley of beer bottles across the room. One of the hippies answers with a chair and soon we've got a major cross-cultural exchange going on. The band keeps playing, thinking that music hath charms to soothe the savage beast. Of course, the bard never heard heavy metal.

The bartender and owner of The Gay '90s is a big blonde bearded guy named Dan. He had been a gunner on a chopper in Vietnam and is smitten with firearms. When the riot breaks out, Dan thinks it might be a good time to try out the .357 magnum rifle he keeps under the counter. Dan grabs his enormous gun and starts firing warning shots into the ceiling, forgetting in his excitement that his wife is upstairs in the bedroom above the bar.

Firing a .357 magnum in a closed room at close range has the effect of instantaneously emptying the bar. Dan's wife is spurred on by several large caliber bullets ripping through the floor around her. She must have thought that her husband had suddenly succumbed to post-Vietnam stress syndrome and would soon be coming up the stairs for her momentarily. So she decides to escape out the second-story window.

Meanwhile the Moly Boys race outside to their pickups, parked across the street, to get their hunting rifles. The hippies get real bad vibes from all these guns and decide not to vacate the bar after all. Some of them are still hallucinating from their acid and moaning, "Bummer! What a bummer!" Dan the bartender is not a man to back down—he sticks his pistol out the cracked door. "I think you boys better go home now!" he yells to the Molys. They keep their rifles aimed.

A turgid silence gripped the crowd.

Suddenly a voice from above—"Help!"

It's Dan's wife in her nightgown hanging from the second-story window ledge, her feet dangling 10 feet above the ground. Dan sees this and is amazed.

Dulcimer Dan and Joe Trumm jamming with friends on the patio at Joe's Restaurant.

Photo by Paul Dembski

"What the hell are you doing?"

"Don't kill me, Dan. Oh God, please don't kill me."

"Hold on, I'm coming!" He dashes upstairs to rescue her.

Jumper looks out the window and sees the situation. Having some expertise in these matters she yells, "Don't let go, honey, or you'll break your ass!"

She then runs across the street to the Moly Boys and starts telling them what to do.

"Quick! Bring a truck over here and get her down." Something about her decisive tone startles them into compliance and they put down their guns. One of them drives his truck up alongside the building. Several others jump in the bed and grab Dan's wife by the feet and try to lower her down.

Dan appears at the upstairs window ready to save his wife. She looks up, sees him standing there still holding his gun, screams in terror and lets go. She tumbles into the bed of the pickup taking a bunch of the Moly Boys with her. Dan sees his scantily clad wife in a Moly-Boy sandwich. He feels compromised by this and yells, "Get your hands off my wife, you bastards."

She yells back to him, "Don't kill me, Dan. Whatever it was, I'll never do it again."

Assuming hostilities are imminent, the driver floors the pickup and roars down the road with Dan's wife in the back, her white nightgown fluttering in the breeze. Dan loses it and starts shooting at the tires. He races downstairs, out the door, jumps into his truck and squeals off in hot pursuit.

Suddenly all is calm. The brilliant stars light up the crystalline New Mexico night. The hippies look at the remaining Moly Boys. The Moly Boys look at the hippies. Everyone goes back inside for a drink on the house. "Hey, hombre, I wasn't really gonna shoot you, man."

"Far out, bro, I know where you're coming from."

Orlando the Dwarf wakes up from his nap and joins us. Jumper feels bad about decking him and offers him a hit of LSD by way of apology, which unfortunately Orlando accepted. But that's another story.

Update:
Marco Perella now lives in Georgetown, Texas, with his wife Diane. He is an actor and teaches film acting. Marco plays in a folk trio called The Melancholy Ramblers. He is the author of a screenplay called "Milarepa Rocks," and has been published in Rolling Stone magazine.

Hispanic girls with Bibles try to save a hippie soul. *Photo by Seth Roffman*

Whatever happened to El Dorado?

by John Nichols

Motive, April/May 1971

Like many other young people, novelist and essayist John Nichols moved to Taos in the late '60s, but his background was left-wing politics with a strong dose of radical environmentalism. Indeed, he called himself a "semi-Marxist-Leninist" who became in Taos "the propaganda arm for a group of quixotic Spanish-speaking septuagenarians locked in mortal combat with the United States government over the preservation of their water rights, their land, their culture, their very historical roots." Thus, he had a different perspective than the hippies or The Taos News *on the "Chicano-Hippie Wars" that troubled the Taos populace in the late '60s and early '70s. In the article that follows, readers will find early seeds of* The Milagro Beanfield War, *Nichols' classic novel about Taos during those times.*

During 1967 and 1968 the word spread around America that somewhere in or around Taos, New Mexico was a kind of hippie El Dorado. Accordingly, an untold number of freaks headed for that small picturesque town at the base of the lovely Sangre de Cristo mountains, and by May of 1969, when I first arrived in Northern New Mexico, a dozen communes were established around Taos, and one real estate office was bragging that it had sold over $500,000 worth of land to the hippies.

Yet almost the first thing I saw when I hit town was a new model Mustang with DESTROY THE HIPPIES taped in white across the side. I stopped in Spivey's Café for a cup of coffee and spotted a sign on the wall over the cash register which read—HELP KEEP AMERICA BEAUTIFUL, TAKE A HIPPIE TO A CAR WASH. That night bricks were thrown through the windows of a hippie free store, and the hippie-owned Seven Paths Macrobiotic Restaurant. Also a hippie vehicle was forced

Hippie establishments were sometimes a target for anger. Eating food grown without chemicals or made without preservatives seemed exotic to many native Taos residents, even though a lot were small farmers already growing their own.

Photo by John Nichols

off the road and fired upon at Horsethief Shorty's corner.

In the morning I picked up a *Taos News*, which was almost hysterical about the hippie "situation." In the first article, I read that the school board considered the hippies a "cancerous epidemic." There was an amazing air of tension about the town, and it looked as if I had arrived just in time for the start of what was being loudly advertised as a Hippie-Chicano war.

But Joe Sage, the owner of the Seven Paths Restaurant was optimistic: "It's just a very small minority doing the roughstuff," he claimed. "Like kids being goaded on by a few parents. But it's all going to be okay. Most of the people in town are wonderful, sympathetic. This thing has gotten blown out of proportion. Everything's going to be all right."

In a way, Joe's optimism, in light of what had been happening to hippies, was pretty far-fetched. Yet it was a typical Taos attitude that more or less denied the problems could be very profound. It denied they might be a lot more than simple and sudden antagonisms, which could just as simply and suddenly be extinguished.

You don't have to look far to find a precedent of Joe's optimism, however. It's in the official line put out by the Taos Chamber of Commerce and other interested citizens, who would have you believe that Taos is an exquisitely beautiful place where three cultures—the Indians, the Chicanos, and the Anglos—live together in absolute harmony. In fact, the propaganda leaflets and advertising would like to give an outsider the impression that Taos is a living epitome of the American Dream.

Word has it that Taos, with its 50-odd art galleries, is the world's third largest art center (after Paris and New York) in terms of volume of paintings sold, but it is also true that one-fourth to one-third of the 2,500 indigenous folk are on welfare. More than half the rural Chicano families in the county live below the old $3,000 poverty level. The per capita income for the county is about $1,300. Unemployment is over 12 percent, and many who are employed work (as do kitchen and cleaning employees at the Taos

Inn) for between one dollar and $1.30 an hour (with no free meals, of course, although an employee is given 15 percent off if he eats at the Inn).

The countryside around Taos is "exquisitely beautiful." The town is a stone's throw from the majestic Río Grande Gorge, and eight trout streams and rivers flow down out of the nearby mountains. Campgrounds in the surrounding Carson National Forest are too numerous to count, yet many of the local people cannot afford to pay the fees for fishing and hunting licenses, or camping permits. Those who can afford to pay often fiercely resent doing so because 100 years ago the land belonged to their grandfathers. Since then they have lost it, first to Anglo thieves who ripped off big tracts of Spanish-American land grants in the last century; later to the Federal Government, which now owns an incredible 44 percent of Taos County; and most recently to the influx of tourist-oriented businessmen (and hippies) who are grabbing anything that's left over.

A swank ski area that *Playboy* magazine recently numbered among the outstanding in America, the Taos Ski Valley is only a 20-minute drive from downtown. Half an hour to 45 minutes away are the Red River Ski Valley and Angel Fire Ski Basin. The parking lots around these areas are always loaded with shiny late-model, largely out-of-state cars that belong to people staying in the Swiss-style chalets (at the Taos Ski Valley) or at the expensive motels that give Taos a definite air of affluence.

But if you travel 40 miles north of Taos to Costilla, you will see numerous old adobe ranch houses going to ruin, and wide fields lying desolate and unused even though Costilla Creek—with enough water to make the town a rich oasis—bubbles right through its center. Ask the residents why Costilla is a ghost town and they will reply bitterly that the state reallocated the water for the big farms "down south," meaning those belonging to the agribusinessmen from Southeast New Mexico and Texas, many of whose cars are parked at the nearby ski resorts or in the scenic camping areas. So the farmers of Costilla have had to go elsewhere; many have become migrants who work in the lettuce and potato fields of the nearby San Luis Valley where, according to the U.S. Civil Rights Commission, Mexican-Americans are sometimes forced to work under conditions "resembling involuntary servitude or peonage."

Into this hypocritical tinderbox came the hippies, largely oblivious to the local situation, looking for an El Dorado. As did Peter Fonda and Dennis Hopper in their film *Easy Rider* (some of which was shot around Taos), many of them blew it. Yet in doing so they brought to light the disparities and divisions in Taos, and there is a good chance that the hippie invasion succeeded in liberating some forces of significant social change in Taos. There is a good chance they left some sort of creative growth behind them.

As Joe Sage predicted, the summer of 1969 ended without any major disasters, but Taos passed the winter with its breath held. Shortly after Christmas, rumors began that there would be up to 25,000 hippies passing through town in the summer of 1970. (A hefty number, considering that the population of all of Northern New Mexico is about 100,000!) And by the end of March so many people had already come into the Taos area that the situation had reached a premature crisis point.

Then, during the first two weeks of April 1970, all the old problems erupted again. Within those two weeks a hippie bus was bombed in Peñasco; a car was bombed in Vadito; a bridge to a hippie community in Pilar was burned; six bullets were pumped through the front window of a house in Pilar; a boy named William Elsea was shot in the leg at the Ponce de

Part restaurant and part community living room/kitchen, Ron and Carols's House of Taos had the best pizza in town. To get their dough just right, they squeezed it through a hand-cranked wringer washing machine.

Photo by John Nichols

Leon Hot Springs a few miles south of Taos; a house and a bridge at the Hot Springs were also burned; an apparent inter-hippie feud erupted near the Lorien Commune 25 miles north of Taos near Questa; four men were fined for assaulting some longhairs and local crafts people in Arroyo Seco; a Chicano girl who was raped in El Prado said her attackers were hippies; and five bullets were shot through the front windows of the new hippie General Store.

After the initial April skirmishes, the hip community suddenly began putting out the word that there was no more room in Taos. Individual communes begged longhairs to stay away during the summer of 1970, and most communes closed their doors to further members; a few got to the point where visitors were allowed only once a week.

What happened during the ensuing months is that the men and women within the hip community began to realize a few facts of life about existence in Northern New Mexico, and perhaps they began to understand the sort of threat they represented to the local residents. They began to realize that although New Mexico is large on the map, hardly a million people can live off its land, and at best that living is doomed to be meager. New Mexico is one of the poorer states in the Union, with a very limited arable land base and access to water. It would probably not be far off the mark to say that for every hippie who arrives and "makes it" in Taos, there is a corresponding Chicano who must give up a last claim to his ancestor's land and become a migrant or move to an urban ghetto.

As the word not to come to Taos started going out, public meetings were called in an attempt to bring about some kind of rapport between the hip community and the local people. Two of the longest, most widely attended meetings were held toward the end of May as part of the White House Conference on Children and Youth. These meetings were chaired by Taos County Juvenile Probation Officer Mary Martinez, who said, "Kids are being involved in the violence going on in Taos, and I don't like it. I don't want kids used to carry out ideas that some of the adults have."

The idea that local people, notably some young Chicanos, were being used as dupes to carry out the violence, surfaced a number of times during the meetings. Eli Herrera, a Vocational Rehabilitation counselor said: "I am a *nativo* of Taos. I am concerned at how some elements are using the Spanish-Americans as scapegoats. As poor people we feel sorry for the hippies, yet if they want to live that way it's their business. But all this talk about 'the natives are very concerned about the hippie influx,'—well, that is a big old fat lie. I've been to some of the meetings in which these pronouncements were decided, and do you know there were only two natives there—me and the Water Commissioner. But as a result of the voting at these meetings, they say, 'The natives are against the hippies.' Well, that is absolutely wrong, and I don't happen to want to see any of our young people killed by hippies who are aroused by these statements. So we've formed a committee to help the kids realize they are being used to achieve the aims of others in the community."

This realization, combined with the hippies' budding awareness of the world around them, caused something both curious and exciting to happen in Taos. As if by magic, the freak immigration slowed to a trickle, and as it did the local people showed the first stirrings of a renewed social and political awareness.

At the end of the summer Luis Valdez' Teatro Campesino, a people's theater which grew out of California's grape strike, came to Taos. Its performance—a strong affirmation of Chicano culture and Chicano pride—was probably the single most creative act that had occurred in Taos for a long time. Although the Town Council refused to let the Teatro give a free performance in the town plaza, money to rent a hall was drummed up from sympathetic Anglos by a small Chicano group working quietly toward local reform, Los Trabajadores de la Raza, and the show went on.

It was a stunning success. Twice the number of people that the hall could seat somehow managed to cram inside. They were lined along the walls, they were seated on the floor in the aisles. The turnout was hard to believe. The people laughed and cheered, and some of them cried, and after each act they joyfully chanted along with Luis Valdez: "Chicano-POWER! Chicano-POWER!" The politics proved to be a little heavy for some Anglos, and at intermission a number of them left.

A few weeks after the Teatro's performance, a small film crew came into Taos to make a documentary about the town, about its people, its problems. Like all artists, writers, photographers, and films crews before them, these young people simply set up and began to shoot. But Los Trabajadores de la Raza made an appearance again, asking what was in the movie for the people of Taos? After some talks an amicable agreement was reached where a certain percentage of the film's profits would go into a non-profit Chicano and Indian educational fund the Trabajadores had set up. In turn, the local people would aid the film crew to find relevant subjects.

Shortly after the film crew departed Taos, I heard the first of many versions of a rumor that I would be hearing for the next couple of months. A local restauranteer called me over to ask nervously if I thought there was any truth to a story that 50 local Chicanos had formed a militia and drawn up an assassination list of the leading Anglo capitalists in town. I said it sounded like bull. The idea seemed preposterous. Of course, it was interesting to think that perhaps the exploited poor in Taos had become sophisticated to a point where they were willing to quit hassling hippies in order to begin harassing people who were more intimately connected with their exploiation.

I almost dismissed the rumor. Nevertheless, I lazily attempted to track it down, and after a while I became a little surprised by the number of people who not only had heard it, but who also halfway believed it.

Around this time, Sen. Clinton B. Anderson. D-NM, was introducing to the U.S. Senate an alternate bill to the Taos Indians' Blue Lake bill. The Indians had been fighting for 65 years to obtain the return of 48,000 acres of sacred land Teddy Roosevelt took away from them during his reign of land grabbing, and they were totally rejecting any settlement except clear title to that land. Anderson thought this would set a very dangerous precedent. (Other Indians might also want the return of land stolen by the U.S.!) So Anderson wanted to make the land a special ranger district supervised by Taos Indians, but still in the hands of the Forest Service.

During the first week of October, two Forest Service signs near Taos were blown to bits by some rather sophisticated explosives. Phone calls to local news media by unidentified persons said, "A response has been given to Sen. Anderson in the form of two Forest Service signs."

Then, on Tuesday night, October 27, a bomb exploded in a Forest Service office in Peñasco, 25 miles south of Taos, causing extensive damage. And later, the wire on a Forest Service corral was cut, allowing three horses to escape. They wandered onto the main highway into Taos, and two of the horses were struck and killed by a car.

Of course, local officials said that the bombings had to be an outside job. But in light of all the hippie-baiting that had been encouraged over the past several years, and in light of the exploitation that has been going on for centuries, one could not help but surmise that the violence the local establishment encouraged had come back upon it at last.

Around this time I came to what I believe was the source of the rumor mentioned earlier; a source which clearly, and rather chillingly, illustrates, I think just how uptight Taos had become. An FBI agent from Albuquerque had gone to at least one of the Anglos—an artist—who'd helped supply rent money for the hall where the Teatro Campesino played. The agent told this artist that some of the people to whom he'd given the money were part of a Chicano militia that planned to assassinate a number of white citizens, including the artist. The agent implicated Los Trabajadores de al Raza, and, playing up to the artist's paranoia, further described the holocaust that was to hit Taos—the militiamen had bought 20 four-wheel drive vehicles which they were going to drive into Taos, armed to the teeth. Once inside the city limits they planned to dynamite all exits leading out of town and take over. As if this weren't enough, the agent went on to insinuate that all this violent activity was partially the result of trips that four people from the area had made to Cuba. The agent then finished his plant by coming down hard on the artist for shelling out some of the rent money for El Teatro Campesino, claiming that things had been running smoothly in Taos until Luis Valdez arrived and started stirring up trouble by making Taos County Chicanos feel proud to be Chicanos.

The sign bomber (or bombers) has not as yet been apprehended, nor has any militia or caches of four-wheel-drive vehicles and dynamite come to light, so what follows is merely conjecture. But if there really was a paramilitary organization bent on murder and mayhem as the agent claimed, it made very little sense for Federal dicks to come in before any arrests were made and lay down all the facts about who they were after. Who would be left around to arrest after letting the cat out of the bag like that?

The evidence that the whole story was a police fabrication intended to make the liberals of Taos uptight to the point where they will shy away from any further reform or dangerous encouragement of Indian and Chicano rebirth makes it difficult to rule out the possibility that some of the attacks against Forest Service installations could have been carried out by establishment provocateurs, in order to scare the local populace, in order to spread fear, confusion, and suspicion, thus discrediting and crippling the fledging local movements for social reform. Such tactics have been used down through the ages to justify repression of anyone trying to change the hideous conditions under which the poor of the earth must live.

What probably happened is that the past three years of hippie-baiting and reactionary violence backfired on the authorities that encouraged them; as Malcolm X said after the death of President Kennedy, "It looks to me like a case of the chickens coming home to roost." The bombings were more likely an outlet for some frustrated persons who have come to realize the numerous ways in which they are victims of a racist and repressive society. Someone, perhaps, has understood fully the hypocrisy of Touristic Taos's American Dream façade, and is determined once and for all to blow the false front to bits.

Whatever the case, as small strides toward political awakening were made in Taos, the Chicano-Hippie feud seemed to die out. And as winter came on, the hippies themselves seemed to have gone elsewhere.

The populations of most communes are way down; some, like the Five Star Farm, no longer exist—only a broken-down house and scraps of junk and clothing attest to the fact that up to 30 or 40 people once lived on the lovely little mesa where the farm was located.

There was a joy and euphoria to the hippie migration at its height; all that is gone now. Those who have survived up until now and who wish to further survive will probably be able to do so only if they integrate themselves with the community and become aware of the social and political struggles going on.

In the spring perhaps there will be a rebirth; perhaps new blood will pour into the communes around Taos. But it feels now as if something has changed, as if now that the migration has been stopped, steps have been made to go beyond the so-called feuding, important steps which will make it impossible to play upon the ignorance of local people to the extent that they will turn their wrath and frustrations upon the hippies in the future.

It is not so clear to me whether the hippies have learned what is perhaps most important to their future survival—that is, how to relate to, and interact with, the local people. Many of the hippies have been notoriously apolitical, essentially disinterested in any trip not of their own liking or making. And although the hip community has laid down a heavy cosmic line about how everybody should be brothers, this line seems often to have been canceled out by some very heavy ego-tripping on the part of a lot of longhairs.

Yet just recently I learned of two men from one of the communes who are coming into town twice a week in order take Spanish lessons from Joe Kelly, a local priest. In that sort of action are the seeds of hope.

MAMA LAMA PRESENTS A
SOLSTICE STOMP
OL' MARTINEZ HALL RANCHOS DE TAOS
WEDS.
JUNE 21
9 PM till 2 AM
ADM. $1.50
NO MINORS
BILL RODGERS HAT BAND
ORIENTAL BLUE STREAKS

Taos Boogie

by Iris Keltz

I'm sitting in the ballroom of the Kachina Lodge watching the two-steppers shuffle in mutually compatible rhythms across the floor. The dress is western; cowboy hats bob on the heads of men wearing stylish-looking Tony Lama boots, tight tight-fitting jeans and cowboy shirts. Twirling around the dance floor in ankle-length ballooning skirts, the women follow their partners. Each couple has their own way of doing the same dance.

The protocol, dress and movement attest to the strictness of the form. Country western dance is appealing yet unfamiliar. In order to dance I need a partner, must follow his lead, wear appropriate attire and pretend high-heeled, pointy-toed cowgirl boots are comfortable. After years of free flow, form is important once again. Between sets, someone offers me a joint. Returning to the ballroom, I have persistent flashes of the old time Taos Boogie. . .

Even before entering ol' Martinez Hall in Ranchos de Taos, I know who's there by the old pickup trucks and cars with the unmistakable signatures of their owner. The brand new four-wheel drives and minivans were still parked at the dealers—we were the generation who had sworn never to buy on the installment plan. No one was in debt yet.

The decrepit exterior of ol' Martinez Hall was in contrast to the grandiose dance hall inside. Huge vigas had been hauled from mountaintops to rest on adobe walls thirty feet high. The smooth hardwood floor creaked and bounced along with the dancers.

The difference between dressing for a peyote meeting and a boogie was a matter of sex appeal. For church, you wanted to look clean, colorful and reverential. For boogies, it was all right to look like a walking wet dream. It was a tribal event, and the look was eclectic—a mix of Native American, gypsy, peasant, western, or simply weird. Our feet were usually bare, or covered by moccasins.

Clothing for boogies was acquired through ingenuity, since most hippies did not have much money. A cornucopia of clothing in the free box by the Co-op in El Prado was a popular place to find treasures. The trading,

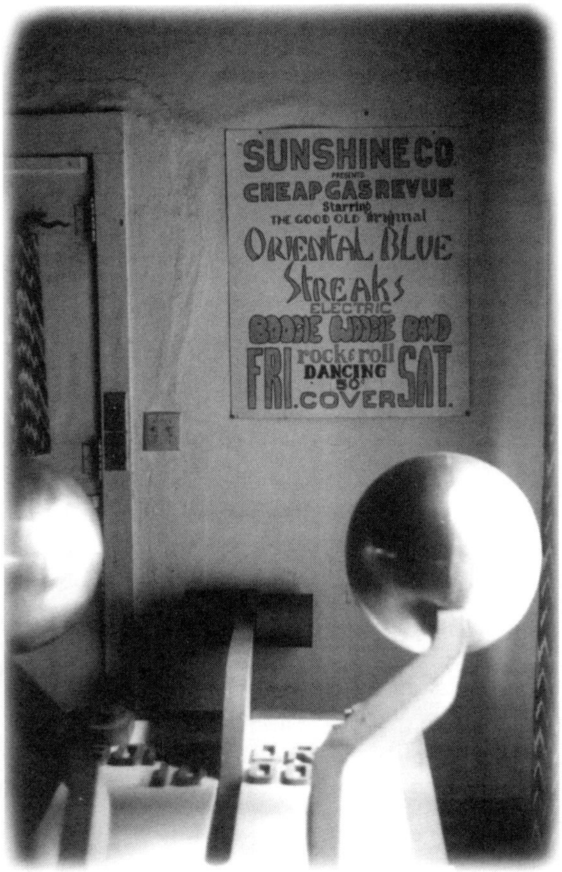

The Oriental Blue Streaks were our favorite boogie band. Does that really say 50 cent cover charge? Photo by Paul Dembski

altering, and sharing that went on when women converged at someone's house had the enthusiasm and bustle of a Third World market.

One day Melinda, my housemate at the time, threw her favorite clothes into a boiling cauldron filled with magenta dye. She invited several women to join her. I tossed in a few blouses, and before we knew it the cauldron was swishing with clothes from Feather, Pilar, Ripple and Seco Sally. For months we mixed and matched clothing, all wearing the same glorious magenta.

As luck would have it, Terry came back from Guatemala with an amazing collection of dresses and hand-embroidered shirts just before a big boogie. Claiming a table and four chairs to display her wares, she hung out at Joe's Restaurant until her merchandise was sold and paid for with cash, food stamps or jewelry.

The silversmith hippies who lived at the Mabel Dodge Luhan house could be spotted by their glut of silver, turquoise and lapis jewelry hanging from every imaginable place. Their concho belts, earrings and squash blossom necklaces gave them the appearance of affluence, but they were really showcases in motion since everything they wore was for sale or trade.

When the Oriental Blue Streaks started to play their music, it was impossible to sit. Our favorite boogie band played with tireless gusto while Sara—their lead singer and every bit as good as Grace Slick from the Jefferson Airplane—belted out our favorite rock 'n roll songs.

I remember one Christmas boogie in particular because everyone seemed to be in an altered state. A huge shipment of blotter acid had just arrived from California and was being passed out on the dance floor. People held out their tongues as if receiving a sacred sacrament. The room was packed, body against sweaty body but there was no sense of claustrophobia. I was a speck of matter bobbing in my personal orbit, randomly colliding with other specks of matter, happy in the knowledge that I was part of the whole.

"An outrageously merry Christmas to you." The chant was tossed around the dance hall like a Frisbee. In fact, when my partner lifted me onto his shoulders, I could see the words bouncing around the room from person to person.

When the chant was fading, one of the diaphanous dancers seized the moment, ran up to the bandstand, grabbed the mike and wailed her personal rendition of "Blue Suede Shoes," fulfilling a lifelong desire.

In between sets of music we visited at tables, at the bar or outside, getting a breath of fresh air. People had traveled a long way to be here. Lots of mating went on, in public and in private. A crowd of people stood around watching Jupiter and Sunshine humping away underneath a table to the rhythm of "Put on Your High Heeled Sneakers." A young man at the bar had an attractive mother draped over one shoulder and her equally attractive pubescent daughter over the other. Like someone caught near a ticking bomb, he hesitated to move. When the music started, the crowd swept back onto the groaning, throbbing, undulating dance floor. The feet of a thousand dancers created a puddle of sweat by midnight.

The definition of a couple was fluid—any combination was possible. Woman freely embraced each other, men danced side-by-side, triads and mini-circles formed spontaneously while lone dancers wove in between like dervishes. Chaos and ever-changing form whirled seamlessly together all night. By the last set, an ecstatic group beat rocked the room, as if ol' Martinez Hall could just lift up and start its own orbit. The Oriental Blue Streaks always closed with the same song, "Smile and Take it With You When You Go."

After the boogie, we hurried to our vehicles and split quickly. Some of the locals, well soused by one o'clock, weren't feeling like part of the "we're-all-one-groovy-tribe" group and waited in their pickup trucks, hoping to get into a good fight. Macho dudes on both sides brought guns, knives and sticks to these rumbles. The following day, the grapevine would abound with stories about what happened after the boogie. "Did ya hear? Tahiti got the crap beat out of him." Or "Preacher's windshield was smashed." No matter how many cops showed up at the end of boogies, there was always time for a rumble in the parking lot, but this never stopped us from showing up for the next boogie, which was anticipated as soon as one ended. We just smiled, took it with us when we left and showed up again.

A mountain momma plays a mean wash basin—chop that wood, wash those clothes, play that wash basin...
Photo by Paul Dembski

y 6, 1976
36 Pages
15¢

The Taos

PLAZA PROPS—Replacing the **puntales** which have been supporting the **portales** in Taos Plaza for the past 40 years are workmen Mark Keltz, right and Philo Sams, employed by the Town of Taos for the past month on the cumbersome — and often delicate — replacement project. The new "vertical vigas," purchased at a cost of $700 with an additional $700 invested by the town in labor, are expected to last at least until the year 2000, and may still be here when the rest of us are gone.

(Staff Photo by Paul C. Merz)

Dope drop case postponed

By MERILEE DANNEMANN

A man accused of dropping 1,750 pounds of marijuana into Taos County from an airplane last fall was given a temporary reprieve this Monday from telling a Taos grand jury where he got it.

Suspect Billy Howard Potts, a resident of Salinas, Calif., was presented with an offer of immunity from prosecution and served with a grand jury subpoena after entering the Taos County Court...

Wright commented later that it was not within the powers of a district attorney to exempt anyone from grand jury subpoena.

Nevertheless, the judge refrained from forcing Potts to testify, and instead granted a month's continuance in the case, instructing the attorneys to "prepare for trial."

The immunity offer was made under a new State Supreme Court ruling...

questions on the grounds that he might incriminate himself.

Rule 58 was described by Kaufman as "a tactical weapon against organized crime, which we of the State Police have been looking forward to with great expectations."

The rule became effective April 1, 1976, and Kaufman believed this was the first time it was to be used.

Brandenburg said he had not...

Trippin'
by Iris Keltz

It was a cold winter's night, somewhere in the heart of January. Cynthia had just thrown a piñon log in the cook stove. A pot of green chile stew simmered on top. It promised to be one of those tranquil winter nights. Outside the world was turning white.

A knock on the door, and out of the blue appeared Helene and Melissa, two friends of ours who had recently discovered each other. After stomping the snow off their hiking boots, a round of clumsy bear hugs and smiles no longer hidden under woolen scarves, we welcomed them in, glad for their company and the burst of fresh air. Curiously, on their shoulders they carried lengths of coiled rope.

Helene, a weaver, lived in a self-built, round stone house in Arroyo Hondo. Melissa, a struggling artist and single mother of two, rented part of an old house on Birch Street in town. She scented the homely rooms with lavender and filled the walls with her paintings of mythic creatures with long flowing hair and muscular bodies. Clay pots with flecks of mica crystals shimmered on top of the shelves.

We soaked up the chile stew with warm tortillas and shared the latest news from around town. Rubbing her fingers in front of the fire, Melissa blurted, "I just had to let you know that a friend from California sent me one hundred hits of pure blotter acid, really pure. Helen and I are going to drop some acid and climb Wheeler Peak tomorrow." I wasn't sure what the connection was between acid and mountain climbing. Maybe the drug coursing through the body worked like wood in a cook stove? Or maybe acid summoned the courage to face a 13,000-foot peak in the middle of winter? Skiers and hikers from around the world were addicted to its vertiginous heights, but neither of my friends were skiers or mountain climbers.

Last July, a friend and I had hiked to Williams Lake, just below the treeless summit. When we weren't looking, heavy storm clouds rolled in and a hot summer's day became a relentless, bone-chilling hailstorm. Shivering, we ran down the mountain. My friends wanted to climb to the peak in January. I admired their courage, but had no desire to join them. Melissa added, "If it's all right with you, we'd like to spend the night here and head up the mountain first thing in the morning."

"Hey, we don't mind," insisted Cynthia quite hospitably.

"Have another bowl of chile and coffee," I added. It turned out that morning was a long ways off. Cynthia and I shared a ramshackle old adobe outside Arroyo Seco in the vicinity known as Dogtown. The back walls had already melted into the earth, threatening the remaining three-foot thick adobe walls like a contagion. The part of the house where we lived felt like a fortress.

"Let's try a hit of acid now," Melissa suggested, flashing her blue eyes at us.

"Sure, why not?" said Cynthia amiably.

"I'm game," added Helene.

If I said no at this point, I would have had to come up with an alternative game plan—which I didn't have.

"It's pure stuff!" reassured Melissa, catching a whiff of hesitancy on my part.

"Let's go for it," said Helene, before anyone could change her mind. We sat around the cook stove chewing white pieces of paper. It may have been a delusional thing to do, but I chewed. Even if I didn't get stoned, I enjoyed the camaraderie.

We told each other stories that must have been hilarious, because we laughed until tears rolled down our faces. It was hard to gauge how long we sat around the cook stove chewing on paper. Cynthia leaned back to grab a piece of wood and fell off her chair, suddenly noticing the backpacks leaning against the wall filled with survival rations and mountain climbing gear—ropes, carabineers, a rock hammer, sunglasses and an *I Ching*. We stretched the ropes from one end of the house to the other to see how long they were.

"Melissa, when did you learn about mountain climbing?" I asked, knowing she'd lived in southern California before moving to New Mexico. She was a self-proclaimed expert on everything from midwifery to aura balancing to detoxifying poultry by soaking it in a marinade of diluted Clorox. Wanting to display her knowledge, she tied special knots in the rope and explained how foot loops and metal stakes were used to ascend and rappel along steep slopes. Melissa was confident, as always. We left the warmth of the cook stove to test her knowledge.

Cynthia's spacious bedroom had huge vigas spanning fourteen-foot walls with slender aspen latillas between the logs. Dirt insulation sifted into the rooms like a chronic spring drizzle. The light had long since faded from the western window where earlier in the day I'd curled up on the blue wooden sill to watch the clouds and listen to the monotonous rhythm of her weaving. Cynthia's room was furnished with an iron bed with ornate brass trim, an old trastero, a chest of drawers, a weaving loom and a blooming geranium.

After throwing a rope across a viga, we tested it for strength. The top of the dresser proved an ideal launching pad and her bed became a perfect landing place. Melissa tied a foot loop in the rope. Cynthia climbed to the top of the dresser, jumped off and went swinging across the room, landing safely on the iron bed. She did it again and started making strange birdlike sounds. We watched, patiently waiting for our turn.

Melissa was next. She went sailing across the room like a pirate swinging from the main mast. Helen closed her eyes and jumped into the abyss. My turn—rush of vertigo as I mounted the dresser, not sure if I could make that leap. All eyes rested on me. I breathed deeply and held my nose as if diving under water and gave myself a thrust. "Ayee! Yeow!" I spontaneously started making those untranslatable bird-like sounds I've come to associate with hang gliders flying around mountaintops.

On my way to the outhouse, I became struck by the quantity and loveliness of the stars spanning the Milky Way like a bridge to infinity. The universe and I were one. More accurately, I was the center of the universe and everything spun around me. In a gesture of thanksgiving, I placed my head on the snowy ground and arched my legs towards the heavens, the one and only time in my life I have been able to stand on my head. From this point of view, the stars above were indistinguishable from the light crystals of snow on the ground. Running inside to share this accomplishment, I noticed Cynthia's silhouette against the house, her legs thrust heavenward. She had found her center of gravity also—an amazing synchronicity!

Melissa was standing by the stove when I came in. She stared into my eyes with an intensity that made me uncomfortable. A long moment passed before she announced her prognosis. "You've got a hole in your gut." She was also an expert in iridology, the art of reading the body's health through patterns in the iris of the eye. I felt a knot in my stomach and went back to the outhouse for a huge bowel movement.

We returned to swinging on the ropes. It was already light outside when we felt hungry. Flying works up the appetite. While eating a bowl of chile stew, tortillas and cowboy coffee, Melissa announced, "I don't feel like climbing a mountain today. How 'bout another hit of acid?" Helen was secretly relieved that she would not have to climb a mountain today and eagerly chewed on a piece of white paper. Cynthia and I looked at each other and said, "Why not?" We were sitting in front of the eastern window watching the sun rise over Taos Mountain.

"I have an idea. Let's go tobogganing up the mountain!" suggested Cynthia. Like a forgotten friend, the wooden toboggan leaned against the outside wall of the house. We climbed into my '56 Chevy wagon and headed over to Llano Quemado, a detour of about 15 miles south. Ralph and Anita, who'd just moved to New Mexico, unsuspectingly invited us in.

Melissa smudging her tarot cards after someone else had used them. *Photo by Paul Dembski*

Before Ralph dropped out of civilization in Chicago, he'd managed to transform an old milk van into the lounge of a Lear Jet. A varnished wooden table, matching benches and a butcher-block counter top contrasted with porcelain walls. They accepted our invitation to go tobogganing in the ski valley. Melissa offered them some blotter acid before they changed their mind. We filled a giant thermos with hot coffee,

That's us with the toboggan after our successful run. I'm the short one in the middle, Anita and Ralph are on the left. Out of control! Early '70s. Paul Dembski is the tall one in the middle.

Group photo by my brother Aaron Devinsky

grabbed strings of dried apples hanging from the ceiling and headed north.

"All aboard," shouted Ralph as he took command in the driver's seat, wearing dark glasses and a brown leather bombardier jacket, looking like a World War I pilot on an important mission. The search for the perfect slope became our quest. The ride to the ski valley could have taken as long as a trip to the moon or been as short as the blink of an eye. Time was measured as moments of cold, hunger, longing, tears, fear or joy. Time was the eternal now. We'd always existed in this moving milk van and always would.

We arrived in a vast and awesome world, brushed with evergreens, aspens, bony-branched trees and steep slopes—a cold world where warm-blooded animals not in hibernation were precious. Heat from our bodies escaped as breath. The warmth of friends was essential. Somewhere in the white void, earth met sky.

That we were from a different tribe than the skiers was obvious. First of all, we had no skis. Secondly, our clothes were gathered from the four corners of the Third World, except for Melissa and Helene who had come prepared to climb a mountain, and Ralph who wore his bombardier jacket. The rest of us were wrapped in layers. My brother Aaron took a photo of us that day. I'm wearing magenta-dyed thermal underwear with a matching turtleneck, and a woolen sweater underneath my burgundy poncho. A Peruvian goat boy hat crowned by a fountain of multicolored threads keeps my head warm. We were neither efficiently nor elegantly dressed, but we were not cold.

As we oriented ourselves to this white world, our senses were heightened, but our judgment was suspended. Fears that should have concerned us, like getting lost or becoming cold, seemed irrelevant. When our leaderless group left the warmth of the van in search of the perfect slope, we had no sense of direction except uphill, downhill, heaven and earth, and the person in front of us. We were in search of the perfect slope. I didn't know where we were going and didn't care. Dragging the toboggan up the mountainside, we plodded along making a trail that was hard to miss. A light snow was falling.

Everything was peaceful and uneventful when all of a sudden an electronic voice boomed from a strategically placed loud speaker, "You people with the toboggan." We knew the invisible voice was watching us.

"You must go no further up the mountain." Now it sounded like someone's father warning us not to be bad. It goaded us on.

"It is slippery and dangerous." Dangerous? This didn't feel dangerous. We kept on going, blatantly ignoring the omniscient voice.

"You could be killed!" Killed? Fear slithered through me. I'm not ready to die. Maybe we should turn back, but I don't because I'm following the person in front of me who is following the person in front of her.

"You will be out of control." Out of control? Out of control! We aspired to be out of control, spontaneous, unencumbered, free. Surely, this was the slope we'd been searching for. We got a second wind. Then, it became quiet again and we forgot about the electronic voice, but the voice had not forgotten about us. The message of doom was carried on every snow crystal and echoed off every boulder, but we were too far up the mountain to turn back.

Wordlessly, we chose a spot and set the toboggan on its downhill course. Someone said, "Bail off quickly if you see anything in our path." We held tight to the person in front of us and cut loose. The first person took a snow bath as we sailed down the mountain shrieking with glee. This was more fun than flying on ropes. Someone shouted, "Bail now!" A plate glass window from the ski chalet loomed in front of us. We leaned and rolled into the soft snow like a litter of kittens.

A cheer went up in the ski lodge when we walked in to warm up. "You're the folks on the toboggan! We were watching. Wow!" They shook their heads in disbelief as we proudly acknowledged our accomplishment. We were safe, victorious, and jubilant. Someone bought us a round of hot chocolate.

I suddenly longed for the quiet of my room and the warmth of the cook stove. A similar wave traveled through the group. We piled back into the van-plane and headed down the mountain.

I'll always remember that as a first-class trip.

THE TAOS NEWS **May 1, 1969**

Marijuana's With Us

by Dave Lucas

As everyone well knows, our Land of Enchantment grows some of the best crops of the weed known as pot.

It abounds wild (and cultivated) throughout New Mexico, along the river banks and arroyos. Properly raised, it also seems that each plant has a potential market value of $500 or more.

Some aspects of smoking pot are similar to the Prohibition period when the law said "no" to liquor, but people said "yes" by their actions.

To this date no apparent harmful effects have been discovered from the use of the weed. Its adherents come from all walks of life—from housewives, businessmen, students and hippies.

Yet, if such is the case that it is presumed to be innocent until proven guilty, why all the fuss? The fact is that in itself it may seem to be harmless, but it can lead to the next step: LSD, Pep Pills or Goof Balls, "Speed," opium, heroin, etc.

An article in the *New Mexico Review* on March 6 quoted one high school student as saying about marijuana: "I get stoned and my eyes get droopy. My neck gets warm and my head feels droopy. You're not out of your mind, actually. It's the music that does it to you mostly."

Another student, asked how he obtained the money for pot, said: "Save up your lunch money. Lie. Tell your parents you are going bowling."

How about it, folks? Is this really part of the search for inner truth that young people need?

The Living Legend of the Rainbow Tribe July 4th, 1973

by Iris Keltz

Every tribe or clan identifies itself with a myth, legend or religion in stories that are passed along the generations. This is the hippie myth.

Somewhere in the foothills of the Grand Teton was a canyon, carved by a winding river, walled by towering rocks artfully etched by time and the elements. The lichen and moss added their green and gold patinas. Everchanging shadow and light from overhead clouds broke the illusion that the rock escarpment was eternal.

This year the Rainbow Tribe, an arc of races, religions and colors from all over the country, gathered here. From coast to coast, an efficient grapevine and posters tacked in hippie watering holes let it be known when and where, like the bulletin board at the Food Co-op in El Prado.

The Rainbow Tribe
will converge, convene and celebrate
July 4th, Grand Teton, Colorado
for the 2nd Annual Celebration
Bring your friends, drums and flutes

Seco Sally and I decided to go on a whim. She was thinking of moving to California, but couldn't make up her mind. "Oh, why not?" she conceded. "I'll decide when we get back." The day we left, a friend gifted me with a homemade wooden rattle the size of my hand. Shaped like a miniature dulcimer, it had three strings stretched across the top. The inside was filled with dried pinto beans, so it twanged and rattled at the same time. With my personal power object resting on the dashboard, our sleeping bags, a bag of trail mix, a few gallons of drinking water and oil for the car, we took off.

The Rainbow Tribe is committed to principles of non-violence and non-hierarchical egalitarianism. They have been holding large non-commercial Gatherings in remote forests since 1972 to demonstrate the viability of a cooperative utopian community living in harmony with the Earth. They govern themselves by a council whose membership is open to all interested people. All decisions are by consensus. Money is not needed, as all necessities are free. The favorite saying is "Welcome Home!"

Photo by Paul Dembski

Due to the advanced age and special needs of my '56 Chevy station wagon, it was slow going. After four days on the road, we turned off the highway in Grand Teton, Wyoming, and began following strategically placed signs. Eventually we found ourselves on a one-lane dirt road, probably an old logging road, in the middle of a pleasant traffic jam—without tension, horn blowing, or cursing. Hitchhikers passed joints between the cars, creeping like snails before catching a ride on hoods and trunks. Drivers abandoned vehicles to walk along the road, letting passengers grab the steering wheel. The procession had no beginning or end.

The road headed steadily down into a canyon. There was no turning back. Finally we came to a huge meadow filled with old beat-up, hand-painted vehicles parked at odd angles. We parked, grabbed our gear, and followed the crowd along a rocky trail. Where or how far we were going didn't seem important. About an hour later, still energetically hiking, I glanced at Seco Sally, who showed no signs of fatigue and hadn't complained, not even once. Eventually the trail opened into a lush valley with miles of grassy meadowland spread out like a ribbon along the banks of a pristine river. The clans and sub-cults were setting up campsites and communal kitchens. Free-floating spirits formed their own spontaneous units. Everyone found a niche—in aspen groves, pine forests, caves in the rocks, or along the riverbank. This was a Woodstock without celebrity or media.

I combed the crowds for the Rainbow Tribe, looking for Pisces Bill, one of their cooks I'd met at the Paradox Restaurant in New York. Six months had passed since that rainy St. Patrick's Day in New York when we found a cave in Central Park and drank drops of water percolating through the plant roots. Shivering and laughing, we warmed each other.

I was about to give up the daunting task of finding him when I saw him working in the Diggers' communal kitchen—they were the group that fed thousands of people for free in Golden Gate Park every Sunday. The Diggers, a commune from California, tended to be older hippies with strong social and political agendas.

Uncombed shoulder-length brown hair framed Bill's pasty face. A blue India-cotton shirt revealed his hairy chest. He was skinnier than I remembered and was missing a front tooth.

"Bill! I hoped you'd be here." I smiled coyly.

"Wouldn't miss it for the world." Did he mean the Rainbow Gathering or seeing me?

"Is Blue or Ami here?" I asked, referring to the managers of the restaurant.

"No, Blue fell in love, but not with Ami so she went back to her husband and children. I'm the only one here from the restaurant." His eyes twinkled when he smiled. "And who is your friend?"

"Seco Sally, Bill. Bill, Seco Sally. We drove from Taos together." His lustful gaze swallowed her from head to foot. Sally was a voluptuous woman with huge breasts, dreamy blue eyes and a crooked front tooth. She smiled innocently, unaware of her effect on him.

"Here, try this." He offered us a sip from his never-empty flask of Irish coffee, half filled with Jim Beam.

"Would you ladies like to camp together?" I wasn't sure. I looked at Seco Sally, who nodded.

"Sounds great," I said.

A grassy spot near the river seemed perfect. Huge black lava rocks separated us from the Hari Krishna encampment. We threw our sleeping bags and backpacks on the ground, took off our clothes and plunged into the river. Then we went to check out the main encampment, never worrying about theft or rain.

Taking full advantage of the volunteer labor force, the Diggers managed to put out two meals a day in a makeshift kitchen, feeding hundreds of hungry people oatmeal in the morning and rice and vegetables at sunset. I chose to exist on almonds and raisins. Raw food appealed to my aesthetics at the moment. Raw was pure, untouched by human hands. Bill and I volunteered to chop vegetables and helped serve rice and veggies to an endless line of half-naked hippies.

The sun had already dipped below the horizon when we meandered back to our campsite. The wail of the Hari Krishna boogies droned on into the night when Sally, Bill and I crawled under the sleeping bags, an inseparable tangle of arms, legs and torsos. I fought against feeling jealous or possessive. Tomorrow night Bill would be mine alone, but tonight nobody would be left out. Secretly I hoped his agony from that day's sunburn rivaled his ecstasy. Exhausted, we fell asleep to the Hari Krishna lullaby.

At first light, we plunged into the icy river for a bath, cupping our hands and drinking the sweet water. None of us gave a thought to bacteria until dysentery set in on the second day and someone asked the Hari Krishnas to move their ashram and their outhouse downstream. Although everyone was aware of their saffron robes weaving in and out of the meadow, they tended to keep to themselves, and when they did mingle it was to tell us about Hari Krishna, whoever he was. They peacefully complied with the request to move their outhouse.

By day we were stoned nymphs and naiads romping through the valley. Seco Sally lay naked on a hot black lava rock, her watermelon breasts turning redder every second. Bill languished nearby, his thin torso and uncircumcised penis also getting sunburned. Bodies glistened from coconut oil. We looked like exotic marine life gone bellies up.

By night, we gathered around neighboring campfires. A main fire near the communal kitchen was ringed with the steady beat of drums and flutes. I was irresistibly drawn into the circle of dancers, hips rotating like the earth in its orbit, arms swinging like trees in the wind. The sound of spring rain came from the rattle in my hand. I was an ancient being dancing around an ancient fire with my tribe, celebrating another year of life! It was hard to believe this instant village, just born, would soon scatter to the four winds. Just before twilight on the 4th of July, as if led

More than 20,000 "Rainbows" from all over the country still gather every 4th of July on pristine and remote public lands. The campfires, drumming, flutes, dancing and visiting go on all night and day. *Photo by Paul Dembski*

by an invisible Pied Piper, hundreds of us were drawn into a hypnotic ascent up a mountain. The slope was steep. The smell of coconut suntan lotion mixed with salty sweat on my skin. My mouth tasted like sawdust. I carried a few almonds, some raisins and my rattle. No water.

We were probably delivering ourselves into the hands of some self-appointed guru, I thought to myself. As if to banish doubt, someone handed me a piece of torn white paper and said, "Blotter acid, chew!" Everyone around me was also chewing paper. One foot in front of the other. No room for thought. When fatigue set in, I reached for the comfort of a human hand.

The sky was darkening as some people wisely turned back to the glowing campfires below. Not everyone was destined to make this ascent. The few people returning from the top said nothing. Perspiration purified my body. Just as the last colors drained from the sky, we reached the summit and I silently blessed us.

Spirits of this mountaintop
Bless this tribe
That climbs at twilight
Half naked
Warming the cold
Lighting the dark with music!

It's loose, it's wild, but afterwards all trash is picked up and the site is restored gratefully to ol' Mother Nature.
Photo by Paul Dembski

Who could fathom why so many people carried drums, guitars and other instruments up this precipitous slope? We had precious little water, no food or sleeping bags and maybe two blankets. A steady wind and a shortage of matches meant no fire. But we had music to keep our energy high not to mention the acid coursing through our collective brains. A fantastic blend of drums, flutes, strings and rattles mixed with the voices and hand-clapping of everyone who had victoriously made it to the top of this mountain.

"Shiva mama, get it on," we wailed around a beautiful buxom blonde woman who had brought her candle-burning-on-the-head dancing act with her. A chiffon scarf floated around her like a mist in the wind. Suddenly someone interrupted the music with an anxious warning.

"It's going to be a cold windy night here without a fire." A flashlight seared the darkness as people followed the light down the mountain. For the briefest moment, I thought of joining them and was relieved when they were gone. The music began again. I turned to Seco Sally, "Lord, what you have to go through for these high cultural experiences." She gave me a Cheshire cat grin through slitted blue eyes floating around black dots.

When the music died down, we huddled into a heap of warm bodies, staring at the myriad of stars in the Milky Way. It was a moonless night. A resonant voice detached itself from the group and began to tell stories and recite poetry. For hours, the disembodied voice held the group in wonder.

"We climbed this mountain because we're waiting. For eons the starships have been visiting Earth, circling, waiting for the right moment to make contact. The aliens are our angels. They will heal the sick and bring peace to this war-torn planet. They are heralds of the Aquarian Age." The steady baritone voice spoke with such assurance that I wondered if he was an alien or if he'd had a close encounter.

Pregnant with expectation, we sat on that mountaintop. Shooting stars and circling satellites were common sights. Sirius glowed like a beacon of light in the southern sky. Every so often someone pointed to an object that seemed to have a random movement. Everyone oohed and aahed. Then it went away. The music resumed, throwing off energy like a fire. The voice continued its incantations, now passionately reciting the poetry of Bob Dylan. It was the first time I heard the lyrics without the music.

Take me on a trip
Upon your magic swirling ship

The voice, unhesitatingly, knew every verse by heart. Pounding images into the black night, he told us of the chimes of freedom flashing, and the roads a man must walk down and about a blue-eyed son. Stripped of the music, the poetry stood strong on its own.

The night passed and the first dappled rose and violet light appeared in the east. When we untangled ourselves from each other's warmth, the disembodied voice melted back into the group. I never found out who he was.

With the sun's first rays, we let out a collective shout of joy. Color bled back into the world. Canyons, mesas and snow-capped peaks loomed all around. I looked at the rushing river below in delirious anticipation of water.

No, the starships had not come for us, but we could wait. Another year of celebrating life. The coming together of the tribe. Maybe next year we wouldn't have to part. We ran down the mountain. Perhaps we would be doing this for thousands of years to come.

"So being a hippie is not a matter of dress, behavior, economic status, or social milieu. It is a philosophical approach to life that emphasizes freedom, peace, love and a respect for others and the earth. The way of the hippie never died. There have always been hippies from the first time society laid down rules, to Jesus, to Henry David Thoreau, to John Lennon, to you and me. I believe there's a little hippie in all of us."—Skip Stone.
Photo by Paul Dembski

A Perennial Aquarian Philosophy

LORETTA PAULSON ⚭ THE FOUNTAIN OF LIGHT, 1970

There is much talk about the New Age or the Aquarian Age. . .a new way of life, but I wonder how many have given very serious consideration as to how this going to come about. We all have a tendency to hope that it will be an "Open Sesame" kind of transition, but I'm afraid the laws of life do not verify this hope or daydream. Do we want the New Age enough to help bring it into existence? If we accept the doctrine of reincarnation, maybe we are more than a little responsible in past lives for many of the problems that are prevalent today. Too long it has been a habit for humans to blame everything and everyone outside of themselves for all of their problems. This is a lack of understanding to a large extent. One of the major changes in attitude which denotes maturity or the maturing process is the ability of the individual to accept full responsibility for his or her own life. Once this step can be taken and the individual desires to continue the process, they are on the way. The only way we can change the world is to change ourselves. When there are enough of us willing to make every effort to change, study the basic laws and principles of Creation, and make them a part of us, then we can affect the outer world. We complain of materiality and the injustices, abuse and misuse of the power structure, but what are we manifesting right in our back yard? Are we contributing to the problem or the solution? If a few of us can make a deep inner decision that we are willing to take the new challenging trip of personal responsibility and work together, we can make an inspirational dent in the wobbly power structure. One of the first principles we need to examine is the power of thought to realize that we are creating with every thought as well as spoken word. It is encouraging indeed to realize we have dominion, control of so much in our lives. We can, if we wish, consciously begin to redirect the creative energy of our words, by rewording thoughts and spoken words. It is a wonderful training in awareness and discipline, and the results are more than worth all the effort. We can have great knowledge, intellectual understanding, but until we apply what we know, it is mere theory and has no practical value in our lives. There is even the factor of intellectual indigestion which is very prevalent today. Many have all the answers when it comes to what the other person should or should not do, but rarely do they take a look at themselves in the same relentless, critical judgement. So here we can come back to the power and nature of our thoughts. If we are critical and unkind in our general thought attitude, we are contributing to the nature of our law of attraction. This is an element in the law of as you sow you reap. It is challenging at first to accept our personal responsibility and the attitude that our problems are opportunities, but once we do we can shift into a whole *new way of life.* And the next important factor is that we can become examples of what we believe and our living will speak far louder than our words. And so we can become a conscious, dedicated link in the continuity of God, and really do our part to bring the New Age. . .

The courtyard of New Buffalo was a great place to celebrate the summer and winter solstice. People came from up and down the valley and then some to catch a tribal rhythm and visit with old friends. At the best of times there was lamb roasting on the fire. At the very least you could count on a chile and beans and tortillas. Living at New Buffalo, I watched the sun roll up and down the mesa during the seasonal changes and to this day it's the only piece of land where I can tell the season from the sun's position on the horizon. *Photo by Paul Dembski*

Last Solstice Celebration New Buffalo, '79

told by Jenny Bird to Iris Keltz

"When I first came to Taos, I was 15 and had just graduated from high school. I was ecstatic to be out of school and away from home—free for the first time in my life. I lived in a little gypsy wagon in the back yard of Dennis' house in Arroyo Hondo. It was very tiny, about the size of a closet.

"Our family had lived in Germany and Belgium when I was growing up, but we moved back to Ohio when I was 14. I couldn't deal with America. It just blew my mind. I came out to visit my sister who was living in Arroyo Hondo and said, 'This is it, this is real.' I made a deal with my folks that if I finished my last year of high school in Ohio I'd be free to come back here to live. And so I did.

"The band Scorch played at the New Buffalo solstice boogie that day. They were my friends and I'd come to the party with them. I'd been back in Taos about a month. At one point, I climbed a ladder to sit on the roof of the southern wing of the pueblo. Lots of people were up there because it was a great view of the band and the dancers.

"It was an ecstatically glorious day with kids running everywhere and people boogying in the courtyard. You could tell by their eyes that they were on acid, pot, peyote, whatever. That was before cocaine got to town. I wasn't on any drugs that day.

"It was just before sunset. The music and dancing had been going on all day and was supposed to go on all night. There was going to be a solstice ceremony. Someone came up to the band and told them to stop playing. Bummer, I thought, why are they telling them to stop? And then it went like wildfire through the crowd, what had happened. Two kids playing on the roof where we'd been sitting had run directly over the skylight and had fallen in together. The girl fell on top of the boy and the glass from the skylight went directly through his heart and killed him instantly. The little girl just tumbled over and was fine. There was a crowd of people inside the room where it happened. They called an ambulance.

"Suddenly it felt like emptiness. There had been this great energy and it simply dissolved into a giant void. I felt moved to go up on stage and sing a song I'd written. It was about the sun. A hush had settled over everyone, like we were sharing a sacred moment.

"The sun was setting in this glorious immense display and I felt this child's soul spreading over the courtyard. There was a palpable sense of his soul departing, a sense of joy and freedom, like it was okay. I stood on stage. Around me were people crying and hugging each other. Along with the grieving was the sense that his soul was rejoicing as the sun was going down. What an amazing moment to go out of your body. There was so much love. Everyone felt incredibly bonded. I did my prayer song and left. This is how it goes.

'We love you, sun.
We know that you're there.
We know you'll rise up and give us our share
of light, sweet light.'

"I sang this song four times to the four directions. It felt awesome. The flashing red lights of the ambulance coming up the driveway jolted us out of that grace-filled moment. Opposing forces blended, the sense of grief and loss, of cosmic ecstasy and the need to deal with the real world. The ambulance left. The sun went down and the people dispersed.

"I don't attribute what happened to drugs. It was a tragic event that could have happened anywhere. Everyone was watchful of the kids.

We all have our own particular beauty and Solstice Celebrations were a place to watch and admire each other's individuality—and perhaps catch someone's eye.
Photo by Paul Dembski

"That was the last great solstice party at New Buffalo. It was an ending. Now there are lots of small ones, it's fragmented. Then everyone was connected, like one huge tribal family. The event was dark but the moment was transcendent. It was '79, the end of a decade, and the energy was shifting."

Update:
Jenny Bird lives with her two daughters, 15 and 11, in Arroyo Hondo, a small village ten miles north of Taos. She is a singer, songwriter and guitarist. She played at the Lillith Fair in 1998. With five CD's out, she supports herself through her music.

Accident Claims Child's Life At Party

By Merilee Dannemann

A five-year-old child is dead after an accidental fall through a skylight at New Buffalo commune in Arroyo Hondo June 21.

Gabriel Fordyce was playing on the roof of a building when the accident took place. According to the official account of the sheriff's office, the child suffered two deep puncture wounds through the chest from pieces of glass when he landed on a stone bedroom floor after falling about 10 feet.

He was the only son of Barbara Fordyce of Taos, a resident of several years who most recently was employed at The Bar.

The fall happened at about 8:15 p.m.—near sundown on the longest day of the year. The child was among some 200 persons attending a party marking the summer solstice.

A companion, three-year-old Mahina Thompson, also fell through the hole in the skylight but reportedly suffered only scratches and bruises.

Though other children had been playing on roofs during the afternoon, most were several years older. Gabriel and Mahina had reportedly been ordered off the roof by Gabriel's mother only moments before the accident, had climbed safely down but then climbed up again unobserved.

The only reported eyewitnesses to the fall itself were other children. The official report states the boy lost his footing when climbing down in response to an order from his mother.

Two nurses and an emergency medical technician were attending the party and began attempts to save the boy's life almost at once. According to a medical account, the child was breathing irregularly and had a faint pulse for several minutes, but was bleeding profusely through one of the puncture wounds. It was believed later that the heart was punctured.

The local medical personnel—nurses John Brinduse and Bill Parker and emergency medic Rachel Finstein—were aided by a stranger who introduced himself as a physician. Though he accompanied the attendants to Holy Cross Hospital, his name was never learned.

Word of the accident spread gradually through the courtyard of the commune, where guests had been enjoying the afternoon and dancing to the music of a local rock band. Several minutes before the ambulance arrived, the band put away its instruments. A woman took over the microphone and led the assembly in the singing of prayer.

Treatment, including mouth-to-mouth breathing and other techniques to restore breath or pulse, continued as Gabriel was carried across the courtyard and driven in the ambulance to Holy Cross Hospital. He was pronounced dead at 10:20 p.m. by assistant medical examiner Ben Tafoya.

The party was the first summer solstice event at New Buffalo in several years, and had been a reunion for old friends, some of whom had come to Taos just to attend the event.

Started as an annual event shortly after the commune was founded in 1967, the parties had continued through 1973. They were halted by commune members concerned about possible damage to crops by visitors unacquainted with farming.

Last week's event was to have marked a revival.

Gabriel's body was buried at New Buffalo Monday.

New Buffalo kids, late '60s—they're almost 40 now. Where did all the time go? *Photo courtesy of Alfred Hobbs*

New Buffalo Ends an Era

by Staci Matlock

The Taos News, January 9, 1997

Joaquin Klein was managing the New Buffalo Bed and Breakfast for his parents one day last year when four Japanese guys in black leather showed up at the former commune's door. They looked tough, mean and spoke almost no English, he told his father, Rick Klein, later. Frightened, Joaquin Klein stepped outside. One of the four kept pointing at the New Buffalo adobe building and repeating two words: "Easy Rider?" Afterward they came inside to sing all the Grateful Dead tunes they had memorized.

Rick and Terry Klein pose under the buffalo carving in the old drumming room of the commune.
Photo by Iris Keltz

For 30 years, New Buffalo has in one form or another impacted the lives of people from all over the world: A place to farm, a place to raise kids, a place to party, a place to relive an era.

Now, New Buffalo is for sale.

Asked why he is selling, Rick Klein said, "We can't hold up the '60s for everybody."

It was 1967, the summer of dreams, of revolution, of possibilities. That was when a group of 25 visionaries such as Rick Klein and Pabla Gonzalez joined together to form a more perfect place. It was the summer of New Buffalo, the first New Mexico commune. Klein, then 25, purchased the property in the rural Arroyo Hondo valley with his money, then donated the land for the commune.

Sweat from the first "family" members built the original adobe dwellings, almost 5,000 square feet, complete with a six-seater outhouse. Hard work sustained the commune for the next 12 years, as hippie farmers grew produce on the 59 acres (24 irrigated) surrounding the commune.

The vision? A place to practice sustainable farming, pick one's own family, "make peace not war." It was to live in a way fundamentally different from the previous generation.

"People have no idea how straight the '50s were," Klein said. "There was a lot of hypocrisy."

Over the years it was visited by such '60s dignitaries as Timothy Leary and the makers of the cult film, *Easy Rider*. Max Finstein was instrumental in founding the commune and coined the term New Buffalo. "The Max," given to winners in the Taos Poetry Circus, is named for Finstein.

For awhile, the commune boasted a solar dairy barn started by long-time member Artie Kopecky. It produced most of its own vegetables, grains and meat. Members shared the tasks from building to cleaning. In the first years, it was a New Buffalo member who served as *mayordomo* of the main *acequia* in Arroyo Hondo.

Still, some things began to drag on members, such as the lack of privacy.

"The whole thing was a courageous experiment, but very naïve," Klein notes now.

His wife, Terry, agrees. "It was not all a bowl of cherries," she said. "In winter it was cold. In summer there were a lot of flies. But for a majority of the time, it was doing what it was supposed to."

The Kleins break New Buffalo's history into distinct periods: the '60s were visionary; the '70s were times of hard work; the early '80s were the time of "wine, heroin and shotguns."

It was during that later period when the Kleins and most of the former New Buffalo members were already gone, moving on to other dreams. The Kleins are reluctant to talk about the period in 1985 when former members, including themselves, had to block a proposed sale of the property by some still living there. It was a painful period for everyone involved.

In 1987, the property was leased to the Sustainable Native Agricultural Center, a non-profit group dedicated to preserving native seeds. New Buffalo's board members felt the seed bank was in keeping with the original vision for the place.

When the seed bank found another home, New Buffalo was left without a caretaker. In 1989, Rick and Terry Klein took back over New Buffalo, finding it in great disrepair. "We actually tried to give it away," Rick Klein said. "We talked to schools, the Hanuman Temple, churches. No one took the offer."

When they decided to open the bed and breakfast, they once again poured thousands of dollars and their own sweat into repairing the huge 18-room adobe building. They added indoor plumbing, 22 skylights and a new roof. They put a conservation easement on part of it through the Taos Land Trust. They tried to bring in modern conveniences without destroying the old feel and architecture of the original buildings.

"The building would have dissolved back into the ground if we hadn't turned it into a bed and breakfast," Klein said.

The New Buffalo Bed and Breakfast opened in December 1992. Before long they had people from around the world coming to visit the historic commune and to relive their adventures there. Members of the original commune family came. Children who had grown up there arrived with maps showing the room they were born in, drawn by their mothers.

A Parisian appeared one day reminiscing about his last trip there two decades before, intensified with a little acid help. Now he is the publisher of a prestigious magazine in France. "People would show up with bibliographies on the place," Klein said. "They knew more about it then we did."

From *The London Times* to *The Denver Post*, 17 articles about the New Buffalo Bed and Breakfast were written in the first two years. But aside from the joys of seeing old friends and the publicity, "it was a

For a time, Rick and Terry Klein turned New Buffalo into an historic bed and breakfast.

Photo by Iris Keltz

thankless job," Terry Klein said. "We were working seven days a week, 365 days a year for little money."

Reliving the '60s began to get old. "During the bed and breakfast, that's what people wanted to do, relive the story," Gonzalez said. The Hondo Fire, which devastated the Lama Foundation and Lama Mountain May 5, was the catalyst for the Kleins deciding to sell New Buffalo. Much of the Kleins' home in Lama was burned, their possessions lost. For more than two weeks after the fire, the Kleins opened the bed and breakfast up as a food and clothing distribution point for victims of the fire. More than 40 people at one point were housed under the New Buffalo roof.

"The fire really caused us to look at our lives, to make some decisions, to realize that we're not going to live forever," Terry Klein said.

Gonzalez, who managed the bed and breakfast for the Kleins, is joining her son in Walsenburg, Colorado where he is opening a restaurant. She is working on a book about the first years at New Buffalo, called *First Family*. "It's time for new horizons and new adventures," Gonzalez said.

Before Christmas, the Kleins held a New Buffalo yard sale. People traveled from miles away to bid on a piece of history. Only a few things are left now, some the Kleins plan to keep: The stuffed bison head and the original commune's American flag, both still hang on the wall of the huge round common room.

The Kleins say they are hoping a school or non-profit group will buy the property. Covenants will keep the property from being developed into a California-style subdivision or worse. The property has been placed in a trust and money from the sale of the property will go into the trust, later to be distributed to non-profit environmental and social groups.

Selling New Buffalo is scary for the Kleins. It has been a defining chapter in their lives. "New Buffalo has been such a part of my life," Rick Klein said. "Next to my kids (Joaquin and Chris), it is the most important thing I've done. It was eccentric to try and create it, and then give it away. I've had to work through all that. It's a big phase of my life, but I feel like this is some closure."

My Last Address to the Troops

Max Finstein

I'm a powermad insatiable american jewish beast
who wants, mostly
in peace, mysterious flowers
of all growths
animal vegetable mineral
that cross my aimless path
upon this whirling living mass
that breeds us
I'm a glory lickin fightin knight in hopeless armor
who believes, kisses in the morning
meaning in the work
better than the flag
more than acclamation
i want to know that i can keep
my nose out of all of it
that i need not pit my star against the tide
Look! we all want something better!
we're all going somewhere else
this can't be all there is!
i mean, call me
i won't call you.

In Memoriam: Max Finstein 1923-1982

by Iris Keltz

"Max Finstein is a man of history, not yet recognized. He probably deserves a monument, a Finstein Memorial, erected in memory of the 1960's, an era that Max Finstein helped to invent and is now perfectly willing to bury. Aren't we all"

— *The Washington Post, May 18th, 1980*

From all over the country we gathered at New Buffalo, where many of us had lived together as hippies, rebels, pacifists, farmers and lost souls. I walked slowly through the newly plowed furrows in the lower meadow, crushing cow pods underfoot, loosening memories. Past the old swimming hole, now dried up, my mind's eye saw tanned naked bodies jump into the cold water on a hot summer afternoon and take a siesta in the shade of an old cottonwood.

I joined hands with the people gathered in the circle to say good-bye to our friend, brother, lover, father, poet and voice of the '60s. We were in one of the upper fields, towards the mesa. Could the circle really have been an acre around? Through his life and his words, Max helped articulate the impossible dream—that somehow we were the critical group to transform society into a Camelot that would last forever.

All that was left of Max's physical remains was in that bag of ashes reverently held by his daughter, Rachael. He was our articulate spokesman for a culture called counter that looked with suspicion on any definition of itself. Max was older than most of us, and we looked to him as one of our few elders. His restlessness, his searching, took him across this country and around the world to Israel and back. Did he ever find what he was looking for? His life touched many lives. Someone once told me that Max's Kansas City in New York was named after him. He was always his own man, his own leader and had friends all over the world.

Rachael emptied the bag of ashes onto the land. Unspoken memories became an enormous silence filling the empty sky. Sadly lacking a ritual, a song, a leader or a rabbi, someone led us in a round of applause. We meandered back to the New Buffalo pueblo, hungry for something, we knew not what, maybe a hippie mystic sign. Suddenly, a flock of wild geese flew overhead in a formation that uncannily resembled the peyote bird. There was an uproarious shouting and cheering as we stood and watched the birds recede on the horizon until they were little black dots in the distance. No one doubted they carried Max's soaring spirit.

Awkwardly we gathered in the kitchen and the old drumming room. Once there had been such intimacy between many of us. Now we were strangers with familiar faces, trying to be in the present without losing our shared past. The circle room was without a fire to warm and gather us up like an old blanket. There were no drummers to invoke the heartbeat of the world and no gypsy clad dancers to express what we all felt.

We milled around as if at a cocktail party. Some showed the disappointments and the ravages of time more than others. An unfamiliar man sat with a bowed head in the shadows of the circle room near a Tibetan monk chanting under a naked light bulb. I wondered how each one knew Max.

I left the strangely quiet circle room and went to get a cold drink in the kitchen that didn't seem to belong to anyone now. The cold, sweet water tasted the same—it had not changed. This was a small comfort. I'd spent many mornings sitting at this very bench around the old wood-planked table swapping stories with fascinating people from all over and watching the clouds roll across the valley.

The sound of Alfred's contagious laughter reached me across the room. Our senior hippie with his white mane and beard was waiting for the rest of us to turn silver like him. He told me his laughter was the glue that held him together and kept life's disappointments in perspective. He laughed again.

A close buddy of Max's was standing near the old cook stove.

"Daddy Dave, do you remember the last time we saw each other?" He shook his head.

"It was up at Ogelvies' Bar," I reminded him. "You and Max came over to say hello. We talked for a while, reminiscing about the past and catching up on the present. Suddenly, Max ran up to a young blond man who currently lived at the commune and proudly introduced the two of us as graduates of New Buffalo." Daddy Dave remembered and smiled.

At home sifting memories that night, my mirror reflects the deepening arroyos on my face and the new silver hairs. A picture of Max reminds me that I am ageless. Folded in the kitchen drawer is an old newspaper article from the *The Washington Post* my mother sent me a couple of years ago—Max is sitting on a park bench in the Santa Fe plaza, a relaxed smile on his face and a twinkle in his eyes, always the renegade philosopher poet. In answer to the journalist's question, Max sounded the battle cry of the 80's—"What do I want to do now? Just make some bread." And he meant the kind you spend, not the kind that rises in the oven.

"Nothing Lasts" from the old Road Hog bus. *Photo by Phaedra Greenwood*

Grateful acknowledgment is made to the following people and organizations for permission to include their work, indicated below, in *Scrapbook of a Taos Hippie.*

» Jenny Bird, for photograph taken at the last solstice celebration, New Buffalo, '79.
» John Brandi, for the commune map of Taos. Copyright © 2000 by John Brandi.
» Bill Davis, for photographs as specified throughout the text. Copyright © 2000 by Bill Davis.
» Paul Dembski, for photographs as specified throughout the text. Copyright © 2000 by Paul Dembski.
» *Fountain of Light*, Jim Levy, Editor, for articles originally printed in the *Fountain of Light*.
» Phaedra Greenwood, for "The Hog Farm—1969." Copyright © 1970 by Phaedra Greenwood and photographs as specified throughout the text. Copyright © 2000 by Phaedra Greenwood.
» Renée Gregorio, for photographs as specified throughout the text, collection of Renée Gregorio.
» Rich Jamison, for photographs as specified throughout the text. Copyright © 2000 by Rich Jamison.
»Marcia Keegan, for the photograph of Taos Pueblo. Copyright © 1999 by Marcia Keegan
» Lisa Law, for photographs "Group Building New Buffalo." Copyright © 1978 by Lisa Law, "Group Om in the New Buffalo Courtyard," copyright © 1978 by Lisa Law, and "Ladies Talking in Courtyard," copyright © 1969 by Lisa Law.
» John Nichols, for "Whatever Happened to El Dorado?" Copyright © 1971 by John Nichols. First appeared in *Motive*, April/May 1971. Used by permission of the author.
» Rosie Pappaianni, for photograph "Rosie's Italian dinner advertisement" (photographer unknown), collection of Rosie Pappaianni.
» Marco Perella, for "An Evening at the Gay 90's." Copyright © 2000 by Marco Perella.
» Seth Roffman, for photographs as specified throughout the text. Copyright © 2000 by Seth Roffman.
» Jennifer Sihvonen, for permission to use "Group Photo of Silversmiths circa '76" (photographer unknown), collection of Jennifer Sihvonen.
» John Stearns, for photographs as specified throughout the text. Copyright © 2000 by John Stearn.
» *The Taos News (El Crepusculo, Inc.)*, George W. Fellows, Publisher, for newspaper stories, editorials, photos originally printed in *The Taos News*.
» Natt Tinker, for photograph "Original Hippie Rake." Copyright © 2000 by Natt Tinker.
» Tony Vinella, for photograph "Little Joe Gomez." Copyright © 2000 by Tony Vinella / Santa Fe.
»Stewart Warren, for photograph of "Phaedra with Old Road Hog." Copyright © 2000 by Stewart Warren.
» Peter Wood, for psychedelic landscape painting, untitled.

Grateful acknowledgment is also made to the following people for permission to use their oral histories, indicated below, as recorded by Iris Keltz in the *Scrapbook of a Taos Hippie.*

» Jenny Bird. "The Last Solstice Celebration: New Buffalo '79."
» Seth Brown. "The Silversmiths at the Mabel Dodge Luhan House."
» Michael Floyd Duncan. "The Eddie Gaudet Story."
» Barbara Durkee. "Mama Lama."
» Rose Gordon. "Morningstar Rose."
» Morgan Haynes. "TLC and the Counterculture: A Kid's Perspective."
» Alfred Hobbs. "From Anthropologist to Native."
» Jean Kenin. "Life at Pilar Hill."
» Charles Lonsdale. "From Capitalist to Communist and Back."
» Lorelei Loveless. "The Silversmiths at the Mabel Dodge Luhan House."
» Ed Morgan. "The Bicentennial Belt."
» Karen Pettit. "How Hanuman Got to Taos."
» David Lee Pratt. "The Founding of Morningstar Commune."
» Joyce Robinson. "Founding Settler of New Buffalo."
» Jennifer Sihvonen. "The Silversmiths at the Mabel Dodge Lujan House."
» Dianna Valdez. "Dixon Before Los Hippies."
With a special thanks to the parents and relatives who made such warm memories possible.
» M. Robert Van Arsdale. "Government Liaison to the Hippies: 1969-70."
» Chris West. "Origins of Pilar Hill."

photographer Paul Dembski now

photographer Rich Jamison now

artist Peter Wood then

Grateful acknowledgments as well for the following photographs:

p. 13 *Edward Sanders. Photo by Miriam Sanders*
p. 23 *Iris Keltz. Photo by Fred Poulos*
p. 35 *Goatyard. Photo by Rich Jamison*
p. 39 *Joyce Robinson. Photo by Iris Keltz*
p. 56 *Gathering of Arroyo Hondo/TLC community. Photo by Seth Roffman*
p. 75 *Dianna Valdez. Photo of Iris Keltz*
p. 87 *Rose Gordon. Photo by Iris Keltz*
p. 99 *Iris Keltz. Photo by Paul Dembski*
p. 121 *Minor Van Arsdale. Photo by Iris Keltz*
p. 127 *Barbara Durkee. Photo by Ayesha Bonnie Henning*
p. 137 *Chris West. Photo by Iris Keltz*
p. 141 *Jean Kenin. Photo by Iris Keltz*
p. 147 *Karen Pettit. Photo by Iris Keltz*
p. 153 *Charles Lonsdale. Photo by Iris Keltz*
p. 169 *Ed Morgan. Photo by Iris Keltz*
p. 188 *Leslie. Photo by Rich Jamison*
p. 195 *Marco Perella. Photo courtesy of Marco Perella*
p. 199 *John Nichols. Photo by Susan Crutchfield*
p. 225 *Jenny Bird. Photo courtesy of Jenny Bird*
p. 216 *Rainbow Drum Men. Photo by Paul Dembski*

Every effort has been made to identify photographers. If by chance we missed you, please accept our apologies. All identified photographs are used with permission.

Poems & Wisdom:

p. 12 *"Refuse to Be Burned Out," by Edward Sanders (P.C.C. Music), recorded by The Fugs on an album of the same name (New Rose Records 56, Paris 1987).*

p. 110 *"Walk Carefully When You Are Among," by Timothy Leary, was published in the* Fountain of Light *but its original publication could not be found.*

p. 135 *Hexagram 27—"The Corners of the Mouth (Providing Nourishment)" from* The I Ching or Book of Changes, *Richard Wilhelm / Cary F. Baynes, translators, (Princeton University Press, Princeton, N.J., 3rd edition, 1967).*

p. 232 *"My Last Farewell Address to the Troops," by Max Finstein was originally published in* There's Always a Moon in America *(Cranium Press, San Francisco 1968).*

Designer Jeff Bryan then